After Ground Zero

After Ground Zero

Everyday Americans and the Unhealed Scars of 9/11

Mike Kelly

BLOOMSBURY ACADEMIC
LONDON • NEW YORK • OXFORD • NEW DELHI • SYDNEY

BLOOMSBURY ACADEMIC
Bloomsbury Publishing Inc, 1359 Broadway, 12th Floor, New York, NY 10018, USA
Bloomsbury Publishing Plc, 50 Bedford Square, London, WC1B 3DP, UK
Bloomsbury Publishing Ireland, 29 Earlsfort Terrace, Dublin 2, D02 AY28, Ireland

BLOOMSBURY, BLOOMSBURY ACADEMIC and the Diana logo are trademarks of Bloomsbury Publishing Plc

First published in the United States of America 2026

Cover Design: Sally Rinehart

Cover image © Gary Hershorn/Corbis News/Getty Images

Library of Congress Cataloging-in-Publication Data Available

ISBN: HB: 979-8-2163-8399-4
ePDF: 979-8-2163-8401-4
eBook: 979-8-2163-8400-7

Typeset by Amnet
Printed and bound in the United States of America

For product safety related questions contact productsafety@bloomsbury.com.

To find out more about our authors and books visit www.bloomsbury.com and sign up for our newsletters.

For my wife, Judy Kelly, and our daughters, Michelle and Anne.
In gratitude for your love that supported me all these years

And . . .

For the 2,977 killed on September 11, 2001

And . . .

The more than 1,000
whose remains have not been identified.

And . . .

The more than 4,000 first responders and survivors
who have died since 9/11 from exposure to toxins at Ground Zero

And . . .

All those who mourn

"The world breaks everyone and afterward many are strong at the broken places."

—ERNEST HEMINGWAY, "*A FAREWELL TO ARMS*"

Contents

Timeline

The Attacks of September 11, 2001

8:46 a.m.: American Airlines Flight 11 strikes North Tower of World Trade Center.

9:03 a.m.: United Airlines Flight 175 strikes South Tower of World Trade Center.

9:37 a.m.: American Airlines Flight 77 strikes Pentagon.

9:59 a.m.: South Tower collapses.

10:03 a.m.: United Airlines Flight 93 crashes in Shanksville, PA.

10:28 a.m.: North Tower collapses.

The Aftermath

October 7, 2001: US war in Afghanistan begins.

October 26, 2001: President George W. Bush signs US Patriot Act.

January 11, 2002: First terrorist captives arrive at detention camp at US Naval Base, Guantanamo Bay, Cuba.

May 30, 2002: Clean-up completed at site of World Trade Center in Manhattan. Police and firefighters form honor guard as final steel beam is removed on flatbed truck.

August 15, 2002: Relatives of 9/11 victims and survivors file $116 trillion lawsuit against a variety of Saudi Arabian businesses, financial institutions, and members of the Saudi royal family.

December 2002: Congressional Joint Inquiry into Intelligence Community Before and After the Terrorist Attacks of September 11, 2001 completes report. Report not released until July 2003. A twenty-eight-page section on alleged links by Saudi officials is kept classified until July 2016.

December 16, 2002: Former New Jersey Governor and Drew University president Thomas Kean named as chairman of 9/11 Commission.

March 19, 2003: US war in Iraq begins.

July 22, 2004: 9/11 Commission releases report.

November 2, 2004: George Bush re-elected president.

January 5, 2006: NYPD Detective James Zadroga dies of respiratory and other ailments brought on by breathing toxins during clean-up of Ground Zero.

February 2, 2006: Countering statements in 2001 by Christine Todd Whitman, head of US Environmental Protection Agency, that Ground Zero air was safe, a federal judge in New York City determines that Ground Zero air and rubble was filled with dangerous toxins released in collapse of World Trade Center twin towers.

September 11, 2008: Dedication of memorial at Pentagon to commemorate 184 people who died there on September 11, 2001—59 of them aboard Flight 77 and 125 in the building.

May 2, 2011: Al-Qaeda leader Osama bin Laden killed by US Navy SEALs in raid in Pakistan.

September 11, 2011: Dedication of 9/11 memorial plaza at site of World Trade Center.

May 21, 2014: 9/11 Museum opens at site of World Trade Center in New York City. Museum's lower level contains repository of remains of more than 1,000 9/11 victims who have never been identified.

November 2014: First tenants begin to move into offices at 1,776-foot-tall "Freedom Tower" at site of World Trade Center's twin towers

September 16, 2015: Justice Against Sponsors of Terrorism Act introduced in US Senate. Known as JASTA, it is meant to counteract immunity claim by Saudi Arabia in lawsuit by 9/11 victims and relatives.

September 29, 2015: Federal judge in New York dismisses lawsuit against Saudi Arabia by 9/11 victims and relatives, citing existing US laws granting immunity to most foreign nations, including Saudi Arabia.

May 17, 2016: US Senate approves Justice Against Sponsors of Terrorism Act (JASTA) which is then transferred to House of Representatives for consideration.

July 2016: Previously classified twenty-eight-page Congressional report examining alleged Saudi links to 9/11 released.

September 9, 2016: House of Representatives approves JASTA with voice vote.

September 23, 2016: President Obama vetoes JASTA.

September 28, 2016: Senate and House vote overwhelmingly to override Obama's veto. JASTA becomes law. Lawsuit by 9/11 families against Saudi Arabia soon reinstated.

September 3, 2021: Under pressure from 9/11 victims and relatives who threaten to protest his attendance at annual memorial ceremony, President Joe Biden orders FBI to declassify reports on possible Saudi links to 9/11 attacks.

July 29–31, 2022: Former President Donald Trump welcomes Saudi-financed LIV golf tournament to his golf club in New Jersey. Critics call the Saudi sponsorship and undisclosed payments to Trump for use of his golf course "sport washing" to improve the kingdom's image. Trump urges golfers to "take the money."

September 2024: Deaths from Ground Zero toxins exceed the nearly 3,000 deaths from 9/11 attacks.

August 28, 2025: Federal judge in New York rejects Saudi legal efforts to dismiss lawsuit by 9/11 families. The lawsuit continues.

The Story Tellers

At the World Trade Center

Doug Brown
Alison Greeley
Stan Kapica
Nancy Karole Kennedy
Jack Kemp
Kathy Kemp
Dereck Lovell
Kevin and Susan Perry
Silvion Ramsundar
Tom Swift

The Search for Truth

Kristen Breitweiser, who lost her husband, Ronald Breitweiser
Brett Eagleson, who lost his father, John Bruce Eagleson
Thomas Kean, chairman, 9/11 Commission
Mark Rossini, FBI agent
Juliette Scauso, who lost her father, Dennis Scauso of FDNY Hazmat 1
Terry Strada, who lost her husband, Thomas Strada

Responders

Antonios Benetatos: probationary firefighter, FDNY
Lawrence "Larry" Byrnes: retired battalion chief, FDNY
Martin Davin: detective, NYPD
David Handschuh: photographer, *The New York Daily News*
Father Brian Jordan: Catholic priest and Ground Zero chaplain
Peter Killeen: psychologist, Port Authority Police
Phil McArdle: firefighter, Hazmat 1, FDNY
John Ryan: lieutenant, Port Authority Police
Frank Silecchia: construction worker

War on Terror

Bert Ammerman: lost brother, Thomas, in Pan Am 103 terror attack, 1988
Joe Connor: lost father, Frank, in Fraunces Tavern bombing, 1975
Tamara Duker Freuman: lost sister, Sara Duker, in Hamas bombing, 1996
James Egan: Captain, US Army, Iraq
Tim Sorbanelli: musician, injured in Boston Marathon terrorist bombing, 2013
James Yee: Captain, US Army chaplain, Guantanamo Bay Naval Base, Cuba

Author's Note

This is a book about death and the indiscriminate murders of nearly 3,000 innocent people by terrorists on September 11, 2001. But this is also a book about life and what took place after the 9/11 attacks as untold numbers of ordinary people struggled to pick up their lives.

Some were lucky enough to survive. Some rushed to the rubble at the World Trade Center in New York City, to the fires at the Pentagon in Northern Virginia, or to the blackened field in southwestern Pennsylvania to try to lend a hand with rescues, or to comfort the injured, and recover the dead. Some dedicated themselves to finding the truth behind what took place. Some lost loved ones and continue to mourn after all these years. Some just wanted to forget but found they could not. Many were left with scars on their bodies and souls that have never really healed.

I can't tell everyone's story here. There are just too many, across America and the world. But I believe that the people depicted in these pages—some of whom I've followed for most of the last two decades—offer a glimpse into the emotional ruins and brokenness left behind in the lives of ordinary people after terrorism strikes. Each of them, in some way, opened a private door into themselves, allowing me to experience the deep sorrow, soul-crushing anger, and head-spinning confusion that continues to wash over them. They trusted me with their hearts. And each time we spoke, I tried to remind myself that the paths they allowed me to walk with them are sacred ground.

This is their journey.

As I came to learn, it became my journey too.

—Mike Kelly

Smoke billows from Lower Manhattan after the World Trade Center's twin towers collapse. Photo by Pat Carroll/NY Daily News Archive via Getty Images.

Prologue

First Steps

No one said a word. How could we really? Looking back, all these years later, there seemed no easy way to describe what we saw that day.

It was almost 1:00 p.m. on September 11, 2001. I leaned against the starboard railing of a tugboat that had just left a dock in Jersey City, New Jersey, and was now churning through the choppy currents of the Hudson River on its way to Lower Manhattan.

A few hours earlier, a team of Islamist zealots, aiming to "wage war on America," hijacked four commercial jetliners. They crashed two planes into the 110-story twin towers of New York City's World Trade Center and another into the Pentagon in northern Virginia, flying the last half-mile over Arlington National Cemetery and the graves of 400,000 US soldiers, including the hillside plot where my father, a Marine major who fought in World War II, Korea, and Vietnam, was buried, and where my mother, one of the first women to enlist in the Marines during World War II, would also be buried years later. A fourth plane, reportedly bound for the US Capitol or the White House, slammed into the grass now growing on the flats of an abandoned strip mine near Shanksville, Pennsylvania, after its passengers, realizing they had been hijacked as part of a suicide mission, revolted and fought back. By the time the tugboat pulled away from its Jersey City berth, the Trade Center's twin towers had collapsed.

To say that America was in shock—indeed, that two of the tallest buildings in the world had been knocked to the ground in just a few hours—was an understatement. Nothing like this had ever happened before in our history.

Surrounding me now on the tugboat deck stood a hastily assembled collection of police officers, firefighters, doctors, nurses, and Roman Catholic priests—our eyes and our collective silence fixed on the untamed mound of gray rubble that was all that remained of the once-gleaming Trade Center's twin towers and several other buildings in the complex. The terrorist's handiwork.

One of the police officers, his voice rising above the tugboat engines, cut into the silence and turned to one of the priests.

"Father, would you lead us in prayer?"

Like the rest of us, Father Kevin Carter, a chaplain of the Jersey City Police Department, had been gazing at the rubble pile across the Hudson. He turned and scanned the faces of the cops and firefighters now surrounding him in a half-circle on the tug's deck. Several officers bowed their heads. Father Carter blessed himself with the Sign of the Cross.

"A great evil has been brought on us today," he began. "Bring some goodness. Bring some life."

It was that kind of day. A day of evil, but also a day when we yearned for life with some measure of goodness. As we stood together that afternoon on the tugboat deck, we all knew a great evil had just invaded what seemed like a peaceful and promising day, when the sun seemed so golden and the sky so perfectly blue. But where would this end? And what would goodness and life look like now?

For me, a newspaper columnist with a deadline only a few hours away, my goal in that moment seemed naively simple: Get across the river on this tugboat and write firsthand and quickly from the scene about what we all sensed would be a turning point in history. I had no idea, however, that this tense and silent crossing of the Hudson would be the first step of a much longer trek into another kind of rubble of pain left behind in the unhealed scars of people's lives after terrorism strikes. What I also did not know is that I would find goodness and life amid all those scars and rubble.

* * *

Histories of terrorism are often conveyed through big-picture lenses, with the narratives framed by the voices of presidents, military generals, scholars, and intelligence experts. Such a focus is entirely understandable, even necessary. Terrorism has altered the politics of nations and transformed the world's power structures. In the 1990s, a series of suicide bombings in Israel by the Palestinian terrorist groups, Hamas and Islamic Jihad, derailed the promising Oslo Peace Accords. Nearly a century earlier, the assassination of an Austrian archduke by a Bosnian Serb revolutionary helped to light the contentious political sparks in Europe that led to World War I.

But the impact of terrorism extends far beyond the broad sweeps of world politics and history. For the most part, the dead are usually just ordinary people going about such ordinary activities as riding a bus, working in an office, praying at a church, catching a plane, attending a class, or shopping at a grocery store. In many instances, these victims were—to use a cruelly harsh but sadly accurate cliché—in the wrong place at the wrong time. Or as a Hamas bombmaker once coldly confessed to me during an interview in an Israeli jail after his murderous handiwork killed more than fifty innocent passengers in a series of brutal bus bombings: They "got in the way."

But what of those who did not perish? For them, another form of pain invades their lives.

Some were witnesses who watched the chaos unfold, and now, stricken with the wounds of guilt, wonder why they lived and others did not, or whether they could have done more to help. Others were first responders like the police officers, firefighters, doctors, nurses, and priests on that Hudson River tugboat, who set aside their fears and rushed in to rescue the living and recover the dead—and now try to live with the memory of what they saw. Still others—the most painful cases of all—were those who lost someone close: a spouse, a parent, a child, a coworker, a friend, or just one of those familiar faces that they saw as they went about their daily routines in the office, in their neighborhoods, or simply walking down the street.

In many instances, I found that the years afterward are filled with a constant throb of heartbreak, confusion—even anger. Emotions boil and percolate without warning. The shadow of trauma never seems to disappear.

Many try to move on, of course—it's only natural. But far too many find there is no escape, no closure. A toxic elixir of cynicism remains a daily companion. And life becomes an ongoing effort to cope with a plethora of questions that remain unanswered and an array of wounds to body and soul that never really heal.

As I stared across the Hudson River from the tugboat on that first day, I had no idea how my own journey into the lives of victims and first responders would unfold. The morning's sky, so cloudless and serene at sunrise, was now smudged by thick and menacing brown smoke. Even a half-mile away, from the middle of the Hudson River, the 16-acre, debris-filled patch of Lower Manhattan that would become known to the world as "Ground Zero" looked foreboding and dangerous.

"That debris pile must be seven stories high," one of the police officers on the tugboat said.

"And look at all that smoke," another shot back. "It looks like someone dropped a bomb."

I wondered how many office workers might be entombed in the crushed concrete and twisted steel. Could it be thousands? Tens of thousands? The Trade Center's skyscrapers were home to more than 400 companies and some 50,000 workers. On any day, another 40,000 or so workers, visitors, and tourists passed through. New York's mayor at the time, Rudolph Giuliani, his face drawn and anxious, conceded in a brief press briefing that the final death toll could be "more than any of us can bear ultimately."

But who really knew? For a second or two, I tried to ponder how America would handle the news that thousands had died in this attack. *Was this the start of a new war?* Then, my eyes were drawn to another building near the debris that was still standing. A 30-foot-long steel beam, weighing several tons, had broken away from one of the Trade Center towers as it collapsed and thrust itself into the side of this other building's twentieth floor like some giant knife stabbing a just-baked turkey.

"What in the world is going on?" I asked myself.

The police officers and firefighters around me seemed to share the same thought.

"My God," one of them said.

* * *

Several hours earlier, throngs of police, firefighters, and emergency medical technicians rushed to the Jersey City waterfront across the Hudson River from the burning Trade Center. I rushed there, too. The first responders, along with teams of doctors and nurses from nearby hospitals, set up triage stations, thinking they might be needed to care for injured office workers who escaped Lower Manhattan on ferries that shuttled commuters from one side of the river to the other. But as it turned out, most of the Trade Center workers who managed to escape from the twin towers headed north on foot into Midtown Manhattan or east over the Brooklyn Bridge. By late morning, the numbers arriving in New Jersey had slowed to just a trickle.

Suddenly, a police detective, his jacket off, his arms raised, and his face streaked with sweat as his pistol dangled and swayed back and forth in his shoulder holster, turned and called out to the first responders on the dock.

"We're going over to help. If you want to come, get on the boat. We're leaving in a few minutes."

I approached the detective and told him I was a journalist.

"Could I hitch a ride on the boat?" I asked.

"I don't care," the detective said, his mind obviously focused on far more important priorities.

I turned and climbed down a ladder that hung off the side of the dock and dropped onto the rear deck of the tug as it bobbed up and down in the river.

For the police, firefighters, EMTs, doctors, nurses, and priests now milling on the deck around me, the task was clear: Once across the river, they would try to rescue survivors and treat the injured. The priests said they would bless the bodies of the dead.

But me? What was I doing here?

I arrived at this moment as a columnist with *The Record*, a medium-sized newspaper in northern New Jersey with a well-deserved reputation for reaching beyond New Jersey to cover national and international events. My impulsive journalistic instincts had pushed me to jump onto the deck of the tug. But now I felt like an interloper—a strange version of a stowaway amid the collection of first responders, each of them trained to offer comfort or first aid.

It was my job to dig beneath the surface of a news event and offer some form of commentary. It didn't matter if the story involved the screwball behavior of a political leader, a down-and-dirty murder in a dank city of despair, or just one of life's weird and occasionally funny twists of fate—like the time an aggressive prosecutor charged a suburban New Jersey homeowner with animal cruelty after he killed a rat that invaded his kitchen.

But the events unfolding before me now seemed surreal, indescribable.

* * *

I reached into my pocket for my cell phone and dialed my wife, Judy, at her office on the Fordham University campus at Lincoln Center in Midtown Manhattan. She had spent much of the morning at an office window, watching fire trucks with sirens blaring and horns honking as they sped south, down five miles of city streets toward the Trade Center.

"How will you get home?" I asked Judy.

"I don't know," she said.

"I'm in Jersey City. I'm going to try to get to the Trade Center on a tugboat," I said.

"How will *you* get home?" Judy asked.

"I don't know," I said.

Little did we know some version of this kind of conversation would be repeated over and over that day between wives and husbands, parents and children, siblings, and friends in all manner of relationships. Suddenly the world that seemed so ordered and scheduled only a few hours before had become unhinged. New York's bridges and tunnels had been shut. Subways and buses ran erratically. Many streets were clogged with frozen lines of traffic—so much so that emergency vehicles had trouble getting through.

That night, Judy would not make it back to our home in New Jersey. She stayed in a dormitory room in Manhattan with our youngest daughter, Anne, then a sophomore at Columbia University's Barnard College. It would be another day before she returned home. I ended up sleeping on the floor of a friend's apartment and didn't come home for two more days.

As I ended the call and pulled the straps tighter on my backpack, I realized how unprepared I was. I was wearing penny loafers, a blue blazer, a light blue shirt with a button-down collar, and khaki pants. Not exactly the wardrobe to cover a disaster.

I had left my laptop at the office and my cell phone charging cord at home. My backpack held just two notebooks, a half-used legal pad, and two pens. No food. No water. I had about thirty dollars in my wallet.

As if all that wasn't bad enough, I soon learned that most of the cellular transmission towers near the Trade Center had been knocked out of commission by the attack and the collapse of the twin towers. I was, for all practical purposes, about to enter an information bubble, unable to receive calls or make them.

My call to Judy would be my last to anyone for many hours.

* * *

Across the arc of my career, I had already covered my share of major stories, from the ugly landscape of American politics big and small to the sharp brambles of America's culture wars over race and religion.

But I found that trying to chronicle the struggles of ordinary people to cope with tragedies or other hardships was the most difficult. As a journalist, how do you suspend your emotions? Amid the carnage, how do you find perspective? Put another way: how do we find the goodness and life that Father Carter had just prayed for with those first responders on the tug?

I had shown up to the scene of a mass murder. I had walked through the rubble of a school cafeteria in Upstate New York after a gust of wind measuring ninety miles per hour knocked down a wall and killed seven children and injured eighteen others. I had visited prisons and hospital wards, courtrooms, and police stations. I spent a day at a home where orphaned children struggled to live after their now-dead mothers passed HIV into their bloodstreams. I spent another day with a colony of homeless men who lived under the boardwalk in Atlantic City. On a cold January morning, I stood on a patch of sidewalk where a homeless army veteran froze to death. I shuffled through the autopsy photographs of a six-year-old boy whose drug-addicted father killed him by burning cigarettes into his skin. I sat with a young mother in a hospital room before she institutionalized her disabled infant.

In short, I thought I knew plenty about the pain that sometimes descends into the lives of far too many people. Indeed, I often told myself that I needed to remember to walk carefully and delicately across the wounded landscape I was privileged to explore as a journalist. And it was my job to honor that ground and the suffering of people there as I wrote about what I saw and heard.

But I had never seen anything like this: majestic buildings that brushed the clouds now reduced to dust. As if they were toys.

I did not consider myself an expert on terrorism. But I was hardly a stranger either to the indiscriminate murders of innocent people by self-righteous and cruel zealots acting in the name religion or politics or bigotry.

In 1975, a bomb planted by Puerto Rican nationalists killed four people at Fraunces Tavern, the Revolutionary-era landmark where George Washington bid farewell to his Continental Army generals after America gained its independence from Britain. Years later, on assignment in Cuba, I took time to track the bomber, Guillermo "Willie" Morales, to an apartment in Havana, where he was hiding under the protection of Fidel Castro's communist regime.

"Leave me alone or I'll call the police," Morales yelled through a locked door.

How ironic, I thought—even weird. Back in New York City, plenty of NYPD detectives would have loved to have been summoned to Morales's apartment to arrest the man who had spent years on the FBI's most wanted list of terrorists.

On an April morning in 1989, I stood outside the White House in Washington, DC, as I followed a protest march by relatives whose loved ones were killed a few months earlier when Libyan intelligence operatives blew up a jumbo Pan Am jetliner over Lockerbie, Scotland.

The group, mostly middle-aged and middle-class, were hardly radical revolutionaries. They merely wanted to speak to President George H.W. Bush to raise concerns that their government had done little to respond to the attack and little else to protect all-too-vulnerable commercial jetliners.

But Bush's aides told the group the president was too busy to talk, so the group left dozens of hand-written messages in the steel fence surrounding the White House. Later that day, Bush relented and agreed to speak with several members of the group. But the meeting hardly soothed the pain from the initial rejection. Sadly, I would learn that this would not be the first time that government officials would set up walls that had to be breached by relatives of terror victims who merely wanted to know what was being done to track down the killers and protect the nation from future attacks.

For years, I stayed in touch with the Lockerbie victims. And over time, I noticed how many seemed to suffer a deep pain that never went away.

A female sculptor from Montauk, New York, who lost her son in the Lockerbie bombing, would later ask many of the women whose children and husbands perished to pose for sculptures in ways that captured their anguish. More than forty women responded, many posing nude, as a way of revealing their most vulnerable and intimate experience of pain. And while the women represented a wide range of ages and races, they all conveyed a similar sense of gut-level torture that they were now forced to live with.

As I wrote about these women and their statues, which were displayed in a variety of outdoor settings, from college campuses to real estate offices, I searched for the right words to chronicle the incessant pain that had taken over their lives. But often, with a deadline facing me, I felt inadequate. *What exactly was the most comprehensive and humane way to describe the impact of terrorism in people's lives?*

In early 1993, after a gang of radical Islamists set off a powerful bomb in the parking garage of the World Trade Center, I found myself again trying to understand the growing problem of terrorism. But this time, the circumstances were different. The terrorists had been arrested, and I was sitting on a bench in a courtroom in Newark, New Jersey to watch how they might respond as they were charged with their crimes. Or would they respond? What exactly would they have to say about what they had just done?

A half-dozen men, all of them handcuffed, entered the courtroom, their leg shackles rattling as they shuffled across the floor. More than a dozen federal agents, many wearing body armor and cradling assault rifles, lined the walls.

Several of the suspects wore Islamic-style clothing—long tunics and skull-fitting kufi hats. But one stood out—and I found myself studying him intensely. He was not dressed in Islamic garb. He wore a sweater, tailored pants, and bookish tortoise-shell glasses. His curly hair was styled. His wife and children sat in the front row of benches. This could have been just another American family.

It turned out that this man was an engineer at a major New Jersey corporation. And yet, he turned out to be the most radical of the group of terrorists. I would later learn, before he was found guilty and dispatched to Colorado and the most secure federal prison in America, that he designed and constructed the bomb that had been set off in the parking garage of the Trade Center.

But why? What caused this man who seemed so settled into American life with a family and a solid career to want to kill in the name of a radicalized—even warped—interpretation of his religion? I never found a good answer to that question.

In 1998, I traveled to Belfast, Northern Ireland, to cover the Good Friday Peace Accords. Belfast brimmed with hope at the possibility that Catholics and Protestants would finally set aside their centuries-old hatred and stop killing each other. But beneath this hopefulness I also sensed a deep distrust that it could take decades—maybe another century—to finally solidify a lasting peace. In Ireland, the graves of those killed on both sides still seemed to hold grudges and speak about revenge.

On assignment in Nairobi, Kenya, in 1999 to write about health care, my driver insisted on taking me to view the rubble of the US Embassy that had been blown up by Osama bin Laden's operatives eight months earlier. At first, I didn't want to go. My assignment, which was two hours away, was to interview American doctors and nurses treating poor Africans in the Great Rift Valley, many of whom suffered from HIV. My time was limited. I wanted to get moving.

But as we turned a corner and I saw the embassy rubble, I understood why my driver wanted me to see it.

"Isn't the destruction shocking?" my driver asked me. "You needed to see this."

"Yes," I mumbled. "I did need to see this."

But once again, I struggled with finding the correct way to place this bombing in some sort of broader context. Was this attack in Nairobi a sign of even worse terror to come or just an event confined to one city, carried out by just a small gang of misguided zealots?

In early 2001, I returned from a reporting project in Israel in which I traced the return of two families—Muslim and Jewish—back to their ancestral Middle East homelands. The families, who lived just five miles apart in northern New Jersey, now resided in separate communities on the West Bank only a few hundred yards apart. And yet, their lives were dominated by violence back and forth between their new towns that seemed to worsen despite efforts to forge a peace.

With the sun setting behind the Judean hills one evening near the Palestinian city of Ramallah, I stood on the side of a road to watch a protest march against the Israeli occupation of the West Bank. Several Palestinian teenage boys started to throw rocks at Israeli soldiers who had been guarding a checkpoint on the road. The soldiers raised their rifles, killing one boy with a shot to the head and wounding another with a bullet that grazed the side of his head.

A few years later, I chronicled the frustrating efforts of Jewish-American parents who lost their children to a series of Palestinian terrorist bombings. One of the victims was a young woman from the New Jersey town where I lived.

* * *

By the summer of 2001, the news in America seemed remarkably uneventful. America seemed to welcome the calm brought by its new president, George W. Bush. Hillary Clinton was now a rookie US Senator from New York, and living with her husband, former President Bill Clinton, in the couple's new home in Chappaqua, New York, about thirty miles north of New York City. With Hillary Clinton in Washington more often, President Clinton spent much of his time in his new home organizing his White House papers and writing a memoir of his upbringing and rise to the presidency. He seemed to miss the press-the-flesh style of politics that he enjoyed as president, though. When I visited Chappaqua to write about how the residents were adjusting to the former president, I found Clinton standing on a corner in the middle of town, shaking hands with passersby.

Back in New Jersey, the state's first female governor, Christine Todd Whitman, a wealthy heiress with a sprawling farm and whose grandfather had built Rockefeller Center, resigned to take a post in Bush's cabinet as director of the Environmental Protection Agency.

Just after Labor Day, I stumbled upon a bizarre tale about a girls' high school field hockey team in one of New Jersey's wealthiest communities that regularly held sexually suggestive hazing rituals with their younger teammates. A producer at MSNBC read my column and called me. Could I appear on the network's show, *Hard Ball,* with its outspoken host, Chris Matthews?

Sure, I answered, then wondered: Didn't MSNBC have something more important to talk about than hazing in girls' high school field hockey? Maybe not.

It was Monday, September 10, 2001. Around 6:00 p.m., I finished a routine column about New Jersey's new governor, Donald DeFrancesco, then drove to an MSNBC satellite studio in Secaucus, New Jersey. A soft rain soaked the New Jersey Turnpike, and I wondered whether the New York Yankees game against the Boston Red Sox would be canceled.

After appearing in a ten-minute segment on *Hard Ball,* I left the studio. The rain had stopped. Puddles glistened in the parking lot.

As I walked to my car, I scanned the Manhattan skyline to the east. Across the Hudson River, the twin towers of the World Trade Center sparkled with a constellation of starry-like bright lights. Every floor seemed alive.

A cloud drifted across the tops of the twin towers. The yellow moon poked its face just above the cloud.

"How beautiful," I thought, opening my car door and slipping behind the wheel to drive home.

By the next morning, the clouds had disappeared, leaving behind a perfect blue-sky dome over the New York region. The air felt cool—a hint of autumn that would arrive in a few weeks.

I decided to start the day early and was at my desk in *The Record's* newsroom in Hackensack, New Jersey, by 8:15 a.m. I listened first to a voicemail recording of Governor DeFrancesco angrily calling to say that he thought my column about him in the newspaper that morning was unfair. Next, I pulled out a stack of letters from readers and jotted down responses on postcards to mail.

Then, just after 8:46 a.m., the morning assignment editor, Susan DeSantis, called out my name from her desk across the newsroom.

"Mike, I just heard a plane hit the World Trade Center."

I turned and looked out the window behind my desk. Thirteen miles away, smoke poured out of the tower known as World Trade Center 1—the North Tower. On many evenings, as the sun set over the New Jersey Meadowlands, the towers took on an orange glow—"like orange popsicles," I often thought.

Now, there was no glow.

"I bet some idiot tried to fly a small plane between the towers and crashed," I mumbled to myself, as I rushed across the newsroom and turned on a TV.

But this was no small plane. The TV images from a news helicopter showed a gaping hole in the upper floors of the North Tower.

"Why don't you try to get to the scene?" Susan suggested.

I grabbed my backpack and ran to my car.

Two hours later, after weaving through back streets and passing the controversial Jersey City mosque where the 1993 Trade Center bombers worshipped, I arrived at the Hudson waterfront and the tugboat that would take me across the river.

* * *

The tug was slowing now as it approached Manhattan. Helicopters darted back and forth along the shore. A lone US Air Force F-16 jet fighter seemed to rip the air as it roared up the Hudson, barely 500 feet above the water. The wind shifted. I breathed in a smell of wet concrete and burnt plastic—and another odor that I later learned was the smell of death. Someone handed me a surgical mask.

As we docked at a pier near Canal Street, about ten blocks north of the Trade Center's rubble, I noticed that police and firefighters were gathering in small knots on a nearby corner. Many appeared exhausted, glum, ghostlike with the gray, talcum powder-like dust that covered them and their uniforms after the twin towers collapsed.

I gazed down West Street—to the blank spot in the city's skyline where the towers once stood.

What in the world happened to us? Where are we going?

In the coming years, those questions would return again and again as I watched the tragic ripples of this day touch the lives of so many ordinary people.

Even then, on that smoke-filled afternoon, I sensed that there would be no easy answers.

I turned and walked toward the rubble.

Part One

Day Becomes Night

"We saw evil at its worst, but goodness at its best."

FATHER BRIAN JORDAN, GROUND ZERO CHAPLAIN

FDNY Assistant Chief Gerard Barbara gazes at the burning twin towers. He later perished when the towers collapsed. Photo by David Handschuh/NY Daily News Archive via Getty Images. Handschuh was also injured when the towers collapsed.

1

Dawn

That morning, Thomas Swift knew exactly where he was going.

Just after dawn, he rolled out of bed in the apartment in Jersey City, New Jersey, that he shared with his wife, Jill. It was another early day at his office on the seventieth floor of the South Tower of the World Trade Center. But he didn't mind. Swift was only thirty years old, and already an assistant vice president with the multi-billion-dollar Morgan Stanley investment firm. Today was another chance to shine. His boss asked him to give a presentation at a quarterly meeting.

Four months earlier, Swift climbed another key step on the ladder to success in the up-and-down world of high-stakes finance. He earned a master's degree in business administration. But Swift did not take a leave of absence from his job at Morgan Stanley to complete his studies. Nor did he tap into his parents' bank account to pay tuition. He worked full days at the Trade Center's South Tower, then took night classes at St. Peter's University in Jersey City. After graduation, Swift's mother was so proud of her son that she purchased a class ring for him as a graduation present.

The ring arrived only a week earlier, and Swift figured that today seemed like the right moment for its debut for his office colleagues, perhaps as yet another reminder of his hard work to establish his career. But what finger should he wear it on?

Swift's left ring finger was home to his wedding band. On his right ring finger, he wore an Irish Claddagh ring.

Swift turned to his wife for guidance. The Claddagh was a present from Jill after they became engaged. Swift loved the ring's image of two hands reaching for one heart. To Swift, it was the first—and most basic—symbol of the love he shared with his wife. Two hands. One heart.

Swift told Jill he wanted to wear his new college ring on his right ring finger but he did not want to leave his Claddagh at home. For just this day, would Jill mind if he replaced his wedding band with the Claddagh?

Jill told her husband to go ahead. She shared his same feelings about the Claddagh, especially since it cemented their relationship before their wedding day five years ago.

Swift placed his wedding ring on the bedroom dresser. He switched the Claddagh to his left ring finger and slipped the St. Peter's ring on his right—then headed out the door. It was not yet 7:00 a.m. He figured he would return his wedding band to his left ring finger that night when he came home.

* * *

Across America, all manner of people assumed they were about to embark on another ordinary Tuesday in September, not knowing that their lives would be permanently changed by the events in the coming hours. Some, like Tom Swift, planned to attend routine office meetings. Others drove trucks, buses, or farm tractors. Still others stayed home with children. Or they showed up at construction sites and factories, grocery stores, police and fire stations, libraries, banks, and coffee shops.

In Middletown, Connecticut, fifteen-year-old Brett Eagleson left for a day of classes as a high school sophomore. His father, John Bruce Eagleson, who supervised shopping malls on the East Coast as a vice president for the Westfield Corporation, was meeting at the World Trade Center to discuss plans to revitalize the mall that had been built under the twin towers.

In Nyack, New York, Marty Davin, a New York City police detective, donned jeans and a T-shirt—his undercover wardrobe—and headed to his assignment with a new anti-drug task force of federal, state, and local cops that operated out of a top-secret building in Lower Manhattan.

In Chatham, New Jersey, Terry Strada was caring for her son, Justin, born just four days earlier, while also trying to help her seven-year-old son, Thomas, and four-year-old daughter, Kaitlyn, dress for school. Her husband, Thomas, a senior vice president specializing in corporate bond trading for the Cantor Fitzgerald investment firm, left before dawn for his office on the 104th floor of the North Tower.

In Dix Hills, Long Island, four-year-old Juliette Scauso figured she would spend the day with her grandfather while her mother, Janlyn, worked at a nearby school and her father, Dennis, a New York City firefighter, worked his normal nine-hour shift with a specialized hazardous materials squad in Maspeth, Queens.

In Washington, DC, Mark Rossini, an FBI counterterrorism agent, drove from his townhouse on Capitol Hill to the headquarters of the CIA in the hills of northern Virginia where he served as the FBI's liaison with a team of CIA intelligence officers that monitored Osama bin Laden's al-Qaeda terrorist network.

In Middletown, New Jersey, Kristen Breitweiser, who was getting ready to take her two-year-old daughter to a speech therapist and then to nursery school, had just hung up the phone from her husband, Ronald, who was checking in from his office on the ninety-fourth floor of the South Tower.

In Midtown Manhattan, Father Brian Jordan, a Roman Catholic priest and member of the Franciscan order of friars, donned his brown robe and headed uptown to a hospital to visit with a girl from the Dominican Republic that he brought to America for surgery. Back at Jordan's rectory at St. Francis of Assisi Catholic Church, his mentor and friend, Father Mychal Judge, readied for another day as the chaplain for New York City's fire department.

In Bedminster, New Jersey, only a few miles from a golf club owned by Donald Trump, Thomas Kean, the state's former Republican governor and now the president of Drew University, a small liberal arts institution, took a sick day. His dental surgery the day before left him with intense pain. "One of my teeth was doing something strange," he told his dentist.

In Chicago, Tamara Duker, who had lost her sister five years earlier in a terrorist bombing in Jerusalem, settled at her desk in an office building across the street from the 1,450-foot-tall Sears Tower that supplanted New York's twin towers as the world's tallest building when it was built in 1974.

In Ridgewood, New Jersey, Nancy Karole Kennedy, a vice president with Morgan Stanley, waited at the town's railroad station for the 7:08 a.m. train, hoping to arrive early for the same staff meeting Tom Swift would be attending on the seventieth floor of the World Trade Center's South Tower. Her boss, Jack Kemp, who normally took the train with her, decided to drive from his Jersey Shore beach house.

In Georgia, at the US Army's Fort Benning, James Egan, a newly minted second lieutenant and recent graduate from his university's ROTC program, finished his morning calisthenics and was about to head to a class in infantry combat training.

In Demarest, New Jersey, Bert Ammerman, a high school principal and former football coach, left his office for a routine meeting with the local district superintendent. Thirteen years earlier, after his brother was killed with some 300 others when a terrorist-planted bomb blew apart a Pan Am jetliner over Lockerbie, Scotland, Ammerman emerged as a persistent critic of what he felt were lax United States defenses against terrorism. Today, his mind was far from terrorism. He hoped to discuss a "back to school night" program for parents to visit their children's classes and meet teachers next week.

In Washington State, at Fort Lewis, an 80,000-acre military base named after Meriwether Lewis of the famed nineteenth century Lewis and Clark expedition, Captain James Yee settled into a new assignment. Yee, a West Point graduate who had commanded an air defense unit in Saudi Arabia during the 1991 Persian Gulf War, had recently been named as one of the first Muslim chaplains in US Army history.

In Fort Lee, New Jersey, David Handschuh, a hard-charging news photographer for *The New York Daily News*, was driving over the George Washington Bridge to Manhattan to teach a photography class at New York University.

In Little Ferry, New Jersey, Frank Silecchia hoped to get a call about a new construction job after spending most of the summer dismantling a defunct power plant. For years, Silecchia, broad-shouldered with hands the size of a baseball catcher's mitt, yearned to trade his hulking tough-guy persona as a construction worker and occasional barroom bouncer at a Manhattan tavern run by the Genovese crime family into full-fledged membership as a mobster—or as the Mafia described it, a "made man." But Silecchia's dream had been scuttled when the Genovese's leaders learned he was half-Jewish and did not meet the age-old Mafia requirement to be fully Italian. A construction job was his fallback plan.

In Clifton, New Jersey, Peter Killeen, a psychotherapist, figured he would spend the day counseling employees at a pharmaceutical company who were struggling with drug and alcohol addiction. He hoped he would not be summoned to his other job as a stress counselor for police officers.

In Seaford, Long Island, John Ryan, a lieutenant who commanded police at New York City's sultry Port Authority Bus Terminal on 42nd Street, was supposed to meet with an undercover officer to discuss the growing threat of street gangs. But Ryan stayed home so he could escort his daughter to her first day of nursery school. He figured he would have time to meet with the officer another day.

In Oakland, New Jersey, Tim Sorbanelli, who would find himself twelve years later watching runners cross the finish line of the Boston Marathon when a terrorist bomb exploded, was beginning just his second week of classes in the third grade at a local elementary school.

* * *

Nationwide, it had been a summer of increasing economic shakiness. By early September, America's financial forecasters—many of them working at the Trade Center or in offices nearby—worried that a trillion-dollar failure earlier in the year of dozens of high-tech companies known as "dot-coms" would trigger a national recession.

In Congress, Republicans and Democrats were mired in an emotionally charged religious and cultural debate over the use of federal funds for stem cell research on human embryos. At the FBI headquarters in Washington, DC, officials were still trying to understand how one of the agency's top counterintelligence agents became a Russian spy.

China signed a twenty-year friendship treaty with Russia. In Macedonia, a British-led invasion force of 4,800 NATO soldiers from thirteen nations struggled to disarm Albanian extremist rebels.

In sports, the International Olympic Committee voted to hold the 2008 summer games in Beijing, and Barry Bonds, a hulking outfielder for the San Francisco Giants baseball team, who would later be exposed for pumping up his muscles with illegal performance-enhancing drugs, closed in on a new home run record.

In New York City, September 11, 2001, was primary election day to select candidates to replace Mayor Rudolph Giuliani, whose two-term tenure was expiring.

In Lower Manhattan, the morning rush hour began before the sun rose on the narrow web of streets surrounding the World Trade Center.

Looming over the area like a giant tuning fork were the Trade Center's centerpiece icons: twin skyscrapers—the "towers" as they were called. Each rose 1,360 feet into the sky and stood less than 200 feet from each other. They were so close that on a hazy August morning in 1974, a self-proclaimed "highwire artist" from France named Philippe Petit, sneaked past the Trade Center's guards and strung a wire between the towers' roofs. Petit then stepped onto the wire, walking back and forth eight times between the towers.

As people gathered below and police rushed to the scene, Petit knelt, danced, and even laid down on the wire, pretending to sleep. He stopped only when police threatened to pluck him off with a helicopter.

The event, dubbed the "artistic crime of the century," became the subject of a documentary film in 2008, *Man on Wire,* which won an Academy Award. Petit, meanwhile, managed to avoid a trial or jail. City police and prosecutors dropped trespassing charges against him after he agreed to perform for children on a tightrope in Central Park.

The blocks near the Trade Center's twin towers, with their growing number of riverside apartments and restaurants, had solidified into one of New York's distinct neighborhoods. The area also had become a financial hub that would rival the older office canyons of Wall Street. Gone were the collection of small electronics stores and radio and TV repair shops that gave the neighborhood its old nickname, "Radio Row." Tucked beneath the towers and next to a multi-story underground parking garage and a web of subway lines, the Trade Center's shopping mall, with some eighty stores, had also become one of the busiest in America. Indeed, the area had become so large and complex that it had its own police force. It also needed two zip codes to process all the mail.

Not surprisingly, days at the Trade Center began early and ended late—if they ended at all.

Each floor of the towers was the size of a football field. And on any of those floors—and in three smaller Trade Center buildings nearby—you could find some of the nation's most powerful banks, investment houses, insurance companies, and law firms, along with such government agencies as the Port Authority of New York and New Jersey, the US Securities and Exchange Commission, the US Department of Labor, and the US Secret Service.

The 106th and 107th floors of the North Tower were even home to a five-star restaurant appropriately named "Windows on the World" where patrons could discuss the latest stock market trends over a martini and a steak or lobster while gazing at ocean liners, barges, and freighters that seemed like small toys a quarter-mile below on the Hudson River. On this day, seventy-three cooks, waiters, dishwashers, and other kitchen workers showed up to serve breakfast to ninety-one customers, some of whom were attending a meeting to discuss technological improvements in the financial industry.

Behind the success that seemed to pulsate from every floor and every pane of glass in the Trade Center, there was always the concern that terrorists would return some day. Was the 1993 attack a warning signal of what might come? Or had the terrorists moved on?

In 1995, after a persistent manhunt, the FBI finally captured Ramzi Yousef, one of the chief planners of the Trade Center bombing two years earlier. Yousef told the FBI that he hoped the bomb in the 1993 attack, a mixture of urea and nitrate weighing 1,200 to 1,500 pounds and driven to the Trade Center parking garage in a rented Ryder van, would be big enough to topple the towers.

The bomb, while certainly large and deadly enough to kill six people, was not powerful enough to bring down the towers or even cause permanent structural damage. According to records kept by the 9/11 Museum, a group of triumphant FBI agents reportedly flew Yousef in a helicopter to his jail cell in New York City to await his trial and passed over the twin towers.

An agent turned to Yousef, pointed to the towers and said: "Still standing."

Yousef seemed to have a ready answer: "They wouldn't be if I had enough money and explosives."

What the FBI did not know is that Yousef's uncle, Khalid Sheikh Mohammed, was already planning an even bolder attack plan with a wealthy Saudi Islamist radical named Osama bin Laden. As the FBI would learn, money would be no object this time.

* * *

It was now almost 7:00 a.m.

As Tom Swift made his way from his Jersey City apartment to the Trade Center's South Tower that morning, another man on the other side of New York's seven-mile-wide harbor left his apartment in Brooklyn. Like Swift, Dereck Lovell was also heading to the South Tower's seventieth floor. He also wanted to arrive early.

Lovell, a ten-dollar-an-hour security guard at the Trade Center, had a new assignment today. The guard who normally handled security on the South Tower's seventieth floor had a dentist appointment. Lovell was told to step in as a replacement.

The move to the seventieth floor was not permanent. Lovell knew that. He normally monitored the comings and goings of workers and visitors on one of the lower floors at the South Tower. But in Lovell's mind, the higher floor meant more prestige and responsibility, especially if it involved Morgan Stanley, whose 2,700 employees occupied twenty-three floors in the South Tower in the skyscraper's midsection—nearly a quarter of the overall office space in the building. Today, he figured, he had another chance to show his value to the company.

Even more importantly, Lovell figured his increased responsibilities might enhance his application to become a US citizen. He moved to America only a year earlier from his native Guyana, a former British colony the size of Kansas on the eastern edge of the Amazon rainforest in South America, between Brazil and Venezuela. Lovell loved his homeland and often smiled as he reminisced about it. But by the time he turned thirty, he knew he needed to leave. Nearly half of Guyana's 830,000 residents lived in poverty. In America, Lovell felt he could build a better life.

It had been a year since Lovell and his wife settled in Brooklyn. He had quickly received a work permit—the so-called "green card"—that allows non-citizens to legally hold a job. But Lovell's primary goal was to become a full-fledged US citizen. He figured that having a solid track record on his job at the Trade Center would surely help.

But this day would test all of Lovell's skills as a security guard. As he later recalled: "I will never forget that morning."

* * *

Eight miles away from the World Trade Center, in the tiny community of Maspeth, Queens, Firefighter Phil McArdle slipped behind the wheel of his black Jeep Grand Cherokee that was parked on a street near a century-old, red brick building that was home to two of the most elite teams in the Fire Department of New York: "Hazmat 1" and "Squad 288."

McArdle, who joined the FDNY two decades earlier, had become a nationally recognized expert in battling chemical fires—indeed, any blaze that involved toxins and other hazardous materials. By this point in his career, he was not just a key member of the Hazmat 1 team, but one of a handful of specialists called to various spots across America to assess all manner of troublesome fires, including possible terrorist bombings.

Five years earlier, McArdle had been dispatched with a group of FDNY firefighters and other first responders from across America to investigate a mysterious explosion of three pipe bombs that had been hidden in a backpack at the Olympic Games in Atlanta, Georgia. The blast was later tied to a domestic terrorist who said he was protesting abortion and what he felt was America's embrace of socialism.

A year before that, McArdle flew to Oklahoma City, Oklahoma, after another domestic terrorist, influenced by neo-Nazi writings and claiming the US government had become tyrannical, set off a massive bomb of ammonium nitrate fertilizer and diesel fuel that had been packed in a truck and parked outside the Alfred P. Murrah federal office building. The blast destroyed the building's façade, killing 168 people including nineteen children at a daycare center.

By the time the sun rose on September 11, 2001, McArdle had already worked most of his usual nine-hour overnight shift with Hazmat 1. He wasn't supposed to leave until 9:00 a.m. But on this day, he was scheduled to meet with his chief, Jack Fanning, at the FDNY training academy nearly seven miles away on Randalls Island in New York's East River to discuss a new instructional program for recruits on how to fight fires containing hazardous materials. The meeting was supposed to start at 9:00 a.m., so McArdle needed another firefighter to come in earlier and work the final hour of his shift.

One of McArdle's Hazmat 1 colleagues, Jonathan Hohmann, a thirteen-year veteran of the FDNY and a trustee at his Christian evangelical church in Staten Island, volunteered to take his place. Hohmann, who drove to Maspeth from his home in Staten Island, walked into the firehouse just after 7:00 a.m. so McArdle could get an early start and beat the rush hour traffic that invariably clogged the nearly seven miles of highways between Maspeth and Randalls Island. But McArdle inadvertently left home in Carmel, New York, without the disc that contained a special computer instructional system that he wanted to show to his chief. McArdle called his wife, Eileen, and that morning she brought the disc to the elementary school in the Bronx where she worked as a secretary. So before heading to Randalls Island and the FDNY academy, McArdle had to drive to the Bronx.

Time was tight. McArdle thanked Hohmann, said good-bye to his Hazmat 1 teammates, including his friend, Dennis Scauso, and headed for his Jeep Grand Cherokee.

It was almost 8:00 a.m.

* * *

Within the next hour, four commercial jetliners would lift off from airports in Boston, northern Virginia, and Newark, New Jersey.

American Airlines Flight 11, a Boeing 767 loaded with approximately 10,000 gallons of jet fuel, was the first. At 7:59 a.m., it left Boston's Logan International Airport, heading to Los Angeles with seventy-six passengers and eleven crew members. Seated unassumingly among the passengers as if they were just normal travelers on a cross-country trek were five Islamist operatives from Osama bin Laden's al-Qaeda terror network. Each planned to die that morning in what they thought would be a religious martyrdom that would guarantee them a spot in a lush and peaceful heavenly paradise.

Fifteen minutes later, at 8:14 a.m., United Airlines Flight 175—another Boeing 767 loaded with almost 10,000 gallons of fuel—took off from Logan International, also heading to Los Angeles with fifty-one passengers, nine crew members, and five more al-Qaeda terrorists.

At 8:20 a.m., at Dulles International Airport outside of Washington, DC, American Airlines Flight 77, a Boeing 757—slightly skinnier than its 767 sister, but nevertheless loaded with 10,000 gallons of fuel—left for Los Angeles with six crew members and five al-Qaeda operatives seated quietly with fifty-three other passengers.

Twenty-two minutes later, at 8:42 a.m., a Boeing 757 with 10,000 gallons of fuel and bound for San Francisco left Newark International Airport in New Jersey with seven crew members and four of bin Laden's terrorists scattered among the thirty-three passengers.

Within ninety minutes, all four flights would be hijacked after the teams of terrorists stabbed flight attendants and pilots to death with box cutters and other knife-like tools they had smuggled on board. In New York City and in Washington, DC—indeed across America and the world—few knew that the deadliest terrorist attack ever on US soil was unfolding.

At one point, Mohamed Atta, the leader of the hijacking team aboard American Airlines Flight 11, made what he thought was just an in-plane announcement to passengers, but, in fact, had been broadcast back to air traffic controllers. Atta told the passengers: "Just stay quiet. Nobody move, please. We are going back to the airport. Don't try to make any stupid moves."

Atta's statement about returning to the airport was, of course, a lie. Minutes after his announcement, flight attendant Betty Ong called airport officials on an in-flight telephone to warn them of the hijacking.

It took another eighteen minutes to mobilize military jets to intercept the plane.

By then, it was too late.

* * *

Back in Lower Manhattan, Joseph Connor, a financial analyst, stepped off a subway under the Trade Center and walked to his office a few blocks away at the J.P. Morgan Bank on Wall Street.

Connor's thoughts were far from banking—or even the subway he had just taken and the delicatessens and stores he passed on his way to his office. The night before, he started writing a memoir about his father, who had been killed in 1975 in a terrorist bombing by Puerto Rican nationalists.

On January 24, 1975, Joe's father, Frank Connor, then a thirty-three-year-old vice president at the Wall Street headquarters of the Morgan Guaranty Trust Company—the forerunner of powerful Wall Street financial institution where

Joe Connor now worked—met several friends for lunch at Fraunces Tavern, the wood-paneled restaurant where George Washington delivered his goodbye speech to his fellow Continental Army generals.

Not surprisingly, Fraunces Tavern, which was only a few blocks from Wall Street, was crowded when Frank arrived that day. It was a Friday. The stock market would soon shut down for the weekend. Connor's group chose a table in the back room. As they chatted, a powerful bomb, planted by members of the Puerto Rican *Fuerzas Armadas de Liberación Nacional*—the so-called "Armed Forces of National Liberation" or FALN—exploded. Frank Connor was killed along with three other financial executives. Another fifty were injured.

Frank Connor's death had hung like a mysterious and unsettling shadow over Joe Connor's life for years.

On that Friday night when his father died, the Connors were planning to celebrate birthdays for nine-year-old Joe and his eleven-year-old brother Tom, who had both been born in January. At the family's home in Fair Lawn, New Jersey, Joe's mother, Mary, an Irish immigrant, spent part of the afternoon making Italian lasagna, a favorite dish of her sons. But the family never ate dinner that night. Mary Connor was summoned to New York City. She later recalled dumping the lasagna in the garbage.

At the time, the bombing had been labeled an act of domestic terrorism—one of hundreds of bombings and shootings in the 1970s by the FALN and other radical groups such as the Weather Underground and the Black Liberation Army. As the radicalism of the 1960s and 1970s faded into the 1980s conservatism that brought about Ronald Reagan's presidency, the tragedy of Fraunces Tavern seemed a mere historical footnote. When the suspected FALN bombmaker Guillermo "Willie" Morales escaped from police custody in New York City and then managed to make his way to Cuba, where Fidel Castro gave him political asylum, there was little demand to bring him back. Even President Ronald Reagan, hardly an admirer of Castro or his communist regime, did not raise much of a huff—certainly not enough to pressure Castro to return Morales and other fugitives such Joanne Chesimard, a Black Liberation Army operative who escaped prison in New Jersey after being convicted of murdering a state trooper in 1973.

By the 1990s, Joe Connor found there was even less interest in solving his father's murder. The string of domestic terror attacks of the 1970s had been eclipsed by yet another series of brutal acts of terrorism, ranging from attacks on the Pan Am Flight 103 jetliner in 1988 and the World Trade Center in 1993, to the Oklahoma City federal building in 1995, and the Atlanta Olympics in 1996.

In high school and college, Joe Connor found himself continually searching—and sometimes struggling—to find the most effective way he could draw attention to his father's death. Why had America been so quick to forget about a blatant attack that resulted in the murder of his father and three others at Fraunces Tavern? Connor did not know. And trying to answer that question frustrated him as he tried to go on with his own life. After college, he quickly landed a job in New York's high-pressure financial world, and soon he got married and started a family of his own. "We talked about my dad all the time. It's not like we forgot," Connor said years later. "We would talk about anniversaries and we would go to church or to the cemetery. But we never really sat down and talked about his murder and what we could do to solve it and bring the killers to justice."

Connor's sense of helplessness and discouragement increased even more as the 1990s ended.

For more than a year Hillary Clinton had been sending none-too-subtle signals that she wanted to run for a US Senate seat in New York. Suddenly, in August 1999, in what election experts felt was a brazen attempt to lure Puerto Rican voters to support his wife's campaign, President Bill Clinton granted clemency to sixteen FALN operatives who had been imprisoned after being linked to the bombings in the 1970s.

None of the FALN members had been convicted specifically for the Fraunces Tavern blast. But it didn't matter. The backlash against Clinton—and his unabashed effort to help his wife—was instantaneous and loud.

Hillary Clinton, while initially praising her husband's clemency offer, abruptly withdrew her support for it. And the US Senate voted 95-2 to signal its overwhelming opposition to the president's decision. But President Clinton, who did not need Congressional approval for offering clemency, went ahead anyway. He explained that the FALN members would receive clemency only if they publicly renounced violence. Fourteen of the sixteen agreed and walked out of prison in early September. But two hardliners refused and remained behind bars.

For Joe Connor, the FALN clemency controversy became a personal wake-up call. He vowed to speak out more on his father's murder and the dangers of terrorism. But the fact that a chorus of protesting voices failed to force President Clinton to withdraw his clemency offer was yet another reminder of the difficult path facing Connor if he hoped to push his government to get serious about the dangers of terrorism and punish those responsible.

In 1999, Joe and his brother, Tom, published an emotional opinion essay in *The Wall Street Journal* that seemed to summarize his family's frustration. "It is our hope and belief," the brothers wrote, "that all New Yorkers will see through this craven political act and send a message to the first family that their votes cannot be bought through the release of those with our father's blood on their hands."

Over the next two years, Joe Connor wondered what he could do—if he could do anything. He eventually decided to write a book. And he figured he would begin writing as he took the train home after work on Monday, September 10, 2001.

Connor felt the time was right. That night, he caught a subway after work at the Trade Center that rolled through a tunnel under the Hudson River and arrived at the waterfront city of Hoboken, New Jersey. From there, he took a train to Bergen County, New Jersey, about twelve miles away. The train followed the same route his father once took when he commuted to the Morgan Guaranty Trust on Wall Street—the same route his father would have taken home on the night of the bombing at Fraunces Tavern.

On his usual after-work commutes, Joe Connor often sat with his cousin, Steven Schlag, a gregarious partner at Cantor Fitzgerald in the North Tower of the Trade Center. Connor's father had been Schlag's godfather. And for the homebound train rides after the usual intensity of their finance jobs, Connor looked forward to the relaxing laughter and companionship from his cousin. Sometimes Schlag picked up a few beers at a store in Hoboken and brought them aboard the train for the ride home. It was something of an unofficial custom that brokers and others in the pressure-packed world of finance often embraced as a way of coping with stress.

But on that night, Connor wanted some quiet time by himself. No laughter. No beer.

Taking a seat in another train car, Connor opened his laptop. He had much he wanted to say, of course—notably, his sense that his government often had been caught flat-footed by terrorists and then seemed remarkably inept at punishing them. But Connor's opening sentence explored his most personal pain—of growing up without his father, his own role now as a husband and father, and how his grandparents must have felt after losing their son to a terrorist attack in 1975. "There is likely no event in a man's life," he began, "as monumental as the birth of his children."

As he settled at his desk the next morning on the thirty-sixth floor of J.P. Morgan, Connor was still pondering what he had written—and what he now felt was his own heartfelt need to tell his father's story and alert America to the dangers of terrorism. He felt inspired and couldn't wait to resume writing on the train ride home that night. But first, there was a day's work to put in. He pulled his laptop from his briefcase and plugged it into a docking station on his desk, then casually looked up. His office window framed the World Trade Center's twin towers where his cousin Steve worked.

Today, the towers shined with a golden hue in the morning sun. Connor took a moment and marveled at their pristine and powerful beauty.

It was now almost 8:30 a.m. He knew he should leave soon if he was going to arrive on time for an appointment in Brooklyn that he had scheduled for 9:00 a.m.

He decided to stay a few more minutes.

* * *

Dereck Lovell had already settled behind the security and reception desk, not far from the central elevator bank on the seventieth floor of the South Tower. On the other side of the floor, past several walls and offices and hallways, Tom Swift walked into a roomy, sun-filled conference room.

Swift didn't sell stocks or bonds. As a member of a marketing team based on the seventieth floor, it was Swift's job to assist the more than 14,000 Morgan Stanley brokers in promoting the firm's investment plans to clients. And it was just the sort of mission that seemed to match Swift's engaging personality and easy mastery over financial data. He was still a junior member of the team and had not yet acquired an office with a view of New York City. But in just a short time, he had developed a reputation as a "go-to-guy," a quick-study problem solver who could troubleshoot almost any challenge in a pinch. At six feet one, with the broad shoulders of a linebacker and a mirthful smile, Swift had grown from a relatively shy beginner into the marketing team's resident comedian who had a unique ability to break the tension of a business meeting by regaling his colleagues with a hilarious story.

His colleagues called him "Swifty." His boss, Jack Kemp, would later say: "I loved this kid with a passion."

Kemp, almost sixty at the time and still trim from his days as a US Army paratrooper, had seen his share of shooting stars during his years on Wall Street—hotshot stock traders who wanted to make their mark quickly. Early on, they might be fueled with youthful exuberance and brimming with ideas. But, in time, many burned out on the climb up the corporate ladder.

Not "Swifty," though. Kemp felt confident his protégé would not slow down. Yes, Swift was willing to put in long hours. But Kemp quickly noticed that Swift possessed the kind of disposition that was a formula for success in the world of high finance. He could shift easily from a back-slapping, joke-filled collegial networking chat with colleagues to a sober discussion of economics.

Kemp also noticed something else: Swift never forgot his working-class roots. He was the first in his family to graduate from college. And after landing a job at Morgan Stanley, Swift didn't move to a posh apartment in Manhattan or a townhouse in one of the hipster neighborhoods across the East River in Brooklyn. He married his high school sweetheart and stayed in Jersey City, not far from his family.

Kemp often told friends how much he admired Swift's work ethic, especially how he stayed on the job at Morgan Stanley during the day, then took night classes for his MBA degree. "Tommy represents all that is good about corporate

America," Kemp said. "You could come in and work hard. You can achieve things and you can climb up the ladder. This was not a kid with a silver spoon. His dad didn't send him away for two years to get the MBA. This is a kid who did it by hard work."

As the summer of 2001 drew to a close, Swift seemed to be on the brink of even more success at Morgan Stanley. He had labored for weeks on a new computerized program that would allow Morgan Stanley's managers to monitor the ebbs and flows of investment packages the firm's clients were choosing.

Keeping track of so many financial plans—and the whims of clients—was a complicated task. But with the right computerized program, Morgan Stanley's small army of economists and brokers could monitor potential investments and trends for new customer portfolios far more easily than just a few years before.

Finally, by September 11, 2001, the program seemed ready to be unveiled. Kemp invited "Swifty" to make a presentation at the quarterly staff meeting that day.

Like Swift, staffers arrived early to the conference room on the southeast corner of the floor. Several sipped their coffee and munched on fruit near the long conference table and its twenty seats. Several others, including a few who had flown in the night before from Morgan Stanley offices in other parts of America, gathered by the room's windows to take in the majestic blue-sky morning panorama that stretched from the Statue of Liberty to the Brooklyn Bridge. All of it bathed in golden sunlight.

Nancy Karole Kennedy, one of Kemp's key vice presidents, found herself gazing out the windows, too, that morning. She had been transfixed by the sweeping vista many times. Window gazing was one of the unavoidable pastimes at the Trade Center, especially on the upper floors where the view on a clear day such as this could stretch for more than fifty miles.

Often, Kennedy would remind herself how fortunate she was to work in such an office, so high above the ground—especially today. The sky seemed remarkably clear in a way Kennedy rarely saw. Years later, Kennedy would remember thinking to herself: "It was what we would call a 'top ten' day. The colors were just popping."

Tom Swift strolled over to the windows, too. He chuckled as he recounted a story about playing golf over the previous weekend. Then, he switched to talking about how disappointed he was that the rainstorm in New York on Monday night had postponed the game between the Boston Red Sox and the New York Yankees, his favorite baseball team.

It was now time for the meeting to begin and for Tom Swift to make his presentation. The chit-chat slowed and the others took seats around the conference table and in chairs lining the walls.

* * *

Several hundred miles to the north, American Airlines Flight 11, with the five hijackers now in control, cruised over the Berkshire Mountains in western Massachusetts. Just beyond Albany, New York, the plane banked sharply left—a nearly ninety-degree turn, flight records would later show—and headed south along the Hudson River toward New York City.

The US military had scrambled several jet fighters in New Jersey and in Massachusetts to intercept the plane, but they were still miles away. American Airlines Flight 11 cruised unimpeded down the Hudson, past West Point and the George Washington Bridge and the fashionable Upper West Side.

Years later, witnesses would recall the high-pitched roar that pulsated from the plane as it flew at a low altitude toward Manhattan's tight grid of streets and buildings. People would say they were startled by the noise that seemed so close at hand. "It sounded like an airport runway," one man said, echoing a common observation by many.

The hijackers at the controls seemed to follow the West Side Highway and West Street which ran along the Hudson River's edge. As the plane reached Lower Manhattan, they dropped the plane to barely 1,000 feet. The FBI and Federal Aviation Administration would later conclude the plane was flying nearly 500 miles per hour or more than 700 feet per second.

The hijackers pointed the plane's nose at the upper floors of the north face of the North Tower.

It was 8:46 a.m.

New York Daily News *photographer David Handschuh, in pain from a broken leg, lies on the floor of delicatessen a block from the World Trade Center after he was rescued from rubble by FDNY Hazmat 1 firefighters Phil McArdle and Jeff Borkowski. Photo by Todd Maisel/NY Daily News Archive via Getty Images.*

2

Collapse

Joe Connor heard a massive thud—"like a concussion" is how he later described it. Instinctively, he looked up from his desk and out the window. A bulbous, orange fireball burst from the North Tower's upper floors. Then, something heavy flew out of the tower. Connor thought it might be an air conditioner.

"The tower seemed to rip apart," Connor recalled.

One of his coworkers said he thought a small plane crashed into the tower. Another said he was sure the plane was much larger—on par with a commercial jetliner.

Connor watched as sheets of paper floated from the hole in the tower. Then he noticed larger objects dropping from the building. "People," he said.

Connor phoned his brother, Tom, who worked at a bank on Broadway, a few blocks from the Trade Center complex. Tom didn't answer.

Connor hung up and thought of his cousin, Steve Schlag, in the Cantor Fitzgerald investment offices that occupied four of the North Tower's uppermost floors. *Was Schlag's office near the spot where the plane struck?*

Connor tried Schlag's office phone. No answer. The call went to voicemail.

"Call me back as soon as you can," Connor remembered saying as he left a brief message.

Connor was frantic now and dialed his brother again. This time Tom picked up.

The brothers compared notes on what they saw, asking each other the same question so many others raised in those early minutes: *What's going on?*

Joe Connor could think of only one answer: Terrorism.

* * *

Across New York, in taxi cabs, buses, apartment penthouses, and tiny bodegas, people seemed to ask the same question. *What just happened?*

Sirens blared from scores of police cars, fire trucks, and ambulances. Like Joe Connor, countless numbers of people reached for their phones and tried to call loved ones or friends—or just about anyone who might have been working near the Trade Center. *Are you okay?*

The Morgan Stanley team, which had started its meeting only a few minutes earlier in the seventieth-floor conference room of the South Tower, also heard the same booming thud.

"What was that?" Nancy Karole Kennedy asked, looking up. Across the conference table, her eyes met those of Jack Kemp, who had just welcomed the staff to the meeting and described the agenda.

"I don't know," Kemp said. "But it was big."

Kennedy's eyes shifted to the windows. A flock of papers blew by. Then, flaming debris. "We're out of here," she announced.

The group moved quickly. Tom Swift grabbed his briefcase and headed for the stairs. Kennedy rushed down a hallway to an office where a young woman who had just returned from maternity leave was still at her desk. Kennedy told her to leave.

Then Kennedy headed to her own office to fetch her purse.

Jack Kemp ran with several staffers down a hallway to the other side of the floor and stepped into the office of Kevin Perry, a Morgan Stanley comptroller, whose window overlooked the North Tower.

Perry stared silently at the scene outside, seemingly unaware at first that Kemp was there. Kemp wondered if Perry was in shock.

He wasn't. Like so many that day, Perry was trying to comprehend what he was seeing.

Perry had been on the phone with his boss at another Morgan Stanley office in Midtown Manhattan when he heard the jetliner's roar. He looked up and saw a flash of silver with the familiar red and blue double-A logo of American Airlines.

A commercial jetliner? Here? Crashing?

Then came the deadening sound. A massive, guttural boom of metal smashing into the metal, glass, and concrete of the North Tower—and then a blast of nearly 10,000 gallons of jet fuel exploding.

"Oh my God," Perry remembers gasping.

Eight floors below in the South Tower, Perry's wife, Susan, was talking to her boss on the phone. She, too, saw the flash of silver, red, and blue.

"Oh, my God," she yelled. "It's an American Airlines jet."

Susan heard the boom of the crash and the explosion. But she couldn't see the fireball. The impact zone between the ninety-third and ninety-ninth floors of the North Tower was too high for her to take in. But within seconds, she saw debris falling. And paper swirling—thousands of sheets. Then, a roll of toilet paper, unraveling as it tumbled through the air.

Susan had survived the 1993 terrorist bombing of the Trade Center in which six Trade Center workers died, but she had long regretted that she delayed her escape by making a phone call. This time, she wasn't taking any chances.

She hung up and headed for the stairs, leaving behind her blue blazer, a briefcase, a cell phone, keys, a wallet with $200, her wedding portrait, and a box with a half-dozen dress shoes. Susan figured she would come back later. She also figured her husband was probably making his way down the South Tower's stairs.

He wasn't.

From his perch on the seventieth floor, Kevin Perry was still transfixed by the scene outside his office window.

A body fell. "It was a man," Perry said. "I figured he was dead already and he got sucked out of the North Tower. He was motionless as he fell."

Seconds later: another man fell.

Perry followed the man's descent as he flailed his arms, as if trying to balance himself. Could the man be alive?

Perry reached for his phone and dialed his wife's office. No answer. Perry figured Susan had already left.

He then phoned his parents, assuring them that he was safe.

Then, he headed for the stairs.

It was almost 9:00 a.m.

* * *

From the Trade Center's twin towers and rippling across America, phone lines and cellular towers suddenly jammed with all manner of people trying to check in on each other. In New York City alone, the 9-1-1 emergency line was overloaded with 3,000 calls. The cellular networks in the city had a 92 percent blockage rate. Eventually the system crashed, only to be partially restored hours later. Across America, especially along the East Coast, phone calls were either delayed or cut abruptly, only to be tried again and again by desperate people watching the TV coverage of the attack.

Spouses and loved ones called each other. So did parents and children. And children and grandparents. And coworkers. And friends. And even those who knew someone vaguely but just wanted to check in. Suddenly the often impersonal modern world had become remarkably intimate in an old-fashioned way. The most common concern in America's fast-paced, tech-obsessed, moneyed culture had suddenly been reduced to one of humanity's most basic, age-old, person-to-person questions, sometimes between people who only distantly knew each other:

Are you okay?

From his office on the 104th floor in the North Tower, Tom Strada phoned his wife, Terry.

Only forty-one, Tom was already a senior vice president for corporate bond trading at the Cantor Fitzgerald investment firm whose nearly 700 employees occupied the top floors of the North Tower. After marrying several years earlier, the couple first lived in an apartment only a few blocks from the Trade Center, in Battery Park City. But, with three children, the family had moved to Chatham, one of New Jersey's most fashionable suburbs.

When the phone rang, the couple's four-day-old son, Justin, was awake. Tom seemed unusually frantic and scared, Terry thought.

"A plane has hit the building," she remembers him saying.

In the background, Terry could hear screaming and what she thought was a "swishing noise." She later assumed it was the wind blowing through the windows near Tom's office that had been punched out when the jetliner exploded.

Tom told Terry he loved her and said he was heading for the building's stairs to escape.

Then he hung up.

From his office across the Trade Center's plaza on the ninety-fourth floor of the South Tower, Ron Breitweiser phoned his wife, Kristen, at the couple's home in Middletown, New Jersey. Like Tom Strada in the North Tower, Ron arrived early for work that day. He caught a 6:00 a.m. ferry from the New Jersey shore town of Atlantic Highlands and was at his desk at the Fiduciary Trust investment firm around 7:00 a.m. He was just thirty-nine. Like Tom Strada, Ron had already risen to senior vice president.

Kristen, a 1996 graduate of Seton Hall Law School, had placed her legal career on hold to raise the couple's daughter, Caroline, now two years old. That morning, Kristen was planning to take Caroline to a speech therapist, then to nursery school.

Ron had already called the house around 8:30 a.m.—just to check in and tell Kristen he was already drinking his second cup of coffee.

Now, just after 8:46 a.m., Ron was calling again. Later, Kristen would write down the conversation word-for-word.

"Sweets, I'm okay. I'm okay," Ron began, using the couple's nickname for each other.

"What are you talking about?" Kristen cut in.

"Don't you know?" Ron said. "Turn on the TV. The building next to mine exploded. It's unbelievable."

Kristen reached for the switch on a small TV on the kitchen counter. A video feed from a TV news helicopter popped on the screen, showing a massive black hole in the upper floors of the North Tower. Plumes of smoke poured out.

"Holy shit," Kristen said. "It's really bad."

"That's why I'm calling you," Ron said. "I didn't want you to worry. I'm fine. I'm okay. Sweetheart, it's not my building."

Kristen asked what happened. Ron said he did not know. He said he was sitting at his desk and felt his face suddenly get warm. He looked up and saw the fireball bursting from the North Tower.

Ron's voice then cracked.

"I am sitting here looking and people are jumping out of the windows," he said. "Right across from me. I can see them. And they are jumping."

Moments later, Ron told Kristen he loved her. He promised to call back when he was safe.

* * *

Twenty-four floors below Ron Breitweiser's office, on the South Tower's seventieth floor, Jack Kemp was relieved. As he walked back to his office, he saw that most of his twenty-six-member staff on the floor had fled. Only Nancy Kennedy and four others lingered behind.

Most importantly, the damage seemed to have been confined to the North Tower. The South Tower seemed safe. Nevertheless, Kemp felt it best to leave, even for just a short time so the firefighters could check the entire building. He figured he could always return and finish the workday.

Kemp remembered that someone pleaded, "Let's go." But Kemp asked if he could take a minute to call his wife, Kathy. The others waited in the hallway, near the elevators and two stairwells.

At the Kemps' beach house in Mantoloking, New Jersey, a community of only 300 residents on a 200-yard-wide barrier island between the Atlantic Ocean and Barnegat Bay, Kathy Kemp was watching the television coverage of the flames in the North Tower when the phone rang.

Standing at his desk, looking south out the windows over New York Harbor toward the Statue of Liberty, Kemp quickly ticked off a litany of what was happening. "Things are pretty bad in the North Tower", he said. But the South Tower was fine and he was about to leave by the stairs.

* * *

Nearly 1,000 feet below, near the corner of West and Liberty Streets, David Handschuh of *The New York Daily News* had been photographing the platoons of firefighters as they rushed into the North Tower and the deathly descents of workers as they jumped or fell from the gaping hole nearly 900 feet above where the jetliner crashed.

Thirty minutes earlier, Handschuh had been driving leisurely down the West Side Highway, then on to West Street. He figured he had an easy morning ahead, free of the hyper-tense pace of a news photographer whose assignments on any day might range from a brutal murder in the Bronx to a star-filled movie premiere in Manhattan.

On this day, Handschuh was on his way to New York University in Greenwich Village to teach a photography class. As he passed Manhattan's Chelsea neighborhood and the pier where the Titanic was supposed to have docked in 1912, American Airlines Flight 11 roared overhead and struck the North Tower.

A plane crashing into one of the world's tallest buildings? On a day when visibility was clear, almost endless?

Handschuh watched the smoke pour out of the hole the plane punched in the tower. He was twenty blocks away—about one mile. This was not going to be an easy day. He reached for his cell phone and dialed the *Daily News* assignment desk. "I'm going to the Trade Center," he said. Next, he dialed New York University and left a message on voicemail: "Professor Handschuh will be late for class."

Traffic slowed. Handschuh knew he needed to move more quickly to the Trade Center or he would be caught in a frozen traffic jam for hours with no photographs to take. Just ahead, a fire truck whipped around a corner from a side street. It was the FDNY's elite Rescue 1 unit, turning on to West Street—but not in the usual right-hand lanes. Rescue 1 headed into the oncoming northbound traffic.

Cars, trucks, and buses moved to the side of the street as Rescue 1 lurched forward, its lights pulsating and sirens blaring. It was the same tactic that the drivers of ambulances, police cruisers, and fire trucks sometimes resorted to in New York City where congestion is considered part of the fabric of life. Just drive down the opposite side of the street.

Handschuh quickly surmised that he ought to try the same move, figuring it was his best chance to beat the impending traffic gridlock. Anyway, he doubted the FDNY brass would object. Just six years ago, Handschuh had been named by the FDNY as its "honorary photographer" in tribute to his many hours chronicling the city's firefighters as they battled any number of blazes. He pushed down on the accelerator in his car and crossed into the oncoming lanes and tucked in behind Rescue 1.

The truck's back door swung open and Handschuh instinctively reached for his Nikon and laid it on the dashboard. With one hand on his steering wheel and his cell phone tucked into his ear, he snapped photographs of the firefighters inside the truck as they slipped into their heavy firefighting coats and strapped air tanks on to their backs. Several recognized Handschuh and waved.

The ride was quick—maybe five minutes. Rescue 1 parked a few blocks north of the Trade Center complex on West Street. Handschuh pulled over, too. He grabbed his two Nikons. Like many experienced news photographers, Handschuh outfitted his cameras with different lenses—one for close-in shots, another for long range. He draped one camera over his left shoulder, the other on his right and walked toward the smoke and flames with the firefighters.

It was now almost 9:00 a.m.

More firefighters flooded the street. The eleven firefighters on the Rescue 1 truck ran into the North Tower. Handschuh stayed back and walked along West Street, looking up at the North Tower and snapping photos. People fell from the upper floors, their bodies pop-pop-popping loudly like small explosions as they slapped, one after the other, on the concrete plaza.

Handschuh tried counting but stopped. There were just too many.

Suddenly, he heard a roar. Instinctively he turned and aimed his Nikon upward and pressed the shutter as a jetliner crashed into the South Tower. A cloud of fire and smoke burst from the tower, with pieces of steel shooting in all directions skyward as if they were toothpicks tossed into the air.

Handschuh had no idea of the extent of carnage that was unfolding. Nor did he realize that he was about to become one of the casualties.

It was 9:03 a.m.

* * *

Kathy Kemp heard the explosion over the phone. On the TV, she saw the fireball burst from the tower's side. She shouted "Jack" into the phone receiver. But on the other end of the line, Jack was not responding.

"I just started screaming," she said. "Just screaming. I'm not that type of person, but I just screamed. It was so horrific."

Jack Kemp would later remember that he was gazing out his office window overlooking New York Harbor as he talked on the phone with Kathy. But he never saw the hijacked United Airlines Flight 175 jetliner bearing down on the South Tower.

The plane had come from the west. It streaked over an industrial scrap yard in Jersey City that would later recycle some of the Trade Center's largest beams, then banked slightly to the left as it passed the Statue of Liberty. When it reached the southern tip of Manhattan and a former Revolutionary War fort known as "The Battery," the plane dipped its left wing slightly as it aimed at an angle at the South Tower. Seconds later the plane's nose slammed into the eighty-fifth floor. Its left wing swept like a massive scythe across the seventy-eighth floor—only eight floors above Kemp's office.

Kemp fell backwards into a bookcase about ten feet away. A dozen books, framed photos, and mementoes fell on his head and shoulders.

Smoke filled his office.

Kemp could see, however. He got to his feet and reached for the phone. Kathy was still on the line.

"I've got to go," he said, then hung up and burst from his office into the hall.

Five of Kemp's closest staff members, including Nancy Kennedy, were waiting by the elevator bank. None had been injured. The rest of the floor was empty.

Kemp stopped at the office refrigerator and stuffed the pockets of his brown-and-green checked sport jacket with bottles of water and diet soda. He then headed with the five others to a stairwell, their feet crunching on the dozens of ceiling tiles that had fallen.

The overhead lights in the hallway were out. Some light still came from the walls of windows on the floor. Otherwise, the group was enveloped in a murky grayness of smoke from small fires that suddenly popped up all around them. Somewhere deep within the steel, glass, and concrete, the building seemed to groan in pain.

Just short of the stairway door, Kemp and the others ran into even more debris from the ceiling, dangling wires, and pipes. They were trapped. The door was blocked.

The group paused to think of alternatives. *Is there an unblocked stairwell somewhere else on the floor?*

Then, from the darkness, they heard a voice.

"If you hear me, follow me. Follow me."

Kemp and the others inched forward toward the voice, stepping in the darkness over wreckage on the floor and ducking past more wires, pipes, and pieces of the ceiling.

They felt their way around a corner and came face-to-face with a man they had never seen before: Dereck Lovell. The substitute security guard.

In one hand Lovell held a bullhorn. In the other, a flashlight. He also knew a way off the floor.

Lovell led Kemp and the others around another corner and down another hallway to a stairwell on the other side of the floor that was not blocked. Like most floors of the South Tower, the seventieth floor was served by only three stairwells—and two of them were already blocked when Kemp's group tried to escape. It's not clear whether they would have found the third stairwell.

Lovell had already scouted the stairs, however. He pushed open a door and the group entered another world. The lights were on. The air was mostly free of smoke and dust.

Lovell held the door for Kemp and the others. Then Lovell turned back into the darkness. He wanted to make another round of the floor.

* * *

Phil McArdle had already picked up the computer program from his wife in the Bronx and was back in his Jeep Grand Cherokee and on the way to his morning meeting at the FDNY training academy when the news broke of the first plane hitting the North Tower.

As usual, McArdle's car radio was tuned to WINS, one of the city's all-news stations whose marketing slogan was "You give us twenty-two minutes, we'll give you the world."

McArdle knew this would be a long day. His Hazmat 1 unit, with his replacement, was likely already on the road to the Trade Center. McArdle wanted to be there, too. "This was not my first rodeo," he later said.

He pulled into FDNY's training academy on Randalls Island just after the second hijacked jetliner struck the South Tower and met another Hazmat 1 firefighter, Jeff Borkowski.

McArdle and Borkowski commandeered one of the FDNY's Chevrolet Suburbans in the academy parking lot. They stuffed air tanks and other gear into the back of the truck, then set off for the Trade Center, crossing into Manhattan and heading south on the FDR Drive. Two trucks from Hazmat

1 had already arrived at the Trade Center, along with two trucks from Squad 288, its sister unit in the Maspeth firehouse.

Seventeen firefighters poured onto the street from the units' trucks, including McArdle's friend, Dennis Scauso, and Jonathan Hohmann, who came to work early so McArdle could depart for his meeting at the fire department academy. Leaving one firefighter with the trucks to take radio calls and fetch special pieces of equipment, the firefighters walked first to the North Tower, witnesses later said. Then several reportedly peeled off and headed toward the South Tower.

Meanwhile, four more firefighters from Hazmat 1 and Squad 288 showed up. They had been at the FDNY's headquarters in Brooklyn for routine medical check-ups. When they heard about the jetliner crashing into the Trade Center, they rushed over the Brooklyn Bridge. The FDNY's chief of hazardous operations, Jack Fanning, also arrived from the academy on Randalls Island.

* * *

Inside the South Tower, Kemp's group of four men and two women tried to walk down the stairs as quickly as possible. The women went first.

Alison Greeley grabbed Nancy Kennedy's hand. Greeley, twenty-nine, was terrified of falling—with good reason. She was pregnant.

None of the others knew, however. Greeley had planned to announce her pregnancy at the staff meeting that morning but never got the chance.

Greeley peered down at the stairs. Someone had spilled coffee and the floor looked slippery. She squeezed Kennedy's hand tighter.

The group covered ten floors, then twenty, then thirty.

"Keep up a steady pace," Kemp called out.

Greeley and Kennedy, still holding hands, started whipping each other around turns—almost like children in a playground game.

They had met years before, growing up in Ridgewood, New Jersey. Both lived on the same street as Kemp. Kennedy sometimes babysat Kemp's two daughters. One of Kemp's daughters was a bridesmaid in Kennedy's wedding.

Neither woman initially aspired to work in a brokerage house. In college, Kennedy first majored in physical therapy, Greeley in art history. But Kemp noticed something in their work habits and personalities that seemed suited for his world of financial marketing and hired them.

Now, here he was, running down stairs to escape a life-threatening emergency and not knowing what dangers awaited them at the bottom—if they made it that far.

"I was kicking myself now for keeping these kids too long," he said of his delay by calling his wife on his office phone.

As the group descended, Kemp's fears heightened. Long cracks began to crease the stairway walls. As the group descended farther, the cracks became wide, V-shaped fissures.

Kemp didn't say anything to the others. "I didn't want to scare them," he said.

Suddenly, a man ran past them, his face crimson and his shirt stained with blood. Two of the men in the group tried to stop him and ask if he needed help. But he pushed past.

"What's your name?" Greeley called out.

"Keith," the man responded.

"Good luck, Keith," Greeley shot back. "We'll see you at the bottom!"

Deeper in the stairway, the group came upon a man in worse shape. Silvion Ramsundar, thirty-two years old and an assistant vice president of an investment bank on the eightieth floor, had a gaping wound in his upper left chest. He looked exhausted and leaned against the stairway's railing.

Before either plane hit, Ramsundar had gone to the forty-fourth floor cafeteria for coffee and a bagel. Then he heard the loud bang from the North Tower resounding through the walls of his own building. "It sounded like a large pot falling," he said.

Minutes later, there was a public address announcement that a plane had struck the North Tower and that South Tower workers should return to their offices and remain calm to await more instructions.

"So that's what I did," Ramsundar said.

Back on the eightieth floor, his office suite was deserted. Ramsundar figured the rest of the staff had escaped, so he, too, headed for the stairs. He walked down two floors to the seventy-eighth floor known as the Sky Lobby, a larger space where he figured he might catch an express elevator that would take him quickly to the building lobby.

It was just before 9:00 a.m. Dozens of workers were also waiting for elevators.

Three minutes later, the second jetliner struck, its wing slicing through the Sky Lobby.

"When the metal hit my chest, it felt warm," Ramsundar said.

But he was alive. He looked around. Bodies were scattered across the lobby. He figured at least fifty, maybe 100.

He gazed down a hallway toward a bright light. It was a hole in the side of the building, cut by the wing.

He got to his feet and found a clear stairway—the same one that Dereck Lovell, the security guard, led Kemp's team to on the seventieth floor.

Ramsundar struggled to make it down several dozen floors. Then he stopped to rest. "I couldn't move my arm," he recalled.

That's when Kemp's staff arrived. One of the men, Stan Kapica, took out a handkerchief and soaked it in water from one of Kemp's water bottles. Another man, Doug Brown, took the handkerchief and pressed it into the hole in Ramsundar's chest.

Kapica and Brown then put their arms around Ramsundar and kept walking down the stairs.

Close to the bottom, another member of Kemp's team, Greg Lowe, came across an overweight man, gasping for breath. Lowe grabbed the man's briefcase and led him down.

At 9:34 a.m., Kemp's staff reached the street.

Three minutes later, in northern Virginia, the third hijacked jetliner, American Airlines Flight 77, slammed into the Pentagon.

* * *

Ten miles from the Pentagon, at CIA headquarters in McLean, Virginia, FBI agent Mark Rossini, sat at his desk in a windowless basement room. Rossini, who had earned his reputation with the FBI investigating a variety of white-collar criminal cases in New York City including financial fraud and political corruption, had spent much of the last year as the bureau's liaison with the CIA's special team of intelligence officers known as "Alec Station," who tracked the whereabouts and machinations of the elusive Saudi-born Islamist, Osama bin Laden and his terrorist network known as al-Qaeda.

Rossini had already spent months on the ground in Nairobi, Kenya, piecing together details of the al-Qaeda bombing of the US embassy there. He was one of two FBI agents with Alec Station now.

That morning, Rossini did not hear the news that a plane had struck the Trade Center from the CIA, the FBI, or even the US military, which had reportedly ordered jet fighters into the sky after airport officials in Boston learned that a plane had been hijacked.

Rossini got the news when a Wall Street contact phoned him.

"Did you hear what happened at the Trade Center?" the contact asked.

Now, with two hijacked jets crashing into the Trade Center's Towers, another into the Pentagon, and a fourth still in the air over Pennsylvania, Rossini instinctively knew that bin Laden's operatives were probably behind it. Rossini and Alec Station had already been tracking two al-Qaeda operatives who had been in the United States for most of the past eighteen months. Were those guys involved?

Rossini feared the worst. Could the FBI and the CIA have stopped these hijackings before they took place?.

* * *

In New York City, Security Guard Dereck Lovell was still in the South Tower. After checking the seventieth floor and finding it was empty, he headed to the same stairwell where he guided Kemp's group to safety.

Lovell knew he had to move fast. He quickly descended ten flights. Then twenty. Then thirty and forty. With almost thirty flights to go, Lovell came upon two elderly men. Lovell recognized them from the Morgan Stanley cafeteria where he occasionally took his breaks. The men walked slowly, their breathing laborious as they leaned on the railing.

Lovell slowed. He wrapped his left arm around one, his right arm around the other and kept walking down with the two men.

Lovell finally reached the bottom around 9:50 a.m. He escorted the men to an ambulance. As he walked away, it occurred to Lovell that he never asked their names. Nor did they ask his. As so often happened that day, strangers reached out to strangers and never knew their names.

Lovell headed north along West Street. Smoke billowed overhead from the North Tower. A block or two away, he heard a series of sharp, thunderous bangs—like a giant jack hammer pounding steel.

Lovell turned. The South Tower was collapsing, each floor pancaking into the one beneath it. One by one. Bang. Bang. Bang. Bang. Bang. As each floor collapsed, a harsh and powerful wind gushed out.

Lovell started to run. Then he sprinted. He covered another block, then ducked into a building.

A cloud of black-gray dust swept up West Street. Chunks of concrete, glass, and steel—and all manner of desks, filing cabinets, chairs, and other office furniture—pummeled the street. Lovell curled up behind a wall.

It was 9:59 a.m.

* * *

David Handschuh, the photographer, also tried to run.

From his spot on West Street where he had been photographing the firefighters running into the tower and the office workers falling from the upper floors, he instinctively turned and tried to find some sort of shelter when he heard the sharp bangs.

He headed toward Liberty Street, which stretched from the Trade Center toward the Hudson River, a block away.

He never made it to the river, though.

The wind from the tower's floor-by-floor collapse pushed up Liberty Street with the same tornado-like power that swept past Dereck Lovell several blocks away. It lifted Handschuh and pushed him along the street. Handschuh stumbled. He couldn't keep his balance and felt as if he were being tossed like some sort of rag doll. Later, the FDNY's report on his experience indicated he had been pushed (or tossed) 20 to 30 feet.

He landed on his back, with his head and shoulders under a parked car, his legs still exposed. Pieces of concrete and steel slammed into his legs.

The crashing continued for nearly a minute. Then silence—except for the snapping of fires and the honk-honk-honking of car alarms.

Several firefighters who had taken cover nearby ran toward Handschuh. "Don't worry brother. We'll get you out," he remembers them saying.

The firefighters pulled Handschuh from under the car and cleared the concrete and pieces of steel from his legs, then ran to save others.

Handschuh tried to move. But his legs were numb. He couldn't see. His glasses were gone—blown off, somewhere.

But he still had his cameras.

And he was alive.

* * *

Phil McArdle and Jeff Borkowski pulled up in the FDNY Chevrolet Suburban and parked on West Street just as the South Tower gave way and fell. A large crowd of office workers ran past them in the opposite direction.

Everything turned black and gray. McArdle and Borkowski could not see beyond the Chevy's windshield. An FDNY report on their actions would later conclude that "visibility was essentially zero."

Pieces of shattered glass, broken pipes, pulverized concrete, and even office equipment slammed into the car's roof and hood. Somehow, the windshield did not cave in. Outside the truck, McArdle and Borkowski heard the slap-slap-slap of people falling as they crashed into other cars or debris that now littered the street.

McArdle and Borkowski waited for the downpour of debris to stop. Then they opened the Suburban's doors and stepped out. "I could barely see my hand," McArdle said.

Neither firefighter had the protective black coats, pants, or helmets that the FDNY's firefighters wore to shield themselves in fires. When they rushed out of the training academy, there were no extra helmets or protective coats—just the air tanks they packed in the Suburban.

McArdle and Borkowski strapped the tanks on their backs, then stepped forward a few feet. West Street was dark, filled with steel beams and concrete from the South Tower. The FDNY report would later say: "While others continued to retreat both firefighters continued to advance into the scene."

They found several bodies. Then they encountered a few others who had been injured but were still alive and trying to run but had difficulty breathing.

McArdle and Borkowski took off their facemasks with hoses that connected to their air tanks and let several people take a fresh breath of clean air.

They turned left on Liberty Street. After feeling their way for another 10 to 15 yards, they noticed a man on the ground amid the rubble.

It was David Handschuh.

He had been lying on the street since the other firefighters pulled him from under the car and moved on to save others who had been buried in the rubble. He couldn't move his legs, though. And he was having trouble breathing.

McArdle and Borkowski, fearing the North Tower might soon collapse and send more debris onto the surrounding streets, knew they had to move Handschuh to a safer spot. But Handschuh balked. He wanted to stay where he was. He didn't have his glasses—and could barely see beyond his outstretched arm. But he was still holding his cameras.

McArdle minced no words. He told Handschuh his life was in danger. Or as the FDNY report on their meeting noted, that this was "a combat situation" and that "he may not survive subsequent attacks if they were to occur."

With that, McArdle and Borkowski lifted Handschuh off the ground—McArdle holding Handschuh's shoulders and Borkowski his legs—and carried him several hundred feet to a delicatessen where others who had been injured had been placed. "Somebody had apparently broken the deli's window," McArdle said. "There is so much debris and stuff in everyone's eyes. They were taking water out of the deli and just pouring it over their heads and into their eyes." An emergency medical technician—no one knows who—gave Handschuh a drink of water and rinsed out his eyes.

Another *Daily News* photographer, Todd Maisel, saw Handschuh and snapped a picture. It showed Handschuh lying by a rack of snack chips and a glass refrigerator door in the delicatessen, his legs bent under him, his arms stretched out and his mouth agape as if crying out in pain. Two bones—the tibula and fibula—in his right leg had shattered. His body was caked with dust.

Handschuh reached for his cameras and handed them to Maisel.

"Take these back to the newsroom," Handschuh said, adding that he thought he had taken some decent photos that documented the attack.

The next day, on page two, the *Daily News* published Handschuh's photograph of the plane as it smashed into the South Tower in the massive fireball. From the delicatessen, Handschuh was ferried by police and EMTs across the Hudson to a hospital in Bayonne, New Jersey where doctors could assess his broken leg. After surgery and several months of recovery, he had to learn to walk again. He would not return to the *Daily News* until early 2002. He told his editors that, for the time being, he wanted to be assigned to photographing feature stories.

"I didn't want to do breaking news," he said. "I wound up taking a lot of feature pictures of food. It was a blessing."

* * *

Hundreds of miles away—and coinciding almost to the minute with the collapse of the South Tower—passengers on the fourth hijacked jetliner were trying to fight back.

United Airlines Flight 93 had taken off from Newark an hour earlier, heading for San Francisco. Over western Ohio, the hijackers seized control of the plane and turned it around. Authorities would later conclude that the hijackers were aiming for either the US Capitol or the White House. But no one really knows for sure.

In this case, the hijackers never made it to their target. Passengers got on their cell phones and called their homes and offices—and learned of the other hijacked jetliners that had already struck the Trade Center's twin towers and the Pentagon. This fourth jetliner was surely on another mission of mass murder. A group of passengers ran up the aisles and charged the cockpit.

So began what authorities concluded was the first counter-attack in the new war against terrorism.

The passengers, including Todd Beamer who was heard saying "let's roll" on a cell phone, tried to push their way through the cockpit door. The hijackers steering the plane, rocked it from side to side, trying to knock the passengers to the floor.

Finally, the hijackers drove the plane into the ground—once again in an enormous fireball. All thirty-three passengers and seven crew members died, along with the four hijackers.

It was 10:03 a.m.

* * *

The delicatessen where Phil McArdle and Jeff Borkowski brought David Handschuh was now beginning to look like a field hospital. Other injured people stumbled in or were carried. All were covered with gray dust—so much so that it was difficult to distinguish firefighters from police officers and office workers.

Several emergency medical technicians tried to tend to the injured. But all they had was water from the deli's refrigerators. Handschuh remembers an EMT trying again to wash out his eyes. But without his glasses, Handschuh still had trouble seeing clearly. McArdle and Borkowski washed out their eyes, then left and walked back toward West Street and the rubble to search for more victims who might still be alive.

McArdle and Borkowski inched forward, staying close to the World Financial Center, a set of four buildings, each rising from thirty-four to fifty-one stories across West Street from the Trade Center. The Financial Center had not been flattened by the Trade Center's debris, but the glass roof of an atrium that connected several buildings had been shattered. The Financial Center's outside walls were gouged with holes from the steel and concrete that had rained down like spears from the South Tower. One of the South Tower's massive beams had been blown off the tower with such force that it was thrust like a giant knife into the side of one of the Financial Center's buildings.

On West Street, squads of firefighters, police, and others tried to pick through the South Tower's rubble in search of victims who might still be alive. But many of the beams and concrete blocks were too heavy.

McArdle glanced toward the top of the North Tower and all the smoke and fire. He wondered if it was about to come apart. Pieces of glass and metal started to fall from the upper floors. They seemed like "sparkles," he thought, as the sunlight reflected off them. Was this another warning that the North Tower would also fall like its sister across the plaza?

For a moment, McArdle found himself thanking God that the North Tower was so tall. He had seen buildings fall before. And the smaller ones fell more quickly. Maybe he would have time to escape if the North Tower fell.

And then McArdle realized that the worst was actually happening: The North Tower was falling. Like the South Tower, the collapse began at the top, with each of the upper floors pounding into the one below it, sending massive puffs of black smoke into the air.

McArdle and Borkowski tried to sprint across the rubble atop West Street to the World Financial Center. They jumped through the frames of the Financial Center's atrium where the glass had been shattered. Inside, they found several large columns that support the Financial Center.

McArdle huddled behind one column with his arms crossed over his chest. "Like a mummy," he said later. Borkowski was behind another column.

Then came the rush of rubble. It began with a "great deafening noise," McArdle said. Like "the world is falling apart."

McArdle pressed his body against the column. Steel, concrete, glass, and other debris crashed through the atrium's frames and pounded into the floor around him. The flood was so fast, violent, and powerful that McArdle felt a "positive wave of energy." Then, a "negative wave" as if a massive vacuum sucked away the air. McArdle pressed himself even harder against the column, hoping that he would not be pulled into the debris still flying past him on each side. He pushed the mask that connects to his air tank over his nose and mouth and tried to breathe. Then came a blast of heat—as if he had suddenly been placed in a giant oven.

Then everything went black.

For Phil McArdle, the day was just beginning.

"I knew immediately we lost a lot of people," he said.

It was 10:28 a.m.

Office workers and residents of nearby apartment buildings run for their lives after the collapse of the World Trade Center's twin towers. Photo by Lorenzo Ciniglio/Sygma/Sygma via Getty Images.

3

Dust

The death of a building is never quiet. Steel slams into steel. Concrete crushes concrete. Foundations split and crack. Windows shatter in their frames. Pipes break. Wires snap.

Then comes the avalanche of debris and a final deafening crash to the ground.

And then—silence.

"When the sound stopped," Phil McArdle said, "I knew the building was down."

For the second time that morning, McArdle had managed to escape the collapse of a 110-story skyscraper. Now he confronted another dilemma. He was entombed in a room of rubble. He couldn't move or see. The narrow space behind the column where he had taken refuge was as dark as a coffin. He wiggled his fingers, flexed his arms, nodded his head, twisted his torso. But when he stretched out an arm, he could not distinguish his hand and fingers.

McArdle quickly realized that if he wanted to escape, he had to find some sort of passage through the rubble to crawl through. A small hole or narrow tunnel would do the job.

But where was such an opening? And how far was "out"? The avalanche of steel and concrete seemed massive. Was his tomb five feet deep? Or ten? Or fifty? Or just one foot?

McArdle had no idea. Nor did he know how many minutes had passed after the North Tower fell or which direction he should take to escape—or if escaping was actually possible in this rubble-strewn landscape.

He took a moment to get his bearings. To the east, on the other side of the pillar that had been his shield: more rubble and fires from the fallen towers. To the west: the Hudson River and possible safety.

He reached to his right, then to his left. A narrow opening. He crawled a few feet over several steel beams and blocks of concrete. He pushed away a smaller piece of steel and a hunk of concrete. He stepped over more steel.

And then: faint light ahead—gray, like the evening twilight.

McArdle shimmied into a larger space. Was he atop the rubble? Or just in a pocket? He had no idea. He inched forward a step or two more, then called out: "Is anyone out there?"

From behind another pillar, Jeff Borkowski answered.

"I'll be there in a minute," McArdle said, crawling toward the voice.

* * *

So began the torturous ordeal of finding survivors and counting the dead and missing.

Is anyone out there?

Those four words became a mantra on that first day across the 16-acre patch of New York City that the world was already calling "Ground Zero." Police and firefighters wandered across the rubble, trying to connect with other colleagues who were still alive or to find those who had been killed. *Is anyone out there?* They came across a few bodies that were intact. But the collapse of the buildings not only killed many, but it dismembered them into fragments that defied identification. In some cases, even gender and race were difficult to determine.

McArdle thought back to another day of mass death and a grim search for survivors. It was April 19, 1995, a Wednesday. A massive bomb made of ammonium nitrate—common farm fertilizer—that had been packed into a Ryder rental truck by two far-right extremists who felt the federal government had become too tyrannical, exploded outside the Alfred P. Murrah federal building in Oklahoma City, Oklahoma. The blast was so powerful that it pulled down the face of the building, exposing offices and conference rooms, and a daycare center. Among the 168 people who died were nineteen children. At the time, it was the deadliest act of terrorism on American soil.

Now at Ground Zero, firefighters passed the word to gather for a roll call a block north of the Trade Center on West Street. Here, the FDNY could get a sense of who lived, who died, or who was missing. But as he arrived at the spot,

McArdle knew there was no need to count. This was another devastating loss of life from terrorism—but far worse than Oklahoma City. "It was obvious," he said later.

Usually, firefighters come and go in the small teams that correspond to a specific ladder truck or engine they are assigned to. But McArdle noticed that the firefighters at the roll call seemed scattered and glum—a few from this ladder truck, a few from another. So many firefighters were missing or dead that no teams seemed intact.

As the afternoon wore on, the numbers emerged—so horrific that they seemed surreal at first. More than 440 of the roughly 1,200 first responders who rushed to the Trade Center that morning had been killed. This included 343 firefighters, twenty-three New York City police officers, and thirty-seven officers from the Port Authority police force. Three courtroom guards who ran from the federal and New York State courthouses at Foley Square a half mile from the attacks were killed. So were an FBI agent and a Secret Service agent.

Among the FDNY's losses was the chief of the entire 11,000-member department, Peter Ganci. Another twenty-three deputy and battalion chiefs were gone too, along with the FDNY's beloved Roman Catholic chaplain, Father Mychal Judge, and the city's deputy fire commissioner, William Meehan.

For the individual FDNY units, some of the losses were especially heavy in part because the attack coincided with a change of the overnight shift to the day shift. Many firefighters who were scheduled to end their shifts around 9:00 a.m., jumped on the trucks with their colleagues and headed to the Trade Center.

The ladder and engine companies based at a fire station near Lincoln Center lost fifteen firefighters. Rescue 1, which had sped down West Street just ahead of photographer David Handschuh, lost eleven. Rescue 5, which rushed across the Verrazzano-Narrows suspension bridge from its base in Staten Island also lost eleven. A ladder company based in the East Village lost eleven more. And a ladder truck based near the South Street Seaport on the lower tip of Manhattan lost eight.

McArdle's firehouse in Maspeth, Queens suffered the worst losses. Nineteen firefighters from Hazmat 1 and Squad 288 had been killed. The dead included Jonathan Hohmann, who had come to work early that morning so McArdle could leave for his training meeting at the FDNY's academy on Randalls

Island. Several other Hazmat 1 and Squad 288 firefighters who perished were supposed to be at routine medical exams at FDNY headquarters in Brooklyn. But when they heard of the attacks, they rushed to the scene on their own.

It was that kind of day. Over and over, police, firefighters, and other first responders were joined by all manner of volunteers who ran toward the fire and rubble to help.

One of those volunteers was Lawrence Byrnes who was sixty-eight years old. He had retired from the FDNY as a battalion chief three years earlier and had just returned from a vacation. When he heard the news about the attack on the Trade Center, Byrnes jumped in his wife's car and drove from his home in Valley Stream, Long Island, to his old firehouse on Duane Street, about six blocks from the Trade Center. The trip normally takes at least forty minutes. Byrnes positioned his car behind a police cruiser with its lights flashing and made it in eighteen minutes.

The two-story brick firehouse was empty as Byrnes walked in—except for a rookie firefighter, Antonios Benetatos, who had been left behind.

Benetatos had graduated from the FDNY academy only a few months earlier and was still working through his on-the-job probationary training. As a "probie," Benetatos had mostly watched how the other firefighters trained and interacted during an emergency. But he had yet to actually "fight" a fire. And when the Trade Center's towers were struck, the other firefighters feared that Benetatos was too inexperienced to come with them, so they told him to stay put and monitor a radio.

Byrnes told Benetatos to grab some protective gear and follow him.

"Stick with me, kid," Byrnes told the rookie.

"He just told me to stay by his side," Benetatos recalled. "And I did."

Byrnes didn't even have protective boots. He wore sneakers. He couldn't find an extra firefighting helmet so he scoured the firehouse and found a white dress cap with a cloth top—the kind that chiefs wear to parades.

Byrnes put on his hat. It surely wouldn't protect him from falling debris. But he figured the other firefighters on the scene would respect a chief rather than just a retired guy with gray hair who was wearing sneakers.

The two ran to the Trade Center and set up a command post and a triage center. It was Benetatos's first fire.

In Arlington, Virginia, at the Pentagon, an Army lieutenant colonel carried a woman through a broken window, then went back inside to rescue a man whose clothes were on fire. "You don't leave your comrades on the battlefield," the lieutenant colonel said later. "To me, this was the battlefield."

An army staff sergeant who worked as a Pentagon cafeteria cook carried out a woman who could not cry for help because of smoke inhalation and was instead clapping so she could be found. She later called the cook her "guardian angel."

Another soldier who was assigned to the Pentagon's tourist office had trained as an emergency medical technician and volunteer firefighter before he enlisted. He ignored signs to stay back and ran around police barricades to assist at a makeshift triage tent. Then he volunteered as part of a six-man team that went back into the Pentagon in search of survivors, walking through calf-deep water and holding wet rags over their noses and mouths to protect themselves from breathing toxic air.

The toll at the Pentagon was shocking, especially for a building that was the heart and soul of the world's most powerful military and, as such, was supposed to be well-defended. The 125 people killed at the Pentagon included seventy civilians, thirty-three navy sailors, twenty-one army soldiers, and the army's deputy chief of staff, Lt. General Timothy Maude.

Back at the Trade Center in Lower Manhattan, Rick Rescoria, a retired US Army colonel who supervised security across the twenty-two floors occupied by the Morgan Stanley investment firm in the South Tower, was credited with helping hundreds of people to safety. He died when he went back into the South Tower to check for stragglers.

Also, in the South Tower, Welles Crowther, an equities trader on the 104th floor and a volunteer firefighter back in his hometown of Upper Nyack, New York, carried an injured woman on his back to safety. Then, returning to the tower's upper floors with a team of FDNY firefighters and covering his nose and mouth with a red bandana as protection against the jet fuel that was burning, he perished in the building's collapse. His heroism became legendary when survivors talked of a man in a red bandana. He was credited with saving at least eighteen people.

These stories of heroism—many emerging within hours of the attacks—became a much-needed balm. But such bravery, as noble as it was, could not mask the inevitable, unavoidable, and heart-wrenching truth of September 11—that so many were dead or missing.

On the four hijacked jetliners, all 246 passengers and crew members had been killed, along with the nineteen hijackers. The youngest to die was a two-year-old girl, flying to Los Angeles with her parents to visit Disneyland. The oldest was an eighty-five-year-old man, heading to San Francisco to attend his son's wedding. Also, among the passengers were David Angell, the co-creator of the TV sitcoms, *Frasier* and *Wings*; Charles Edward Jones, an astronaut; Mari-Rae Sopper, a college gymnastics coach; and Barbara Olson, a TV commentator and wife of US Solicitor General Ted Olson.

At the Trade Center, it would take months to fully tabulate the missing and dead, in part because more than 1,000 victims simply vanished without a trace, their bodies vaporized or dismembered in the violent collapse of the buildings. But within hours on that first day, it became clear that the toll would be long and tragic—especially for those firms on the uppermost floors.

In the North Tower, the Cantor Fitzgerald brokerage house lost 658 staffers, including Tom Strada. The Marsh McLennan management firm, whose offices were just a few floors below Cantor Fitzgerald's, lost another 358 workers and consultants. In the South Tower, the Aon Corporation lost 176. Fiduciary Trust International lost ninety-eight, including Ron Breitweiser.

The Trade Center even lost its new security chief, John O'Neill, who had retired only two weeks earlier from the FBI, where he was regarded as one of the nation's top counterterrorism experts.

A year earlier, O'Neill joined other FBI agents and NYPD detectives at the Trade Center's Windows on the World restaurant to celebrate the twentieth anniversary of New York City's special Joint Terrorism Task Force that investigated the 1993 Trade Center terrorist bombing. Mark Rossini made a point of coming. Rossini admired O'Neill as not just a mentor but an inspiration. O'Neill, in turn, considered Rossini to be one of a talented team of FBI agents who he expected to become influential leaders in the growing war against terrorism. Indeed, O'Neill had personally assigned Rossini to be the FBI's liaison with the CIA's unit that monitored Osama bin Laden's al-Qaeda network.

The night was filled with boisterous banter from law enforcement colleagues who had devoted years to the murky job of tracking international terrorists.

And at one point, Rossini remembers gazing out the restaurant's window, hoping to take in what otherwise would be a majestic view of New York harbor and the city lights. But on this night, there was no view. Clouds had enveloped the top of the North Tower. It was as if someone had hung gray curtains on the restaurant's wall of windows. "You couldn't see out the windows which made me feel a bit uneasy," Rossini recalled years later. "I said to myself that a pilot in a plane couldn't see us either. It's kind of creepy to think about."

* * *

As he walked across the jagged rubble, McArdle struggled to stay focused on the job at hand. He tried to keep his mind off the horrific numbers of dead and missing. But he soon learned news he could not ignore. His brother, John, a retired veteran of the NYPD's elite emergency services unit, put his uniform back on that morning and rushed to the Trade Center. So did another brother, Brendan, a civilian operating engineer at several Manhattan buildings who was also a member of one of New York City's volunteer fire units.

Were his brothers okay? McArdle did not learn until hours later that they were safe. In the meantime, McArdle focused his attention on the rubble, wondering if dangerous toxins or other hazardous materials had been released when the buildings collapsed.

McArdle needed only a few minutes and just a short walk back to the rubble to reach the conclusion he feared in his gut: The air and land were indeed now filled with toxins.

The long-term impact of those toxins would return later to sicken McArdle and thousands of others.

* * *

Across the New York metropolitan region and, from there, across America in emotional ripples, relatives contacted other relatives, and friends contacted friends—all in search of the smallest morsel of news about someone they knew at the Trade Center or at the Pentagon or perhaps flying on one of the hijacked jetliners.

For many, the phone did not ring. In Chatham, New Jersey, Terry Strada spent the day hoping for another call from her husband, Tom. But it never came. The same was true in Middletown, New Jersey, for Kristen Breitweiser. No call from her husband, Ron, either.

At her beach house in the Jersey Shore town of Mantoloking, Kathy Kemp spent most of the morning watching the televised horror.

"It was surreal," Kathy said later. "You couldn't believe what you were watching."

The night before had been so peaceful. Jack and Kathy had gone to dinner at their favorite lobster restaurant. That morning, Jack loaded his blue Mercedes sports car with his suits and headed north. The relaxed pace of summer was over, Jack figured. After working that day at the Trade Center, he planned to head to the couple's home in Ridgewood, New Jersey. Kathy planned to stay at the beach house for a few more days, then join him.

Now, with her comfortable beach life suddenly in turmoil, Kathy's worries deepened considerably. It had been three hours since she heard from Jack in that rushed phone call as the plane struck the South Tower. Where was he?

After a terrorist bomb exploded at the Trade Center in 1993, she remembered that Jack needed ninety minutes to make his way down the stairs to safety. This time, Kathy feared that her husband would not have enough time. The South Tower had already fallen—in less than an hour.

Kathy thought of the couple's oldest daughter, Kristin, who was five months pregnant and had already endured one miscarriage. Kathy wondered if Jack would ever see his first grandchild.

Then Kathy screamed. "Noises were coming out of my mouth that I couldn't believe," she said later.

Just after 11:00 a.m., she walked outside the house to a wooden dock on the edge of the bay to call Kristin. As she spoke to her daughter, Kathy's cell phone beeped with a call-waiting signal.

It was Jack—finally.

"Kath, I'm alive."

* * *

In Chicago, Tamara Duker looked out her office window at the Sears Tower, a 110-story skyscraper that was a Midwestern rival to New York's World Trade

Center. Duker, who had lost her sister, Sara, in 1996 when a Palestinian suicide bomber blew up a bus in downtown Jerusalem, suddenly felt a need to be far away from any skyscrapers and another terrorist bombing. She left work and went to her apartment. She needed a refuge, someplace protected, someplace far from possible danger.

In Demarest, New Jersey, Bert Ammerman, a high school principal, thought back to the day in 1988 when he heard the news his brother had been killed by a terrorist bomb aboard a Pan Am jetliner flying from London to New York for the Christmas holidays. Ammerman knew the students and staff would be upset and fearful even though they might not have lost any relatives or friends at the Trade Center or the Pentagon. He quickly started planning for a memorial service.

In Dix Hills, Long Island, four-year-old Juliette Scauso could not imagine her father, Dennis, a firefighter with Hazmat 1, not walking through the door after work—as usual. She was only four years old. But with so many relatives and neighbors now arriving at her parents' home, she sensed that something awful had just happened.

In Middletown, Connecticut, Brett Eagleson, a fifteen-year-old high school sophomore, also tried to make sense of the news that his father, John Bruce Eagleson, an executive with a corporation that ran shopping malls who went to the Trade Center that morning for a meeting to discuss the center's underground mall, also might not be coming home. Like Juliette, it was hard to imagine that his father might have disappeared from his life. Even more broadly, what would this mean for his family?

Eagleson felt numb as he tried to imagine the possibilities.

* * *

In his office at the CIA, FBI counterterrorism agent Mark Rossini also found himself wrestling with his own set of imagined possibilities. How would the bureau face down terrorist threats without John O'Neill? It seemed impossible, Rossini thought. O'Neill always seemed bigger than life and even indestructable. From his assignment in Nairobi, Kenya, Rossini knew first-hand how devastating a terrorist bomb could be on unsuspecting people at "soft targets" such as offices. Had those same terrorists who attacked Nairobi now killed O'Neill?

Rossini had no time to dive into that question—or the rising anguish and anger that crept into his thoughts. He tried to focus. Right now, he couldn't think of the loss of his friend. He tried to busy himself in collecting information on the attacks. He figured he would wait for a list of passengers on the hijacked flights, including the hijackers. Maybe he would find a clue there.

* * *

In Midtown Manhattan, a block from Madison Square Garden, Father Brian Jordan walked into his church, St. Francis of Assisi, and came upon a scene he rarely witnessed in the middle of a weekday. The church was packed. Many were frightened at what had taken place at the Trade Center. Others wondered how they might get to their homes in the suburbs or other parts of the city.

The community of Franciscan priests who ran the parish let people use the church's restrooms. The priests and others passed out water and even attempted to offer some words of comfort.

Jordan felt restless. He removed the sandals that he and other Franciscans often wore with their iconic brown robes and slipped into a pair of running shoes he used to train for 26.2-mile marathons. He grabbed a bottle of Holy Water and headed for the door. As he was about to leave, another Franciscan priest stopped Jordan to pass on the news that Father Mychal Judge had been killed when the buildings fell.

"I was stunned and speechless," Jordan recalled. "I can't believe it. How can this be?"

Like John O'Neill had been to scores of new FBI agents, Judge had been a mentor to a generation of younger Franciscan priests. When Jordan was a student and a rough-and-tumble rugby player at Siena College in Upstate New York, it was Judge who personally invited him to join the Franciscans. But now, Judge was dead? From terrorism?

Jordan felt he had to make a choice. "And I had to make it right away," he later said. He could "sit on my backside" and "cry for my loss." Or he could head to the Trade Center and "minister among the people like Mychal Judge was doing."

He left and started walking the three miles to the Trade Center.

* * *

John Ryan also walked that day from midtown to the Trade Center.

Ryan, a lieutenant on the Port Authority police force that monitors the bus terminal on 42nd Street, had taken the day off to escort his daughter to her first day of nursery school. But when he heard that the Trade Center—another Port Authority police responsibility—had been attacked, he headed to Manhattan from his home in Seaford, Long Island. He stopped at the bus terminal to change into his police uniform. Then, after finding no cars to take him to the Trade Center, he started walking.

Like Jordan, Ryan was a marathon runner so he had no trouble covering the distance to the Trade Center.

As he arrived, Ryan came upon a scene that was both frighteningly desperate and heroically inspirational. Scores of police officers, firefighters, and others had formed lines at the top of the rubble pile, searching for possible survivors. Those at the front of the lines dug with their hands or with small shovels, and filled plastic buckets with almost anything they could lift. Concrete. Steel. Glass. Then they passed the buckets, hand-to-hand, one-after-another down the line as other empty plastic buckets were funneled back to the top of the pile.

Ryan joined what would later be called "the bucket brigade." So did Father Jordan when he arrived.

The routine continued for hours—even a few days—until construction crews arrived with motorized backhoes. But the bucket brigade had little success in trying to find many survivors who might be alive under the rubble. The collapse had been too violent.

Only 200 whole bodies were found in the rubble. And only twenty people were pulled out alive—with Genelle Guzman-McMillan, a Port Authority office worker on the thirteenth floor of the North Tower, being the last. Guzman laid in the rubble for twenty-seven hours, her head wedged between two steel beams and pain shooting through her legs and torso. Only her left hand was free.

Finally, one of the bucket brigade workers spotted her hand. She spent another month in the hospital, recovering from four surgeries that were needed to save one of her legs and heal the burns that covered her face.

* * *

Several blocks north of the rubble, NYPD Detective Marty Davin leaned against a concrete barrier and stood guard over West Street.

That morning, Davin left his home in Nyack, New York, and drove toward the George Washington Bridge to cross into Manhattan and spend the day on assignment with a special anti-drug task force of NYPD detectives and state and federal agents. The group was so secret that its headquarters was a non-descript building that Davin and others nicknamed "The Bat Cave" after the mysterious lair where the Batman comic book character kept his disguise and souped-up car.

Davin's role was to go undercover. So that morning, he wore his usual jeans and T-shirt. When he arrived at "The Bat Cave," however, he was told to put on his NYPD uniform that he stored in his locker. There would be no need for undercover detectives.

For today at least, Davin was returning to the work he knew well. Once more, he would be a beat cop.

Davin dressed quickly. Then, his supervisor told him to head down West Street toward the Trade Center rubble.

All morning, Davin had listened to reports. Cops and firefighters missing. Office workers running in a panic—some of them jumping to their deaths from the top floors. Suddenly, what seemed like a perfect morning had turned dark.

And empty, too.

Davin made his way to the corner of Murray and West Streets. A block away, a piece of the North Tower still stood, tilting to one side as if it was about to make a final, humbling fall. Its windows were broken out and it looked like a decrepit version of a paper doll cutout.

It was now early afternoon. An inch or two of gray dust covered the street, along with thousands of pieces of paper—memos, stock reports, receipts—that had been blown by the squall-like gusts of wind from offices when the towers collapsed. Stuyvesant High School, the elite public institution that accepts only 800 of 30,000 applicants each year, was empty. So was a nearby outdoor basketball court.

Few cars or trucks rolled by. Even fewer people milled on the sidewalks—just another police officer warning passersby to avoid a building that was on fire and a firefighter who staggered from the Trade Center rubble with a gash across his face.

Then Davin saw me.

I had just walked the ten blocks from Canal Street where a tugboat dropped me and several dozen police officers and firefighters, along with several Catholic priests.

I approached Davin, asking him what he thought. Both of us looked down West Street toward the rubble.

"I've never seen anything like this," he said. "I don't think our grandchildren will see anything like this."

I jotted the comments in a notebook and asked his name.

"Marty Davin," he said. "NYPD."

Then I kept walking.

It was the kind of brief encounter journalists have all the time when reporting a major disaster. Some call it "man-on-the-street" reporting. Others refer to it as just collecting random observations.

I didn't even use Davin's comments in the column I dictated over a phone line I managed to find that connected me to my newsroom in New Jersey. I offered Davin's observations—ordinary as they were—to a long news story that was being compiled from dozens of staff contributions.

Then, I forgot about Davin.

Until twenty-three years later.

That brief encounter on West Street would turn out to be life-changing for Marty Davin.

* * *

Joe Connor made it back to New Jersey that night and rushed to the home of his cousin, Steve Schlag. No one had heard from Schlag since the first hijacked jetliner struck the North Tower.

Schlag's wife turned to Connor and asked a favor. That morning, Steve had driven to a rail station in Fair Lawn, New Jersey, to catch a commuter train. Could Connor bring Steve's car home?

Suddenly, Connor thought of his father, Frank, and another act of terrorism. Twenty-six years earlier, before being killed by another terrorist attack during lunch at Fraunces Tavern in Lower Manhattan, Frank Connor caught his final train to work from that same station.

Joe Connor tried not to focus on the loss of his father, but it was difficult as he slipped behind the wheel of his cousin's car in the train station's parking lot. What would this mean for his cousin's family? Would the killers ever be brought to justice?

Out of respect and wanting to preserve his cousin's memory, Connor did not adjust the seat to fit his shorter frame as he drove the eight miles back to his cousin's home. He also left the car radio tuned to the same station, WCBS. It would be days later before authorities confirmed his cousin's death.

* * *

Less than four miles away from the train station where Connor picked up his cousin's car, Nancy Kennedy was at her home in Ridgewood, New Jersey, studying the list of home telephone numbers for the twenty-six colleagues who worked with her Morgan Stanley marketing team on the seventieth floor of the South Tower.

After escaping from the Tower, she made her way to the Hudson River with her boss, Jack Kemp, and caught a ferry to Jersey City. Kemp had left his car in a Jersey City parking garage. The two were home by early afternoon.

But Kennedy now faced a difficult task. Did everyone else get home?

She picked up her phone and started calling. By 10:00 p.m., she had connected with everyone in the department—except one.

Tom Swift was missing.

It would be weeks before Kennedy and her fellow Morgan Stanley staffers were able to piece together some fragmented details about what may have happened to the colleague who had become such a positive force of energy and laughter in their office.

After the first jetliner struck the neighboring North Tower that morning and as the staff meeting broke up, Swift made a dash for the stairs. He was likely ahead of most others on the South Tower's seventieth floor. But when he had reached the fifty-ninth floor, he stopped. An announcement on the building's public address system advised all South Tower workers to return to their offices where they would be safe from falling debris on the outside plaza.

Swift opened a door on the stairwell and walked into a nearby office to find a phone.

He first dialed his wife, Jill, at work and left a voice message when she didn't answer:

"I'm fine. It wasn't my building. We're being evacuated. I'll call you when I can."

Then he phoned his mother, Frances.

"Mom, I'm alright," he said when she picked up. "Just do me a favor. Call Jill."

Then, for just a second or two, Tom was silent.

"Oh, my God," he said. "Something just went flying past the window. Oh, my God. It looked like a body."

Two workers later told representatives from Morgan Stanley that Swift hung up the phone but did not return to the stairs. He headed for the elevator bank and got on.

It's not clear whether Swift pressed a button to ride up to his office or down to the lobby. But it is clear that seconds after the elevator door closed on Swift, the jetliner struck the South Tower.

Authorities would later conclude that a fireball of jet fuel ripped down the elevator shafts of the South Tower. Dozens were instantly killed. One of them was likely Tom Swift.

As midnight approached, Frances Swift still wondered what had happened to her son. Forty years before, she had lost her firstborn—a five-year-old son—to leukemia. She had never recovered emotionally from that loss, she said. Now her youngest was missing.

With her daughter and son-in-law, Frances headed into Manhattan and started walking from hospital to hospital, asking about unidentified patients. They checked with nurses and doctors at St. Vincent's, Bellevue, and Mount Sinai hospitals. At every one, Frances described her son—six feet one, about 200 pounds.

But there was no sign of Tom.

At home, the Swifts learned that Morgan Stanley had set up a hotline where its Trade Center workers could call for information on fellow staffers.

Swift's brother, Peter, dialed the number and was told that Tom had called in. He was alive.

Jill Swift then called the hotline and was told her husband was still missing.

Peter Swift tried again and an operator said Tom was fine but did not know his whereabouts.

"It went on like this about five times," Peter later said.

After another day, the Swifts gave up.

* * *

As the night lengthened, more police and firefighters tried to make their way to Ground Zero. Many came from New Jersey, Connecticut, and Long Island.

It was the same scene at the Pentagon in northern Virginia.

As word spread of the attacks and the toll of casualties, thousands of people wanted to help. In the coming weeks, some of New York City's best chefs would stand over makeshift ovens at Ground Zero. The city's therapists would come to help with the grieving. Even masseuses would show up to rub sore backs.

That first night, Phil McArdle needed his eyes washed.

He had already poured water into his eyes after rescuing photographer David Handschuh. But hours later, after wandering amid the smoke without any protective goggles, McArdle felt blinded by the amount of grime that had caked into his eyes.

A firefighter drove him to the Maspeth firehouse. But McArdle couldn't clean his eyes well enough so he was taken to Elmhurst Hospital in Queens. After four hours of doctors and nurses washing his eyes, McArdle could finally see clearly again.

As he left, a doctor offered advice: Don't go back to Ground Zero. You may end up blind.

McArdle nodded, seeming to agree. In his heart, however, he knew he could not stay away from the spot where so many friends died.

* * *

At his desk in the basement office in northern Virginia where the CIA monitored Osama bin Laden and his al-Qaeda network, Mark Rossini worked late, too.

The questions mounted for him and the other investigators and intelligence analysts with the top-secret team called "Alec Station." How did the terrorists smoothly pull off this complicated plan to hijack four commercial jetliners?

Was airline security *that* bad? How had the terrorists remained hidden inside the United States? And didn't anyone from the FBI, the CIA, or even the National Security Agency, which monitors cellular calls, radio transmissions, and other electronic communications across the globe, notice that something ominous seemed to be emerging that summer? Weren't there any hints that something bad might be afoot? It turns out that there were plenty of hints.

Late in the day, Alec Station got its hands on the list of passengers. Rossini studied his copy closely, his eyes running up and down the names—and finally settling on two who had been on the jetliner that struck the Pentagon.

Khalid al-Mihdar and Nawaf al-Hazmi.

Rossini knew those names. In fact, he knew of them all too well.

Both were well-known members of al-Qaeda. The CIA team that Rossini worked with as an FBI liaison had been tracking al-Mihdhar and al-Hazmi for more than a year. In fact, the CIA and Rossini knew that both terrorists had first traveled from the Middle East to Kuala Lumpur, Malaysia, where they met with a small group of al-Qaeda members who were based in Southeast Asia.

The CIA secretly monitored that meeting. The agency also followed al-Mihdhar and al-Hazmi to Bangkok, Thailand. And then, knowing that the two had obtained US travel visas, the CIA tracked them on a flight to Los Angeles, California.

It was mid-January 2000—some twenty months before the 9/11 attacks—when al-Mihdhar and al-Hazmi set foot on American soil. But the CIA did not sound any alarms. Federal regulations prevented the CIA from spying on people within the US borders—even known terrorists. That was the job of the FBI. But the CIA did not pass the word to the FBI that al-Mihdhar and al-Hazmi had arrived in Los Angeles.

Rossini found himself becoming deeply bothered at the CIA's refusal to reach out to the FBI as several months passed by. Why keep this information secret within the CIA? He asked his CIA supervisor if he could tell the FBI that two well-known al-Qaeda terrorists had come to the US. Surely, the bureau's counterintelligence agents—especially John O'Neill—would insist on monitoring them and possibly arresting them.

More months passed. Rossini's concerns grew. Who was monitoring these al-Qaeda operatives in the US? But as it did when al-Mihdar and al-Hazmi first arrived, the CIA continued to hold off telling the FBI. And when Rossini and another FBI agent assigned to Alec Station formally objected, they were officially ordered not to tell anyone at the FBI about al-Mihdhar and al-Hazmi.

Rossini kept his mouth shut.

But now, looking at the passenger lists, Rossini felt sick. It had been a long and painful day. Midnight was approaching.

He busied himself at his desk until most everyone had left. Around 3:00 a.m., he drove to his Capitol Hill townhouse.

His wife asked how he was holding up as he climbed into bed.

Rossini didn't want to talk. He just wanted to sleep.

But before he closed his eyes, he turned to his wife.

"We knew who these guys were."

Part Two

Fire and Rubble

"Foolishly, I assumed my government was doing its job in keeping us safe and protected."

KRISTEN BREITWEISER, 9/11 WIDOW

Rubble from the World Trade Center's twin towers in Lower Manhattan still smolders weeks after the 9/11 attacks as rescue teams search for the remains of the dead. Photo by Mike Segar/AFP via Getty Images.

4

Ground Zero

The morning of September 12 seemed as peaceful as the morning before. A golden sun. A perfect blue sky. A soft and crisp breeze. But the quiet tranquility of another dawn was an illusion. America was now a very different country. Whether life would change permanently—and how much it would change—was an open question. You could almost hear the entire population ask: *Now what?* What *should* America do in response to the deadliest terrorist attack ever on its soil? What *could* it do?

There was, of course, the inevitable measuring of what happened. We counted the dead and injured. We tabulated the financial losses. We tried to predict how long it might take to recover and rebuild. We wondered how many soldiers might be deployed if America embarked on another war in another distant land. Wall Street forecasters took a deep breath and wondered whether the nation would plunge into an economic downturn. Relatives of the more than 1,000 people listed as missing at the Trade Center plastered light poles and construction fences with posters showing faces from happier times and the question: "Have you seen this person?"

A collective sorrow seemed to hover over almost every activity. For many in the New York region and in the tight-knit, government-focused communities of Washington, DC, Virginia, and Maryland that were home to thousands of military families and other Pentagon workers, the loss was personal and close. Many knew victims—or they knew of someone who knew a victim, or someone who was listed as missing. In other parts of the nation, the loss, while less personal, nevertheless left deep wounds in America's national pride and confidence. Normal life in almost every community seemed altered.

Not surprisingly, President George W. Bush quickly promised to track down the leaders of the plot that already had been given a simple moniker that needed no explanation: "9/11." Just like the words "Pearl Harbor" became a shorthand reminder to a generation of Americans of the horrific attack on the US Naval Base in Hawaii that led the nation into World War II sixty years earlier, the numbers "9/11" were all that was needed now to sum up the death, outrage, sadness, shock, fear, and confusion that rippled across the United States.

In a televised address to the nation on the evening of the attacks, Bush declared that "the search is underway for those who are behind these evil acts." But as the nation awoke from the shock of September 11, it realized that finding the right answers to the question of what *should* be done—or *could* be done—in the aftermath of the deadliest terrorist attack ever on US soil was far more complicated. Responding to the attack was not so much a matter of dropping bombs on terrorists' bases, making arrests, punishing the guilty, or patching the wounds of victims and then moving on with some sort of "closure." The entire nation seemed to know that the wound it had just suffered would take time to heal.

* * *

From his office at a school in New Jersey, Bert Ammerman knew all too well how difficult it could be to navigate the fragile, mysterious, and sometimes meandering path of healing. He also understood that no one could really place a time limit on how long that healing might take.

As the weeks passed after 9/11, Ammerman, the principal of Northern Valley Regional High School in Demarest, New Jersey, was continually reminded of his family's experience with terrorism when Libyan agents planted a bomb aboard a Pan American jetliner flying from London to New York four days before Christmas in 1988. He knew all about the instant anguish that swept through his own family with the news that his brother, Thomas, was among the 259 people who died aboard the plane. He knew that the incident—like the 9/11 attacks—would be quickly reduced in the media to an easily digestible moniker that would explain much about what happened and yet skip over so much of the anger and confusion that became part of life for the families of the dead. The 1988 attack on the airplane became known simply as "Pan Am 103" for the name and number of the flight or just the "Lockerbie bombing" for the Scottish town where the plane crashed and killed eleven residents.

He also understood all too well and personally, that the relatives of the victims needed to hear some sort of confident promise from their government leaders that the United States would actively investigate this attack. That it would find the killers. And make necessary changes to prevent the next attack. And, perhaps most important, that the government would be transparent and honest about what mistakes had been made.

Finally, Ammerman knew that the relatives of the victims needed time to mourn, sometimes in ways that could not be easily explained. "Don't use the word 'closure,'" he would say years later as he reflected on the 9/11 attacks. "There is no closure."

Often during the months after 9/11, Ammerman found himself turning his thoughts to a Saturday in October 1993, when he stood on the grounds of Arlington National Cemetery in the hills of northern Virginia that overlook Washington, DC, with scores of other relatives of victims of Pan Am 103.

It had been a frustrating five years since Ammerman's brother, a thirty-six-year-old marketing manager for a shipping firm, had died when the Pan Am jumbo jetliner carrying him home to his wife and two daughters, blew apart in the nighttime skies over Scotland.

United States and British investigators quickly determined who was responsible. In some ways, that was easy. The trail of evidence was filled with clues. The path to justice had been filled with obstacles, however.

Two Libyan intelligence officials had been indicted by British and American authorities. But Libya's leader, Muammar Gaddafi, refused to turn them over so they could stand trial. The United Nations, in an effort to pressure Gaddafi, imposed sanctions on Libya such as a ban on its citizens from traveling, a freeze on its financial assets, and a ban on other nations selling parts or machinery for Libya's oil production.

Gaddafi did his best to ignore the sanctions. Libya's oil production slowed but not enough to cripple its economy. And when repairs were needed, Gaddafi turned to the black market or rogue nations for parts. The bombers, meanwhile, remained free.

Ammerman understood firsthand how difficult it could be for any victim of terror to persuade his own nation to face down a tin-horn dictator such as Gaddafi. Ammerman had taken time from his career to lobby Congress. He was even part of a small group that met with President George H.W. Bush not long after the bombing.

The families of victims, however, had made little headway. Whether it was Congress or the White House, or the US military, or the nation's intelligence agencies, Ammerman felt hemmed in by the stranglehold of bureaucracy and the nation's short attention span.

The families achieved one significant victory, however. Congress was planning to appropriate funds to build a memorial at Arlington National Cemetery for the Pan Am 103 victims. So Ammerman and a group of victims' relatives and friends decided to gather at the cemetery before any memorial was built to once again try to draw attention to their plight.

Ammerman feared that the window of time for punishing Libya and the killers seemed to be closing. A new president, Bill Clinton, had taken office eight months earlier with a promise to fix the economy, not to start a war against terrorism, especially in the volatile Middle East amid a noticeable uptick in radical Islamism that even struck fear into many of the region's more traditional and stable Muslim leaders in Saudi Arabia and Egypt. And while a memorial to the Pan Am victims at America's most hallowed cemetery was clearly a kind gesture by Congress, Ammerman felt it was far more important to hold the killers accountable and make the necessary changes to stop the next terrorist attack. Indeed, just eight months earlier—only a month after Clinton took office—Islamist zealots had set off a bomb in the garage of New York's World Trade Center. But even that attack, Ammerman felt, had not been enough to galvanize the nation to make major changes.

For the ceremony at Arlington, he had typed out a speech of just 550 words. But they summed up much of the frustration he felt over the previous five years.

"Terrorism, the mere word, sends shock waves of fear and revulsion through the hearts and minds of all freedom loving individuals," Ammerman began. "We are assembled here today to remember those Americans who died in acts of terrorism. With the mention of each atrocity, feelings of anguish, vulnerability, and rage rush in. Who can forget?"

He recited a litany of terrorist attacks that had swept through the world since the 1970s—bombings in Lebanon, hostage taking in Iran, "and, yes, for me, the most personally tragic, the bombing of Pan Am Flight 103, which underscored that Americans are vulnerable to attack anywhere in the world."

Ammerman also told the mourners that "defeat begins in the heart" and that "we must guarantee a future in which all Americans will know the joys of liberty and the pursuit of happiness."

As he looked back on that speech in the weeks and years after the 9/11 attacks, he worried that his words on that October Saturday in 1993 in Arlington had been a warning of the unfortunate trap that would snare America's newest relatives of terrorism victims.

Ammerman knew all too well how "defeat begins in the heart." He had fought that kind of emotional battle within himself ever since Lockerbie. For relatives of 9/11 victims, Ammerman knew the healing process would be long and perhaps as unending as his was.

"I learned from Pan Am 103 and Lockerbie," he said.

* * *

Throughout its history, America had dealt with all manner of calamities, from natural disasters to wars—even a civil war that sent more than 600,000 Union and Confederate soldiers to their graves. And in recent decades, attacks by terrorists against overseas American targets had become so common that they seemed like an expected part of life in a modern world where it had become far easier for terrorists in even the most backward nations to obtain advanced weapons that could kill or injure hundreds. In the 1980s, foreign terrorists staged two notable mass casualty attacks, setting off a powerful and sophisticated bomb at the US Marine encampment in Beirut, Lebanon, and then using a much smaller explosive device hidden in a suitcase to cause a Pan Am jumbo jetliner to crash in the tiny Scottish town of Lockerbie.

Then came other high-profile attacks. But even the bombings of New York's World Trade Center in 1993, a US military barracks in Saudi Arabia in 1996, US embassies in Africa in 1998, and a US Navy destroyer in Yemen in 2000, along with the bombings in Atlanta and Oklahoma City that law enforcement officials categorized as a new form of "domestic terrorism," failed to capture the nation's attention in any lasting manner.

In the months after 9/11, the mood seemed different. The previous attacks were either overseas or, if they took place in America, were the work of just one extremist or a small and often disorganized group of zealots. The reality that America confronted after 9/11 is that terrorism had now become far more sophisticated. What's more, terrorists had taken advantage of the kind of freedoms of coming and going—and just living in America—that the nation had long tried to protect.

The facts behind the 9/11 attacks shocking: Nineteen members of the Islamist al-Qaeda terrorist group easily entered America with tourist visas. They didn't arm themselves with sophisticated weapons or bombs. Yet they managed to elude the defenses of the world's most technologically sophisticated and militarily powerful nation.

In some ways, 9/11 confirmed America's worst fears—actually fears that should have gained far more attention after terrorists, who had come to America as seemingly peaceful visitors, had set off the bomb at New York City's World Trade Center in 1993. Foreign terrorists did not need to attack US targets overseas anymore. They had now breached supposedly well-defended American borders and staged a major attack here.

We soon learned that none of the hijackers had ever previously set foot in America. None spoke or read English well. And yet, they blended seamlessly into American life. They rented apartments, cars, and postal boxes. They opened bank accounts and utilized ATMs. They joined exercise gyms, purchased sunglasses, took flying lessons, and even flew to Las Vegas for a pre-attack romp in "sin city," the center of many of the cultural transgressions that they seemed to hate about America.

America also discovered that the nation's counterterrorism system was "blinking red" with warnings that Islamist terrorists affiliated with Osama bin Laden's al-Qaeda network might strike, possibly with commercial jetliners. And yet, America's vaunted intelligence bureaucracy, including its ability to monitor phone calls from around the world, had not paid enough attention. Indeed, the harsh and painful truth that emerged soon after the attacks is that the nation's defenses had been neglected. Whether it was carelessness, arrogance, or just the fact that America's attention was focused on other worries or on an unwarranted belief that the country was impregnable, the nation had left itself defenseless in ways that were enraging and embarrassing.

The hijackers were hardly trained commandos, on par with the US Army's Delta Force or the US Navy's SEAL teams. But they eluded America's intelligence and law enforcement services. They passed effortlessly through airport security, then, armed with the kind of box cutters and other tools that carpenters carry in their toolboxes, seized control of defenseless commercial jetliners and crashed them into some of the nation's most iconic targets—the World Trade Center's twin towers that symbolized America's economic might and the Pentagon that symbolized its military prowess. The fourth jetliner, which was brought down by the courage of its passengers, reportedly had been heading to the White House or the US Capitol.

Understandably, many asked whether terrorism—and even the fear it could take place anywhere—had become a "new normal" for America. Indeed, in the months after 9/11, much of America wondered whether the insecurity they felt for those first months would ever disappear. Polls showed a dramatic increase in fear of flying, gathering in large groups, working in tall office buildings, and just taking a bus or train.

But this rising apprehension was not just confined to New York City, Washington, DC, or even the farm fields of Shanksville, Pennsylvania, where destruction and death from the attacks was most obvious. A Gallup survey taken in the months after the attacks found that nearly half of Americans—45 percent—had decided to permanently change the way they live because of a rising fear of terrorism and the feeling that an attack could take place any time, in any community. Even more alarming perhaps, a Gallup survey twenty years later found that 64 percent had changed their lives because of a continuing fear of terrorism.

In those initial months after 9/11, America seemed stunned—as if the entire nation was staggering after a hard punch in the nose and was struggling to figure out what to do about it.

Commercial airlines and the federal government tried to beef up security. Congress took only a few weeks to draw up the Patriot Act to expand surveillance and investigative powers of law enforcement and the Aviation and Transportation Security Act that set up a system in which passengers were routinely patted down, asked to empty their pockets and remove their belts and shoes, and submit to searches of their luggage before they were allowed to set foot on commercial flights.

Concrete barriers were set up outside prominent buildings. Traffic patterns were reconfigured. "Watch lists" were created of suspected terrorists, some of whom were under suspicion merely because they had an Arabic name. Schools canceled classes. Malls, tall office buildings, and even bridges and tunnels used by thousands of commuters were suddenly considered danger zones. Police who spent large portions of their days handing out traffic tickets or just patrolling residential streets in search of burglars were now assigned with National Guard soldiers to guard bridges and airports and be on the lookout for terrorists.

It seemed clear that America needed a road to recovery. But how?

The counting of the dead and the national sense of mourning coincided, sometimes clumsily, with efforts to return to normal life. For example, while battalions of electricians laid miles of wires across Lower Manhattan to quickly restore the power grid for Wall Street and the nation's financial industry, almost every available wall and light pole in the same neighborhood was smothered with posters pleading for help in finding the thousands of victims who were listed as "missing."

Amid the sadness and the constant drip-drip-drip of worrisome news, something uplifting took place, however. People from all manner of income levels and racial and ethnic backgrounds, in communities large and small, actively tried to set aside their differences and forge some sort of civic unity. They hung flags on their porches and doorways. They gathered in community parks and churches or on the steps of libraries and city halls to light candles and sing the National Anthem. In New York City's Greenwich Village, one of the most progressive neighborhoods in America, teams of ad hoc "cheerleaders" gathered for months on street corners along West Street each morning to hold signs and shout encouragement to first responders from across the nation who drove by their community on the way Ground Zero to hunt for victims' remains. Across New York City, residents delivered food to firehouses and police precincts. And the New York Yankees initiated a new tradition by pausing during the seventh inning of their home games at Yankee Stadium to line up outside their dugout and join the crowd in singing "God Bless America."

The desire to bolster unity and find common ground even extended to politics. From Congress to local school boards, political warriors who had proudly devoted much of their careers to fighting each other now pledged to lay down their partisan swords and work together. Most notably, Congressional Republicans and Democrats gathered on the Capitol Steps on the evening of September 11 to sing "God Bless America." Days later, the House and Senate overwhelmingly passed a $40 billion emergency response package and pledged additional funds for recovery efforts, especially in New York City.

Not everyone embraced the new political détente, however. The urge to point fingers—even at the wrong targets—was just too ingrained in the national political vibe.

The attacks sparked an immediate wave of hatred against Muslims. Local and federal law enforcement authorities investigated more than 100 anti-Muslim bias incidents in just the week after 9/11. In Ohio, vigilantes tried to burn down a mosque. In Texas, police reported that bullets had been fired into a mosque.

In some cases, the anti-Muslim fervor was stoked by unverified reports of Muslims cheering in the streets of their neighborhoods after the attacks—notably in Paterson, New Jersey, where some of the hijackers lived in the months leading up to 9/11, and in Jersey City where the 1993 Trade Center bombers had resided before they were arrested. While such reports were never confirmed, the rumors nevertheless persisted for years.

The finger pointing was not just directed at Muslims, though.

Two days after the attacks, one of the most outspoken figures in the nation's conservative Christian political movement, the Rev. Jerry Falwell, the founder of The Moral Majority, suggested that God allowed the 9/11 attacks to take place as punishment for America's support for abortion and gay rights.

In what he later tried to categorize as a "long theological discussion," on the popular evangelical Christian television program, *The 700 Club*, Falwell warned that "what we saw on Tuesday (September 11), as terrible as it is, could be minuscule if, in fact, God continues to lift the curtain and allow the enemies of America to give us probably what we deserve."

The host of *The 700 Club*, Pat Robertson, another influential evangelical Christian with deep ties to the conservative wing of the Republican Party, agreed.

"Jerry, that's my feeling," Robertson said. "I think we've just seen the antechamber to terror. We haven't even begun to see what they can do to the major population."

With that, Falwell added: "The abortionists have got to bear some burden for this because God will not be mocked. And when we destroy 40 million little innocent babies, we make God mad. I really believe that the pagans, and the abortionists, and the feminists, and the gays, and the lesbians who are actively trying to make that an alternative lifestyle, the ACLU, People for the American Way, all of them who have tried to secularize America, I point the finger in their face and say, 'You helped this happen.'"

"Well, I totally concur," Robertson said. "And the problem is we have adopted that agenda at the highest levels of our government."

A tidal wave of criticism, from Christian theologians, civil rights advocates, and even a few conservative political figures, swept over Falwell and Robertson. Even the White House, which fancied itself as an ally of Christian evangelicals, called Falwell's remarks "inappropriate" and that President Bush "believes that terrorists are responsible for these acts."

Two days later, Falwell tried to back away from his harsh finger-pointing, claiming that his words had been taken out of context. "I would never blame any human being except the terrorists, and if I left that impression with gays or lesbians, or anyone else, I apologize," he said.

Whether Falwell's sudden apology convinced anyone was difficult to determine. His remarks were rooted in a long-standing theological belief that was popular among the most tradition-bound conservative evangelicals—and largely rejected by Roman Catholic, mainline Christian, and Jewish scholars—that God started wars and even created storms and floods to punish entire nations who allegedly strayed into what was seen as sinful behavior.

If nothing else, the tempest Falwell unleashed—however brief—was a reminder that America was still deeply divided, culturally and politically. In the coming decades, those divisions would not only return but would widen considerably.

If there was a sought-after balm to soothe the divisiveness and pain in those early weeks and months, it was a common desire to tell the stories of heroes and find meaningful symbols that either reminded the nation of its basic goodness or offered some measure of hope that the darkness of the moment could be overcome.

One of the first heroes to emerge was a software account manager from a suburban New Jersey town. Todd Beamer had been flying to San Francisco from Newark on United Flight 93. After it was hijacked, he reached for a plane-to-ground "air phone" that was common in jetliners at the time. Beamer connected with Lisa Jefferson, a supervisor at Verizon that managed in-flight calls. The thirteen-minute recorded call quickly became a reminder of the bravery that emerged even from those who knew they were about to die.

With the FBI listening in, Beamer calmly told Jefferson that at least one passenger had been murdered, that the pilot and co-pilot were incapacitated, and that hijackers had taken over the cockpit. He asked Jefferson to tell his pregnant wife, Lisa, and the couple's two sons that he loved them. Then he asked her to recite the Lord's Prayer with him and explained that he and other passengers were about to revolt and try to take back control of the plane. Just before he hung up, he was recorded as telling other passengers: "Are you ready? Okay. Let's roll."

Beamer's invocation to "let's roll" quickly became a symbol of resolve in the face of death and a rallying cry across the nation, from military units preparing to track down Osama bin Laden to the throngs of firefighters, police, and other volunteers who flocked to Ground Zero.

Also playing a large role in helping to preserve America's unity and inherent toughness was a photograph, taken late in the afternoon of September 11 by photographer, Thomas Franklin of *The Record*. The photograph showed three gritty FDNY firefighters raising a US flag over the rubble of the Trade Center's twin towers. Several other photographers at Ground Zero that day witnessed the same flag raising, but none were able to capture the firefighters' resolute faces.

Franklin's photo, along with Todd Beamer's in-flight "let's roll" command, emerged as vital symbols of how ordinary people were capable of extraordinary actions in a crisis.

In those days and weeks after 9/11, America badly needed heroes and symbols.

* * *

On the day after the attacks, Frank Silecchia, a construction laborer who specialized in basic "pick and shovel work," walked into the rubble of Ground Zero. He did not feel any urge to find symbols that would bring unity or inspiration to America. Nor was he expecting to do anything extraordinary. Certainly, nothing heroic. He just wanted a job.

Silecchia soon became famous, however, for discovering one of the most extraordinarily meaningful yet ultimately controversial symbols of America's resiliency after 9/11: a 17-foot-high cross of steel beams that had managed to somehow remain upright in the rubble as the twin towers collapsed around it.

Silecchia had no idea, however, of the role the rusted pieces of steel would ultimately play, even in his own life. He remembers falling to his knees with tears rolling down his cheeks when he discovered the cross standing in a hollow space that seemed grotto-like amid the broken steel and concrete. "I couldn't stop the tears," he said later. "I cried like a baby."

Silecchia grew up in the close-knit Bensonhurst section of Brooklyn where street-smart toughness was a way of life. As he reached his twenties, he befriended several low-level members of the Genovese crime family. With muscled arms and shoulders that could easily toss a bag of cement or a cinder block, Silecchia was soon hired as a bouncer at bars owned by the Genovese gang.

He started first in several Brooklyn clubs, then moved to fancier spots in Midtown Manhattan. "I walked the streets of New York with respect," he told me years later. "I demanded it, and I had it."

But Silecchia soon learned that the bouncer's life—and the respect he thought he had—was mostly a dead-end path to even minimal happiness. Yes, the work was steady. He even figured his rough style might lead to him to a promotion as an official member of the Genovese crime syndicate—a "made man" as the Mafia termed such an upgrade.

"I was wearing the shoes but I was not wearing the coat," Silecchia told me, using a term that describes how the Mafia often lets ordinary street toughs perform some rudimentary jobs but delays giving them any sort of official status and the money that comes with that status.

Silecchia said he desperately wanted to "wear the coat" of a mobster—to become "made" in a secret ceremony where he took an oath of *omerta* in which he promised never to tell law enforcement authorities of crimes by fellow Mafia members. He was even mentored by Vincent "The Chin" Gigante, then a noted Genovese enforcer who ran the family after its boss, Anthony "Fat Tony" Salerno, was sent to prison in the mid-1980s with several other leaders of the "Mafia Commission."

Gigante became a legendary figure in New York in his own right and was dubbed "The Odd-Father" and the "Enigma in the Bathrobe" by local newspapers after his years of escaping suspicion of his criminal activities by feigning dementia when he appeared in public. Most notably, Gigante would be seen mumbling to himself and wearing a bathrobe during his daily walks near the Genovese's headquarters in Little Italy's section of Manhattan.

In 1990, Gigante escaped prosecution when a judge declared him mentally unfit to stand trial. But several years later, federal prosecutors finally caught up to Gigante and his play-acting scheme. They secretly recorded his telephone calls and discovered that he never mumbled or seemed hampered by any cognitive disorder when he discussed crimes with his fellow mobsters.

Gigante was in prison when the 9/11 attacks took place. Already, however, Frank Silecchia was having second thoughts about wanting to follow Gigante's path into the life of a mobster.

At this point, Silecchia's life consisted of him working nights and trying to make ends meet on his bouncer's paycheck. Was this his future? Silecchia was troubled.

His concerns intensified one night when he quietly took the rap for vandalizing a taxi cab even though he was innocent. The cab drove down a dead-end street in Brooklyn. One of Silecchia's neighbors got into an argument with the taxi driver and smashed one of the cab's windows.

Police arrested Silecchia. He spent only one night in jail. But he had to pay to fix the cab's window.

Not long afterwards, Silecchia concluded that he needed to change his life. What's more, his road to official membership in the Genovese family was blocked by something he could not change.

Silecchia's mother was Jewish. And while his father was Italian—and had been counted on by the Genovese's to help with low-level crimes now and then—the Mafia required that their "made men" be fully Italian.

Silecchia joined a construction union. He found work at a few building project sites in Manhattan. But the jobs were never steady. He might work a few months at one site, then be home looking for a job for several more months.

During the summer of 2001, Silecchia commuted from his home in Little Ferry, New Jersey, to a job dismantling a defunct power station. But when the twin towers fell on September 11, 2001, Silecchia was officially unemployed and trying to regularly attend Sunday services at an evangelical Christian church.

On September 11, he was watching the live TV coverage when the second hijacked plane struck the Trade Center's South Tower. Then he watched the towers fall.

The next day, after hearing that construction laborers were needed at the World Trade Center site to help search and rescue teams make their way through the debris, Silecchia headed to Lower Manhattan.

"My city was hurting," he said later. "I couldn't get there fast enough."

Silecchia arrived at Ground Zero late in the afternoon of September 12. Like so many in America who remained transfixed to their TV's, he thought he had a good idea of what to expect. "But that didn't prepare me for the reality," he said.

Years later, Silecchia would describe the scene as "hell on earth." Fires burned in hollow pockets of twisted steel and broken concrete, their flames spitting into the air like the thermal vents of a volcano. Fire trucks, police cruisers, ambulances, and scores of private vehicles littered the streets, some of them crushed by debris. Almost every inch was blanketed by a blizzard of gray dust. Breathing was arduous in the choking stench that permeated the air.

Few of the firefighters or volunteers had masks to protect themselves from the toxic air—that sort of protective gear would not begin to arrive for several days. Silecchia soaked a bandana with water and wrapped it around his head to cover his nose and mouth. And for a moment, he found himself stopping and asking: How would he get through this?

He quickly put the question out of his mind. A search team of firefighters asked him to join them that night. The group headed for an opening in World Trade Center Six on the northwest corner of the site.

At eight stories, Building 6 was the shortest in the Trade Center's complex. For nearly three decades it had been home to such federal agencies as the US Customs Service, the Departments of Labor and Commerce, and the Bureau of Alcohol, Tobacco and Firearms. On September 11, it was pummeled with debris from the collapsing 110-story North Tower next door. All of the windows in Building 6 were blown out. Fires destroyed the walls. Only a few pieces of the steel structure remained standing.

Silecchia's team first headed to a section of the Trade Center's parking garage. A stairway was still intact. But it was filled with smoke and as dark as midnight.

The firefighters and Silecchia shined flashlights as they descended several levels of the garage, calling out for survivors. "But there were no signs of life, no cries for help," Silecchia said.

The firefighters spray-painted orange "X's" on doors and hallways in the garage as a message that the area had been searched and to mark their path so they could find their way back to the surface.

After twelve hours, the group found three bodies.

It was now almost 5:00 a.m. on September 13—Thursday. Silecchia felt exhausted as he climbed the stairs from the garage and walked into the debris field. Another clear and golden day dawned. The sun's rays streaked through the surrounding office buildings and across the ragged rubble.

As the search team walked past the remains of Building 6, Silecchia told the firefighters that he wanted to "take a look over there."

He picked his way through debris then found himself in what he later described as a grotto that had not been flattened by the North Tower's torrent of broken steel and concrete. Instead, a series of cross-shaped beams from North Tower were standing upright, each seeming to have been shot by some sort of massive crossbow.

"A field of crosses," Silecchia would say later.

The largest and most noticeable stood 17-feet tall and weighed several tons. Its foot-square beams seemed rusty and a ragged piece of silver ventilation duct was draped over one of its cross beams as if a shroud had been tossed there as some sort of memorial talisman.

Silecchia remembered feeling a "strange sense of peace and stillness" as he knelt in the debris at the foot of the cross and cried. "I could almost hear God saying, 'The terrible thing done at this site was meant for evil. But I will turn it into good. Have faith. I am here.'"

After a few minutes, Silecchia got up and walked to the front of the atrium and spray-painted "God's House" on a hunk of debris.

In the coming days, the former atrium with the cross became a meditation space for Ground Zero workers to relax and allow themselves a few minutes of peace from the horrific task of combing through the rubble for human remains.

The importance of the cross in the life of Ground Zero soon took a dramatic turn. Twelve days after the attacks—a Sunday—Father Brian Jordan presided at an open-air Mass near the NYPD command center that he organized for Ground Zero workers. After helping with the bucket brigade on the day of the attacks, Jordan decided to come back the following day. And the day after that. And, then, more days. Soon, he was regarded as one of the regulars.

Jordan had quickly discovered that the firefighters, police, construction workers, and other volunteers who had come to Ground Zero needed a chaplain to speak to about their sorrows, worries, or just the mental drain of working amid so much death and destruction. It didn't matter what religion anyone followed—if they followed a formal religion at all. Jordan felt he had been spiritually called to lend a hand, especially after the death of his friend and Franciscan colleague, Father Mychal Judge, who had served as the chaplain for New York's firefighters.

Jordan started by just showing up and approaching workers to introduce himself and to ask how they were holding up. He was definitely noticeable in his brown Franciscan robe. Then came the outdoor Mass. Jordan remembers that only about twenty-five people showed up including cops, firefighters, and others from the medical and counseling units that were working from a series of hastily constructed plywood shacks along the edge of the rubble.

After Mass, Jordan had a few Communion hosts left. He walked around the piles of debris asking if anyone would like one.

It was almost 11:00 a.m., Jordan recalled, and a "tall hulking figure dressed in a hard hat, blue overalls, construction boots, and a bright yellow vest" walked up.

It was Frank Silecchia and he had a question for Jordan: "Do you want to see God's House?"

Jordan remembers thinking that Silecchia might be an escaped mental patient from Bellevue Psychiatric Hospital or just a guy looking for a church to visit.

Jordan started to explain that there was a Catholic church a few blocks away—St. Peter's. Father Mychal Judge's body had been carried there by anguished police and firefighters and laid in front of the altar on the afternoon of September 11. A photograph of the group holding Judge's limp body as they rushed from the smoke and rubble was later compared to Michaelangelo's *Pietà,* which depicts the body of Jesus Christ being embraced by his mother, Mary, after his crucifixion.

Jordan started to offer directions to St. Peter's, but Silecchia interrupted him.

"No. No," Silecchia said. "I don't mean some built church from the past. I want to show you God's House in the present."

Silecchia turned and walked toward the remains of Building 6. Jordan followed behind but remembers keeping his distance, wondering whether Silecchia had "truly gone mad," perhaps overcome with the emotion of working in such proximity to so much death.

They walked past the spray-painted "God's House" sign, then entered. It was dark. Two firefighters walked past them in silence, as if they were leaving a real church. Silecchia told Jordan to look closely into the space.

And there it was—the cross with the sheet of ventilation duct hanging on the side.

Jordan remembers being so stunned that he couldn't speak. He stood in silence for at least three minutes. Then he turned to Silecchia and said that "God was truly present."

So began a new friendship—the tough-guy-bouncer-would-be-mobster-turned-construction laborer and the Catholic priest. Both had one thing in common: They had been raised in Brooklyn.

Jordan wanted more Ground Zero workers and the throngs of volunteers at the site to see the cross. With Silecchia lining up a construction crane and

Jordan getting permission from city officials, the cross was lifted out of the debris and placed on a concrete pedestal on West Street.

Jordan held a formal blessing of the cross on October 4, the feast day of St. Francis of Assisi, who not only founded the Franciscan order of priests, but is widely considered a patron saint of peace.

More than 400 people assembled on West Street, just steps from the rubble and with the fires still burning underground. Construction workers stood with police officers, firefighters, nuns, and volunteers who served food. To many Ground Zero workers—indeed, countless visitors—the cross had already become one of the few emblems of positivity in an otherwise dismal time and place.

Names of some of Ground Zero's dead had already been etched into the cross along with a more general message, "God Bless Our Fallen Brothers." Father Jordan stepped into a cherry picker bucket and a crane lifted him over the cross as bagpipers played, "Amazing Grace." He sprinkled holy water over the beams and prayed aloud: "By the grace and love of Almighty God, to the north, I bless this cross in the name of the Father, the Son and the Holy Spirit." He then repeated the blessing for east, west, and south.

"Keep playing bagpipes," Father Jordan shouted.

Some onlookers prayed silently as they dragged on cigarettes and leaned against shovels and rakes. A few, holding hands, sang "God Bless America."

Father Jordan blessed two dogs, Atlas and Keifer, who were part of a growing herd of specially trained search and rescue canines who rambled across the rubble in those first months in search of human remains.

The crowd repeatedly cheered "USA . . . USA . . . USA."

Father Jordan announced that "you can never destroy the spirit of America."

In that moment and with those words by Father Jordan, the cross had become one of the most unifying and uplifting symbols of dedication and resilience for Ground Zero's workers—and, as the photos of the cross spread, for a wounded nation.

The cross, however, would also become the center of a debate—and even a federal court case—over religious expression that would take years to resolve.

On New York City's Fifth Avenue, firefighters stand atop a fire engine as it carries the flag-draped casket of FDNY Lt. Dennis Mojica after a funeral mass at St. Patrick's Cathedral. Mojica, a member of the FDNY's elite Rescue 1 Company, was among 343 firefighters killed on September 11, 2001. Photo by Joe Raedle/Gettyimages.

5

Twenty-five Funerals a Day

One evening in October, not long after Father Jordan blessed the cross at Ground Zero, two police officers knocked on the back door of Kristen Breitweiser's home in Middletown, New Jersey.

It was almost 9:30 p.m. Kristen had just put her daughter to bed. Her dog, Sam, started barking.

Kristen peered through a window and saw the officers standing on her porch. Both seemed dejected. Kristen immediately sensed they had come with bad news. She opened the door and started to cry.

In the month since the 9/11 attacks, Kristen had heard nothing more from her husband or even second-hand information about what happened to him after he had telephoned her from his office at the Fiduciary Trust on the ninety-fourth floor of the Trade Center's South Tower. After that phone call, Ron had essentially vanished.

In the most rational corners of her heart, Kristen sensed the worst—that Ron had perished when the tower collapsed. But search teams had not found his body—not even any personal items such as a wallet. As was the case with many of the relatives of more than 1,000 other victims whose remains had not been found—and would continue to remain unidentified for the next two decades—she did not know for sure. On many days, Kristen found herself trying to control or at least make sense of the emotions that swirled inside her.

In those first weeks, she found herself imagining that Ron might be alive, and she would dial his phone number, letting it ring over and over. "I didn't expect him to answer, but I wanted to keep alive the possibility that he might," she wrote later in a memoir, *Wake Up Call: The Political Education of a 9/11 Widow.*

At one point, she pictured Ron being treated in a hospital burn ward where no one could recognize him and he could not speak. Or perhaps he had been struck in the head by debris and was stuck in a hospital room with amnesia. She heard a rumor about a man surviving by riding a steel beam down the cascading flood of debris when the towers collapsed. Could that be him?

Rumors constantly emerged in the early weeks. For example, a firefighter said he carried an office worker to safety sliding down a steel beam after one of the twin towers collapsed. In another case, a man said he had been blown out of the towers by the wind of the collapsing floors and somehow landed on his feet with barely a scrape or two.

Kristen figured that if anyone could find a way out of the maelstrom of 9/11, it was Ron. She was sure of that—and kept trying to remind herself to remain confident. After all, one of Ron's favorite expressions said much about his innate confidence in facing any sort of challenge: "Bad shit doesn't happen to me."

At the same time, however, she could not ignore the grisly questions that popped into her thoughts. What if Ron lost his legs? Or an arm? Or that his body was covered with burns? It didn't matter, Kristen told herself. She and Ron would still love each other. At least he would be with her.

But as much as she tried to cling to even the slightest hope that Ron was still alive, Kristen's logical and fact-based training as a lawyer would ultimately kick in, and she could not stop herself from facing an all-too-obvious reality. Ron was, in fact, gone and the two-year-old daughter she was raising with him would now have to grow up without a father.

As she drifted between feelings of loss and hope—along with roller-coaster bouts of confusion, rage, and deep sadness, Kristen also faced some practical duties as what she would come to describe as "the bureaucracy of death." With her sister, she had to pick up Ron's car from the lot by the ferry where he took his last morning commuter trek to Lower Manhattan. She filled out pages of forms to apply for financial help from the Red Cross, the United Way, and Catholic Charities. To help the New York City medical examiner identify Ron's body if it was found, she turned over samples of DNA from his razor, his contact lenses, and his comb. She made a detailed list of what he wore that day: Calvin Klein boxer briefs, Ralph Lauren beige pants, a brown Cole

Haan belt, brown Cole Haan suede shoes, a brown Ralph Lauren sweater vest, a beige linen dress shirt. In her records, she found the serial number for Ron's Breitling aviator's watch. She retrieved copies of his dental records. She even turned over a photograph of a scar on Ron's stomach.

As if that wasn't enough, Kristen was facing her own bout with mortality. Before the 9/11 attacks, she discovered a tumor in her breast. A biopsy had been scheduled for September 21. Ron had promised he would accompany her to the hospital, explaining when the fear of death crept into her thoughts: "You're not going anywhere, and I'm not going anywhere."

But with Ron now among the 9/11 missing, Kristen's father came with her to the hospital. Afterward, Kristen fought off the depressing feeling of not caring whether she lived or died as she waited another ten days for the biopsy results. And then, finally, some good news: The tumor was benign.

She remembers thinking that she and Ron would have celebrated. Not now, however. "I was relieved," Kristen wrote, "but that was about it."

As a source of comfort, she clung to as many memories as she could. She purchased a small recorder at a local Radio Shack store so she could preserve Ron's last voice message on the home answering machine. She chuckled when she opened a door to the kitchen pantry and saw a restaurant-sized jar of peanuts that Ron had purchased over her objections. She wrote a letter to her daughter, describing how much her father loved her—a letter that was not only a gift to her daughter, but a reminder to herself of the deep love she shared with Ron. "I just know in my heart that he tried so hard to get home to us. I just know he did," said Kristen in the letter. "But oh, my God, honey, he didn't have a chance."

And now, after weeks of hoping for news of some sort, here were two police officers at her door.

One of the officers started to speak, but Kristen held up a hand, motioning him to stop. She reached for the phone and called her friend, Paul, whom she had known since almost the day she had met Ron at a Jersey Shore beach bar. Paul's uncle ran a local funeral home.

In the month since the attacks, as she sunk deeper into the emotional quicksand of trying to go through life as the widow of a 9/11 victim, Kristen had begun to feel an unexpected sense of tension and apprehension during even the most ordinary aspects of her day. Whether it was related to the fear that Ron's body would be found and he would be officially categorized as "deceased," she did not know.

Kristen's memoir offers a revealing and painfully personal, day-by-day account of the mental and emotional battles that waged within her. Outwardly, she tried to remain calm—a dutiful mother and a hopeful wife. But she often spent large portions of her days "paralyzed by fear" with a "serious phobia of everything." Even walking down aisles of a grocery store, she found herself imagining that the food was poisoned.

Increasingly, Kristen turned to a favorite place—the woods. Before 9/11, Ron and Kristen often took long walks in the thick groves of trees near their home. With the leaves on the trees now sprouting their autumnal palate of reds, oranges, and yellows, Kristen found some comfort in taking those long walks with her daughter Caroline.

"It was gentle and pure beauty," she wrote. On some days, when the sunlight glistened through the trees, she even felt her husband's embrace.

"I'm surviving because of this," she told a neighbor who happened to meet her on one of those afternoon walks in the forest and asked how she was doing. "Every single bit of sparkle in these woods is Ron's love surrounding us."

But now, Kristen had come face-to-face with a reality she had done her best to ignore. With her friend Paul now on the other end of the telephone call with her, one of the officers started to speak again. She overheard the officer say something about "remains." Kristen screamed. She handed the phone to the officer and walked outside and stood on her deck.

She could not see Ground Zero. But she could smell it. Even more than forty miles away from the peace and quiet of her woodsy neighborhood in Middletown, New Jersey, across Sandy Hook Bay and the shipping channels into New York Harbor, the acrid stench of fires in the rubble that had become her husband's grave managed to invade Kristen's life. In that moment, she wrote that the "pilot light of hope" that Ron was alive had suddenly extinguished.

She looked through the window into her kitchen. With Paul still on the phone, the officers shuffled through some official forms. She took another breath of the bitter air and walked back inside.

A search team had found Ron's left arm with some clothes still on it and a wedding band on his ring finger. Even days later, Kristen would suggest to Paul that some sort of mistake had been made—that this ring might belong to someone else. But the New York City Medical Examiner's research team that was trying to sort through the first batches of what would eventually become more than 19,000 pieces of unidentified remains had also been able to confirm Ron's fingerprints. There was no doubt that Ron was gone. Now it was official.

Kristen asked for Ron's wedding ring. His left arm was sent directly to the funeral home where it was cremated.

Three years later, the medical examiner's office called again. DNA technicians had identified Ron's right arm and part of his shoulder. Kristen could hardly bear to hear the news. She asked that the arm and shoulder be sent to the funeral home and cremated.

Before hanging up, however, the medical examiner staffer mentioned another gruesome detail that would remain as an open wound with Kristen for years. DNA detection had improved greatly, the staffer said. And now that technicians had identified Ron's arms, they would likely be able to identify other parts of his body.

Kristen tried to imagine what this meant. Would there be a call about Ron's leg? His torso? His head?

The thought sickened her—as it would hundreds of other families who were placed in the situation of not knowing when the phone might ring with news that yet another piece of a loved one's body had been identified. And it did not help that some of these messages were passed with all of the sensitivity of a real estate transfer.

"You should be expecting more," the staffer said.

Kristen would later say in interviews that she realized as she spoke that day on the phone with the medical examiner's staff that she faced an unknown path that might not ever end. There was, in fact, no time limit on the process of trying to identify body parts—some as small as a penny and so charred by fire or crushed by debris that they were almost unrecognizable. Nor was there any way of softening the message that a finger or a foot might be identified. Who knew when the medical examiner might call again?

Kristen then made the kind of decision that hundreds of other families would face in the coming years. She had to accept that her husband's body would probably never be fully identified.

* * *

The search for bodies, or just pieces of bodies, amid the Ground Zero rubble that would be stored in refrigerated trucks in a parking lot behind the New York Medical Examiner's office would become one of the most sensitive aspects of 9/11 that still persist a quarter-century later.

The dilemma began with a basic reality of the attacks: only a handful of intact bodies were recovered. Most victims' remains were mangled, dismembered, or burned beyond recognition in the churning and fiery collapse of the twin towers or vaporized in the massive explosions when the jetliners crashed.

Early on, families of victims wanted to conduct a funeral and erect a tombstone by a grave, if only to find some measure of closure and to give their loved ones one of humankind's most basic gifts—a final resting place.

But the attacks of September 11, 2001, did not result in normal deaths. In many cases, families were burying or cremating only a small piece of a loved one—sometimes the size of a finger. Then, like Kristen Breitweiser, they had to make a choice on what to do about other remains that might be identified in the future.

Others worried that pieces of their relatives' bodies might inadvertently be tossed with other debris into a landfill or shipped to a recycling mill. That fear worsened after news spread months after the attacks that workers at a metal scrap yard in Jersey City found someone's severed foot amid the thicket of twisted pipes and beams that had been trucked there to be chopped up and shipped to India or Malaysia where they would be melted down in a steel mill and recycled. Working in that same scrap yard during the summer of 2002, an engineer looking for clues among the twisted beams on why the twin towers collapsed so quickly, found office Christmas decorations and even a dust-covered FDNY firehose with its nozzles engraved with the numbers of a specific fire truck. Concerned that the dust on the hose contained human remains and that its engraved nozzle might be pulled from the pile by a souvenir hunter and sold as a 9/11 relic on the internet, the engineer removed the hose from the pile and delivered it to the FDNY for safekeeping.

Now, more than two decades later, as scientists have found ways to extract DNA from small or badly damaged remains, the medical examiner is still managing to identify victims. But more than 1,000 victims have never been identified. Not only has there been no resting place for many who died, there has been no rest for their families and friends who mourn them. For the relatives of those victims, it meant trying to conduct a funeral without the usual coffin or urn—or even a grave or a spot in a mausoleum.

For those working at Ground Zero, this was especially troubling. They had to make difficult decisions that would affect the lives of countless people in mourning and also move rubble out of the way. At the same time, they worried about their own health. Even though Christine Todd Whitman, the chief administrator of the US Environmental Protection Agency, proclaimed just three days after the attacks that the air was "safe to breathe" and that there was "no need for the general public to be concerned," many who worked at Ground Zero or lived nearby found that the air sickened them. Within months, many workers complained of a "Ground Zero cough."

By December 2001, a NYPD detective, James Zadroga, would emerge as a shocking reminder of how dangerous it had become to even venture into Ground Zero's rubble.

Soon after the 9/11 attacks, Zadroga was assigned to a search and rescue team at Ground Zero. But after putting in some 500 hours at Ground Zero he had trouble breathing. Even walking became a chore.

As a precaution, police officials pulled Zadroga away from the rubble and assigned him to the NYPD homicide investigative squad at Manhattan's midtown south precinct. But his condition worsened. By 2004, after being forced to retire on a disability, Zadroga was confined to a wheelchair and needed oxygen to breathe. His death two years later set off a decades-long battle within the US Congress to set aside funding to pay health-care costs for the tens of thousands of Ground Zero first responders and nearby residents and office workers who would become sick with a variety of respiratory ailments and cancers.

In those early months before hearing of Zadroga's respiratory problems, many first responders ignored the health warnings. For police and firefighters, the need to help with the searches at Ground Zero became part of their unspoken code of never abandoning one of their colleagues. This included finding the bodies of the dead.

Within days, first responders were equipped with construction hard hats and respirators that looked like military gas masks. Even psychiatric counselors, cooks, truck drivers, clergy, and journalists were given hats and respirators. But the smells of Ground Zero along with the rubble's fires were a clear signal that this was a dangerous place.

Marty Davin, the NYPD detective who stood guard on a street corner a block north of the Trade Center's rubble on the afternoon of September 11, sensed that. So did John Ryan, the Port Authority police lieutenant who walked several miles to get to the rubble on September 11. So did Phil McArdle, the firefighter who rescued *New York Daily News* photographer David Handschuh from the rubble and had been warned that he might lose his eyesight if he continued to return to Ground Zero. And so did Frank Silecchia, the construction worker who found the Ground Zero cross.

To Marty Davin, the rubble seemed like a giant ant hill. And when he finally climbed to the top and peered into a chasm of steel and concrete, he remembers thinking that he was staring into the "gates of hell." The fires below seemed to burn endlessly. It didn't matter how much water the fire department's trucks sprayed or how many tons of concrete and steel were removed by the dozen cranes that were brought to the site. The damage was deep—seemingly endless.

Still, the police and firefighters kept coming. "I think a lot of guys were just trying to do something to help," Davin said years later. "There was a feeling of 'let me try.'"

At the same time, Davin's experience as a detective told him early on that finding anyone alive was almost impossible. The damage was too extensive and harsh. Even when Davin was sent with a team of police officers to climb onto nearby rooftops in search of rubble, he sensed that they would find little besides the dust. But he went anyway. Every available spot in the three-square-mile section of Lower Manhattan that would eventually be described as "exposed" had to be searched.

One morning, Lieutenant John Ryan of the Port Authority police led a team on a search of the underground parking garages at the Trade Center. It was a ghostly trek into a silent and dark world. The team descended a staircase where doors and corridors had been marked with orange "X's"—the sign that other teams had already searched the area. Finally, the team found the garage. Several officers scanned the darkness with flashlights. Beams of light illuminated dust particles suspended in the air over dozens of parked cars that looked as if they were well-preserved wrecks that had sunk deep into a darkened ocean.

The team moved to another staircase that led to the underground shopping mall—and more dust that covered dolls in a toy store. In a bookstore, a poster-sized sign still stood by the door, announcing an upcoming appearance and book-signing by Jack Welch, the former chairman of General Electric who had just released his autobiography. Near one of the bookstore's cash registers, someone had left a wristwatch that was still ticking.

Back on the surface of the rubble pile, the searchers faced another sort of emotional balancing act. Teams of construction workers, who knew how to operate backhoes to move heavy debris and welders' torches, ended up working side by side with police and firefighters who showed up—often after working all day in a patrol car or firehouse—to search at night for the bodies of their friends and colleagues.

Within days, the construction workers, cops, and firefighters fell into a search and recovery system. The cops and firefighters would walk ahead of a backhoe as if they were trying to delicately find buried landmines. Some officers and firefighters pulled and scratched at the debris with their bare hands or garden rakes and shovels. The construction teams, in turn, lifted the heavy concrete or cut through the tangled pipes and beams.

If they found something—a hand, a leg, an office worker's dress, a police officer's handcuffs, or a firefighter's helmet and fireproof coat—work stopped. Construction workers shut off their machines and, with the police and firefighters, would remove their protective hard hats and stand in silence as a stretcher carried the flag-draped remains or other items out of the rubble to a temporary morgue that had been constructed on the site.

One afternoon, a firefighter reached into the dust and picked up a charred ear. Another firefighter found what seemed to be a blackened stick that turned out to be a bone from someone's leg. Yet another firefighter found a small album of wedding photos that had somehow survived the fires. He stared in silence at the photos, holding the album as if it was a prayer book.

On another section of the pile that day, a female Port Authority officer crawled on her knees, slowly sifting through the pulverized concrete wearing knee pads, a hard hat, a respirator, and gardening gloves for women from a collection marketed by Martha Stewart.

She explained later that the cartons of men's gloves donated to the Ground Zero teams were too big for her hands, so she brought her own. And when she discovered that the truckload of donated boots were made to fit men, she wore her own boots. (Learning that more women like her were helping at Ground Zero, a shoe company sent a truck full of women's boots.)

The needs of many Ground Zero workers extended far beyond boots, gloves, and brief moments of silence, however. The attacks had killed many of the searchers' colleagues. Some of those who survived developed survivor's guilt. Others felt the guilt that they had not done enough on the day of the attacks—or now, at the rubble pile.

On the day of the attacks, Peter Killeen, the stress management counselor for the union that represents the Port Authority Police Department's 1,200 officers, sensed that he would be facing a tidal wave of emotional problems.

Killeen knew firsthand what it was like to be a cop. His father served on the Port Authority force. Then Peter signed on. But after two years, he left to follow another calling. He joined the Franciscan friars, the Roman Catholic order of priests that Fathers Brian Jordan and Mychal Judge also joined.

Killeen spent another eight years with the Franciscans before discovering that the life of a priest was not for him. From there, however, he decided to become a psychologist. And, with his police officer's background, he was quickly hired as a therapist for Port Authority officers.

Beginning with the day of the attacks, Killeen felt as if he had been on a non-stop emotional treadmill as he tried to offer help for the officers. Many told him they felt psychologically and physically exhausted. He even found one hiding in a closet—a refuge of sorts to get away from the reminders that he had survived but some of his colleagues had not.

Killeen's cell phone pinged constantly with calls for help with officers at the George Washington Bridge, the Lincoln and Holland Tunnels, even the airports that were patrolled by the Port Authority police.

But the most troubling spot was Ground Zero. Early on, Killeen noticed some officers just staring blankly as they went about their tasks. To Killeen, it was the first sign of post-traumatic stress disorder (PTSD), similar to what soldiers sometimes experience after an intense period of time in a combat zone.

"Some officers are not functioning well, and I have to tell a commander to send them home," Killeen said a few weeks after the attacks. "Everybody is very eager to help and be supportive to everyone who has suffered a loss. In the meantime, they are trying to carry on as police officers."

Like NYPD officers and New York firefighters, many of the Port Authority cops were putting in twelve-hour shifts at Ground Zero while also working their normal police shifts. Killeen found that this kind of schedule was basically a prescription for problems. "They go home but they want to be here [at the site] so they can pull out their coworkers for better or worse," Killeen said. "That way, they know they did everything possible to rescue their friends."

Marriages frayed. So did the psyches and patience of otherwise stable officers. Many slept only three or four hours between shifts.

Killeen was seen as the primary healing balm. And yet, he knew the wounds he was seeing in the officers' emotions would likely not heal for years—if they ever healed.

As if that was not enough, Killeen also found himself counseling the spouses of officers who were missing. One afternoon, after meeting with officers all day to discuss their PTSD symptoms, he drove to a gathering at a Port Authority office near the George Washington Bridge to listen to the heartbreaking stories of a dozen spouses of missing officers.

In those sorrowful and vulnerable conversations with spouses of missing officers or even with those officers who survived, when despair seemed to permeate every word, Killeen said he tried to instill just a flicker of hope that someone might miraculously be found in the Ground Zero rubble—or at least identifiable remains would be quickly found. "Otherwise," he said, "it would be too devastating, impossible for them to function."

But he knew the reality facing the surviving officers and the spouses who mourned the missing. It was the same reality he faced as he tried to offer advice.

Few bodies would ever be found. Even planning a funeral became a difficult struggle because remains were so difficult to identify. In the end, most victims' relatives and friends would be left trying to preserve the memories of the missing.

* * *

Four weeks after the attacks of September 11, the friends and family of Tom Swift gathered at St. Aloysius Catholic Church on the western edge of Jersey City.

Swift was the only worker from South Tower's seventieth floor who was still classified as missing. No one had heard anything from him—or about him—since he telephoned his wife and mother and stepped into an elevator.

Tom's wife, Jill, had already reached the painful conclusion that Tom had perished. As was the case with many victims, Tom's remains had not been found. But Jill did not want to continue with the agonizing wait-and-see routine of waiting for a confirmation of some sort. She felt it was time to memorialize him.

Tom's parents, Peter and Frances, refused to come—at first. As with many victims' relatives, they tried to keep some measure of hope alive. It's not that they expected their son to unexpectedly reappear with a remarkable tale of how he survived but had been in hiding or in some sort of coma for the past month. It's just that different people sometimes follow different paths in accepting that someone close has died. With the 9/11 attacks, that process of acceptance was made all the more painful and challenging because so many victims simply vanished.

Five minutes before the service began, however, Peter and Frances walked into the church, through the front portico made of Indiana limestone and up the main aisle under the 100-feet-high arched ceiling that was meant to evoke the same French Gothic Renaissance design as several churches in Paris.

St. Aloysius Church was, in some ways, a fitting place for Tom's memorial service. More than a century before, it had been built with the piecemeal donations of Jersey City's Irish working-class immigrants who unloaded the ships that docked in Hoboken or built the web of roads across New Jersey and New York. As the first in his family to attend college and become a rising star at the Trade Center, Tom represented the best of what those immigrants once hoped for. And the grandeur of St. Aloysius, in many ways, also symbolized that immigrant pride.

A few blocks beyond the church, on West Side Avenue, Holy Name Cemetery, with its forest of stone angels and crosses, was home to the graves of many of those immigrants. Beyond that, like a steady soundtrack, the hum of cars and trucks echoed from the Pulaski Skyway, a five-mile labyrinth of steel and pillars that was considered the first of America's superhighways when it opened in 1932.

Tom Swift's boss on the seventieth floor in the South Tower, Jack Kemp, stepped up to a microphone. Kemp, who ran the twenty-six-member marketing team for the Morgan Stanley investment house, had given eulogies before—but always for friends and colleagues who were his age or older. "Swifty," as Kemp called Tom, was young enough to be a son.

As he looked over the pews that included the staffers who escaped the South Tower with him, Kemp felt his throat tighten. Coming to the church that morning had been an emotional step for Kemp and the others from Morgan Stanley. As life-threatening as the 9/11 attacks had been for them, they had survived. Here now, in the pews were Nancy Kennedy and Alison Greeley, who had held hands as they descended the South Tower stairs. Sitting nearby were Doug Brown and Stan Kapica who carried a severely injured man to safety.

"Often when people ask Wall Streeters what they do for a living, they struggle for an answer to describe their actual jobs," Kemp began. "As an example, when my daughters were young, they would see the twin towers of the World Trade Center and proudly say that 'they' were 'Daddy's work'. I am certain that many of you who have grown up here in the shadow of those towers have often described them with similar vagueness. But now, with the events of September 11, we are all more aware of what the WTC towers meant to us and are more intimately aware of the lives that were spent in those towers by the people who worked there. Tom Swift was one of those people. His career with us at Morgan Stanley is what the American dream is all about: dedication, hard work, teamwork, ambition, recognition, and success. Tommy lived that dream."

Kemp went on to speak about Swift's devotion to the New York Yankees baseball team, how he amused his colleagues with stories about his weekend exploits, how he was "such a caring and giving person: a true friend."

And then Kemp turned to his own feelings. For weeks, Kemp had felt the heaviness of Swift's disappearance and probable death. For him, the loss was personal.

"Since the first time I learned that 'Swifty' was missing," Kemp said, "I have thought daily of the times that Tom and I have spent both at work and play."

In those sad moments, Kemp said he took some comfort by reminding himself of an observation by Helen Keller: "With every friend I love who has been taken into the brown bosom of the Earth, a part of me has been buried there."

With that, he finished. As he stepped away from the microphone, Kemp felt his eyes filling with tears.

* * *

On the Monday after Thanksgiving, Phil McArdle stood at a podium and looked across the pews at St. Elizabeth of Hungary Catholic Church in Melville, Long Island. McArdle had already attended a dozen or more funerals and memorial services for the 343 firefighters who were missing. Sometimes, there were twenty-five in just one day. He couldn't attend each of them. No one could. So sometimes he would stay for half of the service, then leave to attend the second half of another.

"I knew many people in the department," McArdle said later. "I lost many friends."

But the memorial that took place on the Monday after Thanksgiving was especially meaningful. Dennis Scauso was one of McArdle's closest colleagues on the Hazmat 1 team.

Every pew was filled with Scauso's family, firefighters, local residents, and many admirers. Even New York City's Mayor Rudolph Giuliani was there.

After his harrowing escape from the collapse of the towers and his rescue of the photographer, David Handschuh, McArdle returned to a horrific reality at his firehouse in Maspeth, Queens. Nineteen firefighters from Hazmat 1 and its sister unit, Squad 288, had perished at the Trade Center or were missing, including Dennis Scauso. Left behind were fifty-one children who would now go through life without their fathers. Scauso had been father to four of those children.

Years later, McArdle said he knew in those early days that he could not remove the pain that was pumping through the remaining firefighters in Hazmat 1 and Squad 288. But he could help the living. He took it upon himself to become a "liaison officer" for the families of the dead or missing.

He helped to create information packets for widows and others that explained how to apply for benefits. When a firefighter's body or remains were found at Ground Zero, McArdle accompanied senior FDNY officers to the homes of the surviving families to break the news. And when a funeral or memorial service was held, it often fell to McArdle to deliver a eulogy.

Dennis Scauso had been one of the most valued firefighters among the talented Hazmat 1 unit. To join the group, firefighters had to study far more than the basics of extinguishing a blaze at a home or apartment building. The hazardous materials that the unit was summoned to handle ranged from bombs to chemical spills. Unlike most FDNY units who arrived at fires in one ladder truck or an engine, Hazmat 1 needed an extra truck to hold all of its specialized chemical detection devices as well as protective clothing.

Scauso, forty-six, had been a commercial charter pilot for nearly a decade before joining the fire department. But what made him so valuable was his talent for fixing almost any machine or device that malfunctioned. The firefighters called him "MacGyver" after the fictional TV character who had a knack for solving technical problems and avoiding crises.

At his home in Dix Hills, Long Island, "Scauso-MacGyver" fixed cars and boats. He built a tree house. He repaired leaky faucets and remodeled rooms, brought injured birds and racoons back to health. He met his wife, Janlyn, when he offered to repair her car. As Janlyn reminded the congregation in a letter to her husband that was printed in the memorial service booklet, he even paused construction on their home so he could save twelve salamanders that he discovered were living in the foundation.

Phil McArdle thought of all of these attributes as he was about to deliver that eight-minute eulogy for Scauso that he had written. There was no coffin. Scauso's remains had not been identified. It would be months before his crushed fire helmet turned up in the pile.

The morning's sunlight beamed through the red and blue and yellow and green stained-glass window on the wall behind the podium. A potted palm stood on one side of the altar sanctuary. An easel holding a large photo of Scauso taken from the side as he looked up from one of his repair jobs stood on the other side.

The church's pastor, Father Bruce Powers, had already spoken of how "God was truly present in Dennis" and others who rushed into the towers. "He was an actual rescuer. He gave himself totally. He gave himself completely," Father Powers said. "He's here. He's with us all. He's with us in spirit, in our hearts. He will not be forgotten."

Mayor Giuliani then stepped forward. Giuliani was nearing the end of his mayoral tenure. His replacement, Michael Bloomberg, the founder of a financial news service that had grown into a billion-dollar enterprise, had already been elected and was set to take office in another month.

For his part, Giuliani had been already touted as "America's Mayor" for his eloquent speeches that helped to calm New York City as well as the rest of the nation during the harrowing days after the 9/11 attacks. Political observers felt it was only a matter of time before Giuliani would take another step up the ladder of public service, perhaps as a US senator or even to the White House. There were no hints yet that Giuliani's otherwise laudable political career would sink amid a series of personal, legal, and political controversies. For now, he commanded wide respect across America.

And on this day, Giuliani displayed his unique ability to combine eloquence and insight while also touching people in a personal way.

"Our country has become stronger and more united and more courageous," Giuliani said. "That did not happen by accident. It happened because of men like Dennis who were there, who were so brave and so courageous that it now requires the rest of us to be that way or at least try to be that way."

Giuliani described how so many in America were now wearing US flag pins or flying the flag from their porches and balconies. "They're deeply moved by feelings," he said. "The reason is because of the way these men acted. Just think for a minute if that same attack had taken place on our country and people had run and trampled over each other. Just think what would have happened to the spirit of this country."

The crowd clapped loudly as Giuliani finished and McArdle stood up and walked to the podium.

His eyes darted across the pews and then finally settled on the first row with Scauso's wife and their four children.

McArdle knew from his other eulogies that one of the most difficult tasks was deciding how to speak to children who had lost a parent. Should he speak of how a man whom the children knew as "daddy" had influenced the world of a firehouse? How he could repair broken devices that detected the presence of dangerous gases or chemicals? Or should he get personal, especially in speaking to a child who might not yet understand that her father was not coming home?

"He talked about each one of you," McArdle said as he looked at the children.

McArdle mentioned how Scauso loved to work on a boat with his son, Donald. How he helped his oldest daughter, Darcie, with her homework even after a long day at the firehouse. How he sat by the side of his daughter, Gabrielle, when she was hospitalized with an acute bout of asthma. Then, to Juliette, he said: "Wasn't your dad the best at piggy back rides?"

At just four years old, Juliette was Scauso's youngest. Wearing a burgundy dress and with several strands of her thick brown hair pulled back in a braid, she grasped her mother's hand as she stood outside the church before the service. The FDNY bagpipe band played the Irish ballad "Going Home." In one hand, Juliette held a doll.

Years later, Juliette would talk of how she found it difficult to understand that her father had perished. For the memorial service booklet, she had written a letter to her father. She recounted how her father would tickle her and how he would pick her up from nursery school and take her to lunch at McDonald's. She remembered how her father would let her ride on his tractor "even when it was bumpy."

Juliette ended with the memory of her father helping her get into bed at night and comforting her so she could fall off to sleep. "You wrap your angel wings around," Juliette wrote. "I miss you, daddy."

McArdle ended his eulogy with a message for the children. "You know what is expected of you. Make your dad proud," he said. "And don't forget to help your mom."

As the memorial service ended, Juliette was still holding her mother's hand as she walked outside to the curb by the church driveway with the entire Scauso family. McArdle and two other firefighters approached and stood at attention and saluted.

One firefighter handed a Hazmat 1 fire helmet to Scauso's son. McArdle handed a US flag that had been folded into a triangle to Scauso's father. The other firefighter started to hand a triangle-folded flag to Scauso's widow, Janlyn.

But Juliette reached for the flag. The bagpipers marched away to the tune of "America the Beautiful." Juliette hugged the flag to her chest.

* * *

Two months later . . .

Phil McArdle was at the podium of another church for another funeral to deliver yet another eulogy.

But this one was even more personal.

McArdle's sixteen-year-old son, Andrew, had been killed when his car skidded off one of the icy roads that twisted through the hills near the family's home in Carmel, New York.

McArdle had moved his family there to get away from New York City's congestion and all the troubles that came with so many people living so close together. And now, he was presented with the kind of tragedy that parents fear most. Still, he felt it was his duty to eulogize his son.

McArdle described how his son had become a top student in his class and how he had become a budding star on the soccer, baseball, and football teams. In fact, he heard that some college scouts were already asking about Andrew.

But then, as he did with Dennis Scauso's children, McArdle delved into some of his most personal feelings. "Most parents, during their life, will talk about what they have taught their children," he said. "While my wife and I had taught our beloved son many things, he has taught us a great deal more. He taught us how important the little things in life were. He was kind, gentle, respectful, humble, and generous."

As he ended, McArdle turned to his fellow firefighters, especially those with Hazmat 1 and Squad 288. "We've lost so much together," he said. "I could not have gotten through this without your help."

McArdle would later tell friends that he would not have been able to speak at his son's funeral if he had not given eulogies at the funerals and memorial services of so many firefighters. But that did not make his task any easier. He realized that the loss of friends and colleagues, the hundreds of funerals, the eulogies he volunteered to give, the visits to the homes of grieving families, and, now, the loss of his own son had taken a toll on him. Soon after, as he spoke to officials who ran the fire department, McArdle said something that would describe why so many first responders carried so much pain for so many years.

"We did a great job taking care of the dead, but a terrible job taking care of the living," McArdle said.

In the coming years, as so many struggled to cope with the reality that the remains of their loved ones and friends had not been identified and so many first responders became sick from Ground Zero's toxins, he would repeat those words many times.

In Washington, DC, attorney Ron Motley, surrounded by relatives of 9/11 victims and survivors of the attacks, as he announces a federal lawsuit against seven international banks, eight Islamic foundations, several individual financiers, the Saudi bin Laden Group, three Saudi Arabian princes, and the government of Sudan for allegedly bank-rolling the 9/11 attacks. Motley's court action, filed on August 15, 2002, was the first of a series of lawsuits which claimed that a variety of international business figures and Saudi Arabian government officials and others with ties to the Saudi government reportedly played a role in assisting the 9/11 terrorists. Photo by Mark Wilson/Getty Images.

6

Let's Take 'em to Court

The sprawling town of Woodbridge, with its web of highways, malls, and warehouses nearly twenty-five miles from Ground Zero in the flatlands of New Jersey, might seem an unlikely place to launch a major lawsuit on behalf of victims of terrorism. But on a Thursday evening in mid-March 2002, nearly fifty relatives of victims of the September 11 attacks gathered in a law firm conference room in Woodbridge to hear about a complex legal action to track down the financial backers of the 9/11 attacks and force them to pay a large financial penalty for the death and destruction they caused. The lawsuit that began to take shape in that meeting—and other similar lawsuits that combined with it later—would become the biggest legal action in the history of the United States.

That night, Terry Strada took one of the seats near the front of the room. She felt pulled to come to the meeting, as if dragged by a magnet. She found a babysitter and slipped behind the wheel of her car for the thirty-minute drive down the highway. It was time, she felt, to hold somebody accountable for the murder of her husband. She was tired of waiting. It was also the first time since September 11 that she had been away from her newborn son and two other small children.

For Strada, the last seven months had been an emotional see-saw.

She felt near-constant internal pressure to remain mentally grounded enough to take care of her infant son, Justin, who was born only four days before the 9/11 attacks. With a newborn in the house, there were diapers to change, feedings to schedule, and naps to monitor, not to mention her own physical and emotional recovery after giving birth. But beneath the strong motherly appearance that she projected for her children and others close to her, Strada wrestled to control a near-constant state of mourning, despair, and anger. The idyllic dream she had longed for, with a loving husband and three children, in the lush New Jersey suburbs had been erased in a few hours on September 11 by an act of terrorism. Her life was not merely turned upside down on that clear blue Tuesday; she felt as if she had been tossed into a swirling storm with no end in sight.

Her husband, Tom, a successful broker at the Cantor Fitzgerald investment firm on the top floors of the World Trade Center's North Tower, was officially still listed as "missing." But Terry knew the truth: Tom was gone.

Knowing her husband's fate was one thing; accepting it was an entirely different emotional challenge. Strada's children—a seven-year-old son named Thomas and a four-year-old daughter named Kaitlyn, along with Baby Justin—were destined to grow up without their father. Just trying to envision what those years would be like for her children saddened Terry deeply. And, meanwhile, at just forty-one years old, she had been put in the position of facing her future with a title she never expected to have at her age: widow.

On that Thursday evening in March, however, when Strada sat down in the tenth-floor conference room at the Wilentz Law firm in Woodbridge, New Jersey, she felt her dark emotions calm a bit. She sensed that she had finally found someone who not only understood the pain and disappointment rippling through her life and the lives of thousands of relatives of 9/11 victims, but he had a plan to do something about it.

He was a lawyer named Ron Motley.

"The ground beneath my grief began to shift toward purpose," Strada later said.

* * *

Ron Motley was already a legend in America's legal circles before he traveled to New Jersey from his home in Mount Pleasant, South Carolina, on that Thursday evening in March 2002.

At 58 years old, Motley had been singled out as one of America's most influential lawyers as the twentieth century folded into the twenty-first. Plain-spoken, with an understated Southern drawl and an innate ability to charm juries with his stories and polite manner, Motley quickly developed a reputation for taking on the big and powerful who seemed immune to legal accountability. After graduating from the University of South Carolina and teaching history in a public high school for several years, Motley headed back to his alma mater to study law. Armed with his law degree, he seemed like a man on a mission. After a few years as a local prosecutor and as a junior attorney with a larger law firm, he set up his own legal practice where he could be the boss. And instead of building his own firm with small cases in his corner of South Carolina, he quickly discovered that he had a knack for looking beyond his state's borders and finding a way to pull together a wide array of clients and other attorneys in massive lawsuits that examined some of the most fundamental problems in America. In short, Ron Motley wanted to make the biggest splash possible.

During the 1980s, he took aim at the nation's multi-billion-dollar asbestos industry and its link to the rising number of deadly cancer cases and other fatal ailments that drained funds from tax-funded public health-care accounts while also bankrupting far too many families who needed years of medical care. But rather than follow the standard path for a small-town lawyer by representing one or two clients and winning judgments of perhaps a few million dollars in courtroom skirmishes that barely made the news, Motley developed a national strategy that would definitely attract attention and possibly change the way America handles health care. After forming an alliance with dozens of other lawyers across America, he won a series of victories with massive financial paybacks from the asbestos industry that could fund the medical costs for the rising number of people suffering from lung cancer, mesothelioma, and other asbestos-related illness. What resulted was the creation of an unprecedented $30 billion trust fund to help asbestos victims cover their health-care bills.

Motley brought the same strategy—with an even larger vision—when he decided to take on the nation's tobacco industry in the 1990s. As with asbestos, Motley's goal was to force America's cigarette makers to shoulder some of the extensive health-care costs of treating millions of cancer patients who had become regular smokers. This wasn't just making a big splash as he did with the asbestos case. Motley wanted an earthquake and a legal tsunami.

For this case, Motley pulled together an even larger alliance. His firm represented twenty-five states and government agencies whose tax-funded coffers had been slowly drained by paying health-care bills for smokers. Lawyers for another twenty states and five US territories joined in, too. And by 1998, Big Tobacco gave up and settled by agreeing to pay a whopping $246 billion over the next quarter century to cover health care for smoking-related diseases. Motley's firm pulled in an estimated $2 billion in fees just from the tobacco settlement.

The case cemented Motley's reputation and place in legal history. The money also helped to bankroll Motley's hard-charging lifestyle. Known as a man who could work twelve hours, then party well past midnight, he married five times. He traveled around the nation on his own plane. He built a mansion on South Carolina's fashionable Kiawah Island and bought a 156-foot yacht that he named "Themis" after the Greek goddess of law who is often depicted in modern culture as a blindfolded "Lady Justice" holding a sword and a set of scales.

Motley also decided to change the direction of his legal career. And now, he had the cash to do it in a big way. In 2002, he formed a new law firm with the expressed goal of taking on causes, not just legal cases. The idea here was to use the law to attack some of America's most fundamental problems that government agencies were unwilling to face—or were just too inept or handcuffed by bureaucracy to handle.

To Motley, the terrorist attack of September 11, 2001, was such a cause. He figured he was just the man for the job.

As Terry Strada watched that evening in the main conference room of the Wilentz, Goldman and Spitzer law firm in Woodbridge, Motley rose and stood behind a mahogany conference table. Before him, in rows of chairs as if they were attending a class, sat the approximately fifty 9/11 victims' relatives.

As a shrewd student of the power lines in American law and culture, Motley knew he was making a statement in selecting this law firm in Woodbridge, New Jersey, as the site of his first meeting. Founded by David Wilentz in 1919, the firm had grown to become one of the most influential in New Jersey. Several of its lawyers were already representing survivors of the attacks and families of victims.

Early in his career, David Wilentz established himself as a power broker in the state's politics that had been dominated for decades by a set of influential party bosses. But like Ron Motley with his legal assault on Big Tobacco, Wilentz also vaulted to national legal fame—and some controversy—with a single case.

As New Jersey's attorney general in 1935, Wilentz led the prosecution of Bruno Richard Hauptmann, who had been charged with the kidnapping and murder of the twenty-month-old infant son of aviation pioneer Charles Lindbergh. In 1927, Lindbergh had been the first to fly solo and nonstop across the Atlantic Ocean and, at the time, he was considered a bona fide national hero. Eight years later, the so-called "Trial of the Century," with Hauptmann cast as the villain who snatched the baby from its crib, and the Lindberghs as the victims, became something of a daily soap opera for Depression-era America. Newspapers and magazines assigned numerous reporters. But radio coverage, then a relatively untested form of media, played a key role in broadcasting near-instantaneous news across America. In the end, Wilentz not only achieved a conviction, but a death sentence in the state's electric chair for Hauptmann.

After World War II, Wilentz's firm became a central figure in major legal cases involving New Jersey's oil and casino industries, as well as land development—notably the waterfront in Jersey City. David's son, Robert, would go on to become chief justice of the New Jersey Supreme Court where he wrote the landmark ruling on the controversial Baby M surrogacy case in the mid-1980s that set the standard for regulating the practice of paying women to bear a child for someone else. By the 1990s, the Wilentz firm's attorneys, following a path set by Ron Motley, won a major ruling in an asbestos case involving ship repair workers at the Brooklyn Navy Yard. In 1998, the firm was also co-counsel in helping New Jersey secure $7.6 billion in the Big Tobacco case that Motley led.

Appropriately for such an influential law firm, the walls of its 50-by-30-foot conference room were lined with paintings of each of the twenty-one county courthouses in New Jersey. By the door, a portrait of David Wilentz looked on. And from a row of windows along the east wall, the crowd that night could look across the various highways, warehouses, apartment complexes, and malls and see all the way to Ground Zero and the spot where their loved ones were killed.

Terry Strada did not look out the window. She suddenly found herself enveloped and focused by a new sense of mission and hope—all inspired by Ron Motley.

As he spoke, Strada felt drawn to Motley's passion and style. His courtly demeanor and soft, South Carolina drawl helped to relax the room. And yet, Strada quickly noticed that a deep passion and intensity lurked under Motley's seemingly easy-going manner. He did not speak in legal complexities. Instead, he seemed adept at reducing the law's often complicated language to easily digestible rhetoric that touched one's heart, mind, and sense of reason. He spoke about trying to achieve justice. And yet, he also seemed sensitive enough to know that the people in the room with him were experiencing intense and unmitigated pain.

In some ways, Motley reminded Strada of both her father and her husband. Motley was short—like her father. But, like her husband, Tom, Motley projected a larger-than-life presence that was captivating, not so much with the theatrics of a TV lawyer but with a down-to-earth authenticity, sincerity, and a belief in basic values like truth and justice. "The moment he began to speak, I sensed I was in the company of brilliance," Strada said later.

Strada was a Republican. She certainly did not consider herself a table-turning radical who demanded major changes in American life. She felt Motley's patriotism and love for America was as deep as hers. And, like Motley, she felt that her own government had misled the nation by implying that the 9/11 plot was a complete surprise. As she entered the meeting that night, Strada suspected that the 9/11 attacks could have been prevented. She was sure of it now after listening to Ron Motley.

As Motley laid out his legal strategy for his lawsuit, it was also clear that he was thinking far beyond Osama bin Laden and his collection of killers in the mountains of Afghanistan. As dangerous as bin Laden and his al-Qaeda network were, Motley was not satisfied in bringing only them to justice. Anyway, when it came to a lawsuit that sought financial compensation for his clients, Motley knew that it might be difficult in forcing bin Laden and al-Qaeda's terrorists to fork over any money. The exception, of course, was bin Laden himself. He was the son of a billionaire contractor in Saudi Arabia. But he reportedly disowned his family—at least publicly. Motley figured that trying to bring him to court amounted to walking into a dark tunnel with no end.

Instead, Motley introduced the group that night to what he had already come to believe was the real culprit behind the 9/11 attacks and years of other terrorist misdeeds.

He said it was Saudi Arabia.

Or more specifically, Motley believed it was the money that flowed from Saudi Arabia's various banks, charities, and rich families into the accounts of al-Qaeda and other terrorist groups.

Saudi Arabia's Islamic-based system of government was thought to have played a leading role in almost every aspect of culture and business in that nation. But was the Saudi Arabian government involved—or at least complicit by ignoring the possibility that the terrorism it publicly condemned was actually funded by people within its borders—and perhaps on the government payroll? If so, how extensive was this inolvement? And how could any of this be proven in an American court with America's laws that provided legal immunity from lawsuits to most foreign governments?

At that early date, Motley did not know. And, certainly, he had no idea of the delicate political and legal squabbles awaiting him and the 9/11 survivors and relatives of victims who signed on to the lawsuit.

* * *

Soon after 9/11, a steady trickle of evidence pointed directly toward Saudi Arabia. These were not just unfounded suspicions or conspiracy theories. Not only were Osama bin Laden and fifteen of the nineteen al-Qaeda operatives who carried out the 9/11 attacks from Saudi Arabia, but US and British investigators suspected that a portion of the funding for the plot passed through several Saudi banks and Islamic charities. Some of that money had reportedly been donated by wealthy and politically connected Saudi citizens including members of the Saudi royal family and possibly by bin Laden's Saudi relatives who had earned their fortunes primarily in building roads and various pieces of the oil production facilities.

Other alarming information also emerged. FBI agents investigating the 9/11 attacks learned that at least one suspected Saudi government intelligence operative living undercover in California and reportedly with links to other intelligence officials at the Saudi embassy in Washington, DC, had met with two Saudi men who turned out to be members of one of the 9/11 hijacking teams when they arrived in Los Angeles. Those two hijackers turned out to be Khalid al-Mihdhar and Nawaf al-Hazmi, the al-Qaeda operatives that the CIA was trailing from Malaysia and Thailand and who had caused the FBI's liason with the CIA, Mark Rossini, to become so worried at the potential danger facing the US that he asked for permission from the CIA to alert his colleagues at the FBI but was prohibited from doing so. Also, a Muslim cleric at a Saudi government-funded mosque in Los Angeles met with the two future hijackers—al-Mihdhar and al-Hazmi—after they arrived. And, in a separate inquiry, US Treasury and National Security officials told Congressional investigators that they believed that a web of Saudi banks and religious-based charities had not just financed the 9/11 attacks, but had become a major nexus of financing a great deal of al-Qaeda's terrorism, which included attacks on US embassies in Africa and a US Navy warship that had docked in Yemen.

Several important questions lurked behind this evidence, however. Did the Saudi government know about the alleged flow of money to al-Qaeda through banks in its nation? If not, why not?

And, in America, why did the low-level Saudi intelligence operative and the Muslim cleric—both of whom presumably had other things to do—bother to meet with al-Mihdhar and al-Hazmi who just happened to arrive in Los Angeles? Did the operative and the cleric know that al-Mihdhar and al-Hazmi were affiliated with al-Qaeda? Did they know a major terrorist plot was afoot? Put another way: Did the Saudi intelligence operative and the cleric ever ask why al-Mihdhar and al-Hazmi were visiting America?

What's more, were the intelligence operative and the cleric ordered by higher-ups in the Saudi government to meet with al-Mihdhar and al-Hazmi? Or were the operative and the cleric just acting on their own? Or, most unlikely but nevertheless worth asking: Did these meetings between the operative, the cleric, and the two future hijackers just happen by accident?

Finally, and perhaps most important to the future of the complex diplomatic relationship between the US and Saudi Arabia: Did Saudi leaders in government or finance just turn a deaf ear to the speculation that Islamist terrorists were using Saudi money to carry out their attacks in America? Or, like the Americans, was Saudi Arabia's government and especially its intelligence apparatus caught by surprise by the 9/11 attacks?

As if those questions were not explosive enough, another concern centered on the extensive US intelligence gathering apparatus: Were American counter-intelligence experts paying enough attention before 9/11 to the rising tide of warnings that a major attack by al-Qaeda was in the works? And if they were, why didn't they either ring alarm bells or take steps to disrupt the plot?

Questions also arose about President George W. Bush's relationship with Saudi Arabia. Just eight days after the 9/11 attacks, Bush gave permission for thirteen of bin Laden's relatives to leave the US on a special chartered jet without being interrogated by the FBI.

The controversial decision, critics said, reflected the Bush family's long history of close ties to Saudi Arabia. Bush's father, President George H.W. Bush, served as an advisor to the Carlyle Group, a private US asset management firm whose investors until 2001 included the Saudi corporation run by bin Laden's family. Also, in Washington, the Saudi ambassador to the US, Prince Bandar bin Sultan al Saud, had developed such close ties to the Bush family and was such a frequent visitor to the White House when Bush's son, George W. Bush, took office that he was sometimes facetiously referred to by the Washington media as "Bandar Bush."

As that long-private Bush-Saudi history began to emerge after the 9/11 attacks, investigators for a joint Senate-House congressional committee had come across a disturbing possibility—that money sent by Prince Bandar's wife, Princess Haifa, to allegedly help pay medical bills of the wife of a Saudi citizen in California may have been passed to another account and used for living expenses for al-Mihdhar and al-Hazmi.

Was this just another coincidence? Or was the alleged transfer of money significant? And, if so, how significant?

The mystery that shadowed the speculation about the meetings with al-Mihdhar and al-Hazmi in California, coupled with the increasing number of questions about whether high level Saudi officials were involved in some aspect of the 9/11 plot, either overtly or inadvertently, were obviously explosive, legally and diplomatically. But for now, those questions remained unanswered, with no clear effort by US or Saudi authorities to explore them.

It's not known whether George W. Bush or his father demanded any explanation from Prince Bandar about the mysterious links to at least two of the 9/11 hijackers. Bandar and his wife denied that they knew any financial contributions might have found their way to the hijackers.

* * *

Terry Strada had never heard of al-Qaeda before 9/11. She knew little about Saudi Arabia except that it was a key player in the world's oil production. And she certainly was not aware of the Bush family's links to the Saudis. Like so many in America, the murky world of international terrorism and its web of mysteries was far from her radar screen. Her focus was her family and building a life for herself, her husband, and their three children.

She had met her husband, Tom, more than two decades earlier. Terry lived in Pompano, Florida, where her father drove harness race carts. In the summers, when he came north to race at tracks in the New York City area, Terry came with him.

It was the summer of 1981. She was a waitress at the posh Meadowbrook Golf Club in Jericho, Long Island. Tom was the assistant golf pro. She was nineteen. He was twenty-one. Tom was handsome and charismatic. They dated that summer and, again, the following summer. But with Terry in Florida during the winters and Tom in New York, their relationship stalled. By 1983, when Tom landed a job on Wall Street, they went their separate ways. However, a few years later they accidentally ran into each other at a Mexican restaurant.

"We've been together ever since," Terry said.

After 9/11, Strada had not thought of contacting a lawyer or filing any kind of lawsuit. Who would she sue anyway? And why? She already was busy caring for her infant son and trying to keep the house calm for her older son and daughter. Despite being the wife of a well-to-do partner at Cantor Fitzgerald, Terry never even bothered to buy a cell phone. Her husband, Tom, didn't own one either.

With Terry at home with a newborn and her husband missing, Terry's mother came from her home in Kentucky to lend a hand. But after several weeks, Terry's mother was ready to head back home. Terry also felt she needed to find some peace outside of her community. So she packed her children into the family's car and drove her mother back to Kentucky.

After returning to New Jersey, Terry brought her children to a memorial service for her husband in her town of Chatham. She also attended a Catholic memorial service for Tom in Long Island. But she found little peace. "I wasn't even watching the news," she said later.

Finally, Terry joined a support group for 9/11 victims' relatives that met in a local church. Chatham had lost thirteen of its residents on 9/11, mostly men who worked in finance. The group consisted primarily of young widows like herself. Several even had small children that they brought.

Besides a chance to speak personally about their emotional struggles and anger after 9/11, the group also brought in several financial and legal advisors, one of whom mentioned a lawsuit led by Ron Motley that was in the works to track the funding for the 9/11 plot.

Motley had already spent millions on an investigation from his firm's fund that was largely bankrolled by its $2 billion in his share of the tobacco settlement. He had also assembled an experienced squad of former US, European, and Asian intelligence analysts who helped him wade through the thicket of information. Motley was so concerned that his investigators might become terrorist targets that he gave them code names, such as "Arnold the Albanian" and "The Muslim."

As he began his presentation in Woodbridge with Terry Strada looking on, Motley told the group that the 9/11 plot was not just a solitary attack on the United States. He talked about how the same players in 9/11 were also involved in a long series of audacious plans for terrorism. At the top of the list was a plot in 1995 called "Bojinka," which consisted of a wide-ranging series of attacks that involved the assassination of Pope John Paul II, the blowing up of eleven commercial jetliners over the Pacific Ocean, and the hijacking of a plane and crashing it into CIA headquarters in Langley, Virginia.

Counterterrorism agents foiled the plot. But the world seemed to turn a blind eye to the ominous warning that al-Qaeda was not just a small-time gang of terrorists. Yes, al-Qaeda operated from a poorly-equipped base in a remote corner of Afghanistan. As a military force it was no match for the United States with its jets, aircraft carriers, legions of tanks and helicopters, and arsenal of weapons that included radar-guided missiles that could strike a small car from thousands of miles away.

Al-Qaeda's leaders did not seem to care how their army—if you could call it that—stacked up against the United States. But its leaders clearly had big ideas. And they seemed well-funded enough to stage major attacks on Western institutions that would make a big splash.

Perhaps the most serious lesson that Western nations ignored was that a key figure in the Bojinka plot was Ramzi Yousef, who had been the architect of the 1993 bombing of the World Trade Center in New York City. Another name that surfaced, Khalid Sheikh Mohammed, was an American-trained engineer who would later become the logistical and tactical mastermind behind 9/11.

As Motley outlined this disturbing history for the group, Strada felt sickened. Her country clearly had plenty of warnings for the past decade—maybe more. But the Clinton administration did little. The same was true of the Bush administration.

"I felt my breath catch," she said later. "Everything Ron was describing contradicted the public posture of the Bush Administration, which insisted no one could have imagined planes being used as weapons in mass-casualty attacks."

Motley steadily outlined the extensive portfolio of facts he knew so far, with a theory that was as clear as it was tragic: The threat against America was not something that evolved in the weeks or months before September 11, 2001, with nineteen al-Qaeda killers who ended up hijacking four American jetliners. The plan had been brewing for years. And the forces behind it were well-funded.

"Ron laid it out plainly," Strada remembered. "He spoke in plain terms about responsibility—not in the abstract." Most importantly, he was not just offering vague bromides meant to soothe her psyche.

Motley's plan to file a lawsuit made sense. Terry Strada knew she could not pick up a rifle and join the fight in Afghanistan, but she could fight in a US courtroom. Where did the 9/11 terrorists get their money? If she could help to answer that question, she might be able to hold someone—or some nation—accountable for killing her husband. And when Motley told the group at the end of his presentation that they could add their names and contact information to a sheet in the back of the conference room, Strada felt a sudden burst of energy, even optimism.

She didn't just walk across the room nonchalantly to add her name to the list. "I charged," she said.

* * *

Five months later . . .

Terry Strada stepped onto a stage in a ballroom at the J.W. Marriott hotel on 14th Street in Washington, DC. Standing with her were nearly twenty other wives, husbands, mothers, fathers, and children who had lost someone they loved on September 11, 2001, or were fortunate to survive the attacks.

A few feet from Strada stood US Army Specialist April Gallop, who held her son, Elisha. On 9/11, Gallop, though injured in the attack at the Pentagon, managed to rescue Elisha, then only two-months-old, who had been buried under rubble in the Pentagon's daycare center. Later, she received a Purple Heart medal, which the military gives to its members who are injured in combat. It was now August 15, 2002. Elisha had just celebrated his first birthday.

Terry Strada had spent months studying the background of the attacks that killed her husband. She now felt it was time to find his killers, and she wanted to help as much as she could.

That morning, Ron Motley had walked into the US District Courthouse across town on Pennsylvania Avenue and filed a 277-page lawsuit on behalf of 600 survivors and relatives of victims in the 9/11 attacks.

His co-counsel was another formidable attorney, Allan Gerson, who had meticulously pursued the government of Libya for orchestrating the Pan Am 103 terrorist bombing. After years of legal maneuvering by Libya and its leader Muammar Gaddafi, Gerson—with the help of the US government and other attorneys who represented victims—negotiated a settlement in which Libya agreed to pay $2.7 billion for the murders of the 270 victims of Pan Am 103, an average of about $10 million per family.

Gerson also played a major role in persuading Congress—and then-President Bill Clinton—to support the 1996 Anti-terrorism and Effective Death Penalty Act that changed the laws of diplomatic immunity and allowed US victims of terrorism to file lawsuits against governments that had been designated by the US as state sponsors of terrorism after they had provided funds or other assistance to terrorist groups. Before the 9/11 attacks, the law had been used by several families of US victims killed in suicide bombings in Israel to win judgments from the government of Iran for its financial support of the Palestinian terror groups Hamas and Islamic Jihad. Collecting money from Iran remained a thorny issue in 2001, however. The US government ended up compensating the victims of Palestinian terrorism with American dollars and then placing a lien of sorts on frozen Iranian assets held by the US.

In their lawsuit, the 9/11 victims hoped to expand that legal path by claiming that they hoped to pursue various financial "interests" connected to the government of Saudi Arabia. Was the Saudi government, and, in particular, members of the royal family, directly involved in 9/11? Or was the financial link the lawsuit hoped to establish a loose combination of wealthy Saudi business owners, Saudi banks, and Islamic charities? In the coming years, such questions—and the difficulty in answering them conclusively—would emerge as some of the most contentious issues in the 9/11 story.

For now, the lawsuit, drawn up primarily by Ron Motley, cited fifteen counts of alleged law breaking. And the defendants he targeted included seven Saudi Arabian banks, eight Saudi charities, three Saudi princes, several wealthy Saudi businessmen, the massive family conglomerate known as the "The bin Laden Group", and the government of Sudan for its role in actively hiding members of al-Qaeda. He said he was seeking $116 trillion in penalties and damages.

Americans can file lawsuits in US courts against citizens of other nations for all kinds of alleged transgressions, from injuries in car accidents to libel and consumer violations. But suing foreign governments in American courts—or entities linked to foreign governments—is a far more complicated legal adventure.

In 1976, Congress passed the Foreign Sovereign Immunities Act, which spares foreign nations from being held accountable for many of the ways they might hurt American citizens. The diplomatic, political, and practical logic behind such a law is grounded in the fear that if US citizens sued other nations, then those nations will, in turn, file all manner of retaliatory lawsuits against the United States and any citizen who travels abroad.

There are exceptions, of course. American firms are allowed to sue government-owned businesses for such transgressions as fraud or copyright theft. Often these kinds of suits involve nations such as China where the government and even the military has some measure of control in hundreds of private firms. Another exception emerges when a foreign government might illegally seize US property.

But for the most part, foreign governments operate with a default across-the-board protection of immunity. And when it came to fighting back against acts of terrorism, Americans could only file lawsuits against nations that had been designated by the US State Department as "state sponsors of terrorism." In 2001, only seven countries had made that notorious list: Iran, Syria, Cuba, North Korea, Iraq, Libya, and Sudan. Saudi Arabia, for all its seemingly backward customs such as public beheadings of criminals and a ban on women driving cars, was viewed as one of America's most friendly and reliable allies in the Islamic world. It was also the world's leading exporter of oil. As many of the relatives of 9/11 victims would soon learn, some of America's most powerful officials feared that any lawsuits against Saudi Arabia might tear into what otherwise was a delicate alliance.

* * *

Like so much about 9/11, Terry Strada was unaware of the legal nuances and intricacies of filing a lawsuit against a foreign government—or even "interests" connected with it. With this particular lawsuit and its links to another nation, it's not clear that Ron Motley saw the full range of obstacles that were about to emerge as Saudi Arabia prepared to defend itself with battalions of lawyers, lobbyists, and public relations specialists.

Terry Strada watched Motley intently as he stepped to the hotel podium with a sign on its front: "Families United to Bankrupt Terrorism." Four easels held posters that detailed the links between the Saudi financiers, the Sudanese government, and Osama bin Laden's al-Qaeda network.

Motley said the group he represented included police and firefighters, flight attendants, and Ground Zero construction workers, as well as military members injured at the Pentagon and passengers killed on the hijacked flights. The clients lived in New York, Virginia, Texas, Connecticut, Massachusetts, Maryland, New Jersey, Pennsylvania, Minnesota, California, Kansas, North Carolina, Georgia, Arizona, the District of Columbia, Arkansas, Nevada, South Carolina, and Kentucky.

He said he expected to increase his client list to more than 1,000 by the following week. Indeed, since the suit had been filed a few hours earlier, another sixty relatives of 9/11 victims or survivors had called his office to be included in the case.

Motley explained that his first client was Thomas Burnett, Sr., a public high school English teacher in Bloomington, Minnesota, whose son, Thomas Jr., was killed on Flight 93.

With his dark suit and white hair, Burnett looked like a judge as he stepped forward to say a few words about why he felt the need to mount a court case. Burnett described how his son, Thomas Jr., a vice president of a California-based medical devices firm, left behind a wife and three daughters. After Flight 93 was in the hands of the al-Qaeda hijackers, Thomas Jr., joined a group of passengers who tried to take back control of the plane. The hijackers, unable to stop the passenger revolt, ended up crashing the plane into the ground near Shanksville, Pennsylvania.

But before teaming up with other passengers to fight the hijackers, Thomas Jr. called his wife, Deena, at their home in California. Hearing from Deena, a former flight attendant that other planes had been crashed into the Trade Center's twin towers and the Pentagon, Thomas Jr. said, "We're going to do something." The group, which included Todd Beamer, who could be heard saying, "Let's roll," then attacked the hijackers.

From the podium in the Marriott ballroom, with his resonant and deep voice cracking, Thomas Burnett Sr. repeated his son's words: "We're going to do something."

"Our son, Thomas E. Burnett, Jr, was a hero on Flight 93," the senior Burnett added. "He was drafted unknowingly as one of the first citizens soldiers of the war on terrorism. And he did serve his country with calm, with decisiveness, with leadership, and with courage."

Burnett went on to say: "In taking this action, we will move terrorist financing schemes out of the shadows and into the light of day . . . leaving those with evil intentions nowhere to hide and no place to escape accountability."

He paused and gazed for a moment across the crowd of journalists in seats arranged in rows across the ballroom, not unlike the arrangement of chairs at the Wilentz Law Firm conference room in Woodbridge, New Jersey, in March. Then he continued. "We will succeed because we have the facts and the law on our side" and "because we have justice and morality on our side."

Several others stepped forward to speak, including April Gallop, who described how she searched in the darkness and reached through debris to pull her son to safety.

Then Strada stepped to the podium. She looked across the room, her eyes darting from side to side. She looked down at her notes and began to speak slowly and firmly, first about the state of her country.

"September 11 was a national tragedy," she said, when "Americans lost their sense of security and fear crept into our hearts."

Then she turned to her own life. She spoke of how she and her husband had just brought a new baby boy into their home and how they looked ahead to years of happiness. "Our lives were complete," she said, "and we had everything to live for. Our lives were rich with love for each other and love for our three young children."

Then she spoke of what had been lost—for her and for her children.

"My children had the best possible father," she said. "He adored them and lived his life for them. They lost it. And the life they were supposed to have. They will never see, play with, or hug their daddy again. My husband will never hold them or watch them grow up. And I will never feel his arms around me again. He made our life fun and happy. Our lives were rich beyond what money could buy. We've had it all."

The message that day from Terry Strada would continue to echo over and over. Terrorism was not just a problem of national security. It was personal in the lives of its victims.

Strada knew this—and had spent many months grieving. Now, in signing her name to the lawsuit, she was ready for the next step.

She looked over the crowd again.

"Terrorism must be seen for what it is," she said. "It is an act of cowardice against innocent people, an act of hatred toward each and every one of us. We must not just speak about it. We must act against it. In filing this lawsuit, we can go after those who killed our loved ones. By taking their assets, the actual dollars that fund al-Qaeda and other terrorists, we can cripple them. We can bankrupt them. We can stop them."

She turned and walked back to her place on the side of the stage.

Little did she know how many years of struggle awaited her.

Kristen Breitweiser (left) studies newly released report by the 9/11 Commission with Lorie Van Auken. Both women lost their husbands in the attack on New York's World Trade Center and went on, with other victims' relatives, to become major advocates for an investigation into the terrorist attacks. Photo by Mark Wilson/Getty Images.

7

What Safety Net?

A month after Ron Motley filed his lawsuit at the federal courthouse in Washington, DC, Kristen Breitweiser walked into the Philip A. Hart Senate Office Building a few hundred yards away on Capitol Hill. Breitweiser had come to the Hart Building's main hearing room to testify before the "Joint Inquiry Into Intelligence Community Activities Before and After the Terrorist Attacks of September 11, 2001," a long and overly-formal name for a special gathering of Senators and members of the House of Representatives who were examining why the elaborate web of US spy agencies who monitor terrorists could not manage to stop the 9/11 attacks or even see those attacks coming.

Breitweiser certainly supported what the Joint Inquiry—as the group came to be known—wanted to do. But she felt it was not enough. Just looking at the 9/11 attacks as a failure of intelligence services would not address the whole story of why the 9/11 attacks were so tragic.

Breitweiser was lobbying for a broad, multi-faceted government investigation that extended far beyond America's spy system—and even the alleged Saudi links that Ron Motley wanted to explore. She wanted to examine an entire spectrum of mistakes, missed chances, and misjudgments. These ranged from US Customs agents at airports who had few security precautions in place or even basic background checks to stop the team of al-Qaeda terrorists from entering the country to the US Air Force jet fighter pilots at bases along the East Coast who were not alerted soon enough to intercept the hijacked planes. It would include the commercial airlines that offered virtually no security other than unarmed flight attendants to deal with unruly passengers on jetliners, as well as the New York police and fire departments who couldn't communicate with each other on 9/11 because they operated their radios on different frequencies. It would even assess what many had come to believe were the haphazard evacuation plans for the tens of thousands of workers at World Trade Center's twin towers. And, finally, Breitweiser wanted this investigation to turn a spotlight on every major federal agency, from the White House and Congress to the CIA and FBI.

In other words, Breitweiser wanted the full story. And her zeal came down to a blunt question that nagged at her conscience and her basic common sense as she studied the calamitous events that led to her husband's death: Why had America's government and security apparatus, along with a litany of other agencies and businesses, failed so miserably in protecting its citizens?

Such was the beginning of what would become the National Commission on Terrorist Attacks Upon the United States—the 9/11 Commission.

It was September 18, 2002. A week earlier, America held a collective moment of silence to commemorate the first anniversary of the 9/11 attacks while also seeming to breathe a collective sigh of relief that no other attacks had taken place on US soil during that year.

For Breitweiser, just entering the Hart hearing room culminated a mission of her own to persuade her government to listen to her and other women. Months earlier, she had begun a steady routine of driving back and forth to Washington with three women from New Jersey who lost their husbands on September 11. The four became fast friends. And during their treks to Washington, they knocked on the doors of offices of senators and congressional representatives. Sometimes they had appointments. Sometimes they did not.

For the four women, the back-and-forth, one-day car rides, starting just after dawn and ending late in the evening, became a very private and soul-connecting time. In the privacy of a car, each had the emotional space to bare their souls to the others about what it was like to lose their husbands, how their children were coping, and how they were trying to reconnect with the world as young widows.

They casually nicknamed their car "the widow mobile."

The four met at a seminar in northern New Jersey where they listened to an explanation of what sort of compensation the federal government wanted to give them as victims of 9/11. Breitweiser spoke that night—largely off the cuff, she said later—about why it was important for the relatives of those killed on

9/11 to "stand up and fight for our rights" as "individuals and then collectively." Little did Breitweiser know in that moment—and in that brief speech—that she would apply that same rhetoric to another campaign that had little to do with how the US government planned to compensate the victims of 9/11. Instead, Breitweiser had been privately wrestling with a deeply painful question that seemed almost unpatriotic to voice at first: Could her government have done more to stop the 9/11 attacks?

Weeks earlier, Breitweiser had befriended another widow from New Jersey, Patty Casazza. The two talked frequently on the telephone, sometimes exchanging jokes or even thoughts about how they each felt their husbands visited them in their dreams. That night, after Breitweiser spoke at the seminar on compensation, Casazza walked up and hugged her. Casazza then introduced Breitweiser to two more widows from New Jersey, Mindy Kleinberg and Lorie Van Auken. Soon the four began attending meetings of widows and other victims' relatives from New York and Connecticut. At one of those meetings, Breitweiser remembers, another widow gave the four a nickname: "The Jersey Girls."

In some ways, the nickname was seen as an homage to the ballad about love and longing, written by the gravely-voiced Tom Waits, that Bruce Springsteen had turned into a much-demanded, sing-a-long crowd favorite during concerts in New Jersey.

But for the women, the song's name also underscored something far beyond a heartfelt sentiment about the Jersey Shore beach scene. It signaled a newfound power and influence that the women would soon have—especially in Washington's power circles.

In the months after their husbands were lost, the four discovered that they each felt frustrated with their government. Their disappointment extended far beyond the notion of how much money they were entitled to receive because they had suddenly joined a class of terrorist victims in what President Bush was now describing as a war. What also bothered them was how inept their government had been in protecting the nation from terrorists in the first place. Or as Breitweiser later wrote: "My husband and the thousands of others in the World Trade Center never signed on the dotted line for a job that placed their lives at risk. . . . I could never have imagined on the morning of September 11 that my husband would be killed while sitting at his desk on the ninety-fourth floor of the WTC while drinking his morning cup of coffee and waiting for the stock market to open."

The women began speaking to each other regularly, often as a group in which they patched together their phone lines in a single call. Their relationship was part therapy as they tried to cope with the deep sorrow each felt. But increasingly, the women felt a collective frustration that coalesced into a question that tormented them to the point of anger: Did their husbands really have to die?

After spending months after the attacks in a state that drifted between mourning, exasperation, and confusion, the four decided they needed to find out what exactly happened on September 11. They did not want to undermine the plan, led by Ron Motley and other widows like Terry Strada, to file lawsuits. The four supported the lawsuits—and why not? As an attorney, Breitweiser knew that the courts could be an enormously effective tool in attacking the financial roots of international terrorism. But the women felt that the courts were only a half measure. And while Ron Motley and the other attorneys involved in that initial legal assault on Saudi Arabia as the alleged financial underpinning of September 11 were certainly capable of all kinds of legal expertise, they could not sue the FBI, the CIA, and even America's military for failing to do their jobs. Also, the lawyers had already been blocked by a special law from suing the airlines.

Soon after the attacks, the Bush administration felt that America's national system of commercial jet traffic that was so important to the economy could be set back and perhaps permanently broken if it was smothered in lawsuits and massive financial penalties. To head off what it expected might be the kind of lawsuits that effectively put such iconic airlines as Pan Am out of business after the Lockerbie terrorist attack, Congress passed the "Air Transportation Safety and System Stabilization Act" that set up a legal wall around the airlines against 9/11-related lawsuits. As a gesture to the 9/11 victims and their families, Congress also set up the Victims Compensation Fund. The practical goal of the VCF was to quickly offer money to 9/11 victims as an alternative to filing lawsuits that could take years to settle. But the fund also hoped to head off the inevitable political criticism that Congress and the Bush administration mainly cared about big business—in this case, the airlines—instead of ordinary people who just happened to be in the wrong place at the wrong time on September 11, 2001.

Meanwhile, the Bush administration ordered the military to attack al-Qaeda's hideouts in Afghanistan, where the CIA began to apprehend a steady stream of alleged terrorists. The arrests were often not made public and the so-called "ghost prisoners" were dispatched to a variety of secret CIA-run "black sites" across the globe, from Thailand and Poland to Lithuania and Northern Africa where some were tortured.

On the increasingly tense homefront, it seemed as if the entire population was on the alert to stop the next terrorist attack. Signs proclaiming, "If you see something, say something," were hung in airports and bus and rail stations. The FBI, armed with new investigative powers from the Patriot Act that had been quickly adopted by Congress and signed into law by President Bush, mounted a nationwide campaign to track down al-Qaeda sympathizers while also foiling several terror plots. Even local police departments were appointing detectives who normally handled robberies to focus on counterterrorism.

In all of this headline-grabbing activity, the Jersey Girls felt something was missing. Since September 11, the federal government had not said much about how a nation that routinely spends hundreds of billions of dollars to defend itself with sophisticated jet fighters, aircraft carriers, computer-guided bombs and missiles, fast-moving tanks, and radar-evading stealth helicopters could be attacked by nineteen religious zealots who were armed only with box cutters and their own guile. In other words, the government, while understandably focused on future terrorist attacks, was not saying much about how it was caught off guard on September 11, 2001.

The Jersey Girls wanted to change that narrative.

The women began by reading everything they could find about the CIA, the FBI, and al-Qaeda. They scoured the internet for news reports—some of them remarkably revealing—about how the Air Force and even the airlines mishandled emergency calls from the hijacked jetliners on 9/11. Then they examined the safety precautions at the World Trade Center, focusing, in particular, on the public address announcement telling workers to remain in place. They even compiled data that chronicled the history of US dependency on foreign oil.

They assembled their research in five, 2-inch binders. Then, after calling in babysitters to watch their children, they would meet at a spot near the New Jersey Turnpike and drive to Washington in the "widow mobile," often stopping on the road or in a parking lot to change their clothes from jeans, sneakers, and T-shirts into skirts, dresses, and pantsuits so they would look professional.

They initially spoke with congressional staffers, then with other members of the government—then with senators and congressional representatives. At first, the women noticed that many of the government officials they encountered agreed to meet with them as something of a public relations gesture. After all, what politician would turn down a meeting with 9/11 widows? Certainly, it was a great "photo op" for politicians looking for positive coverage.

Breitweiser remembered that some officials displayed a patronizing view of the women, underestimating their ability to master complicated facts about national security and their lack of fear in confronting some officials. It was as if the officials wanted to pat the women on their heads and usher them out the door with a few verbal bromides about how difficult life must be and how the rest of the nation admired their courage and wanted to support them in this difficult time.

But the Jersey Girls quickly set a tone that they were not to be ignored. "We didn't want empathy," Breitweiser later wrote. "We wanted action in fixing the gaping holes in our national security. The only way to get that action was to build support and argue the most compelling case we could for a 9/11 independent commission."

As a typical meeting would begin, the women would deliberately plunk their three-ring binders on a conference table as a signal that they had done their homework. And if an official said something they found questionable, it was not uncommon for one of the women—sometimes all of them at once—to thumb through the binders and then offer a contradiction or correction.

From those initial meetings, the women sensed that they would have to leap a series of bureaucratic hurdles that had been erected over time to stymie the kinds of ground-level, populist challenges the women were presenting. In some ways, theirs was an assault on what they found to be a debilitating code of behavior in Washington in which far too many officials, especially in the intelligence services, thought of themselves as the "experts" who were not accustomed to being contradicted, especially by women who compiled their own research and did not back down from asking why their government—and especially those allegedly smart intelligence experts—seemed so unprepared for the attacks of 9/11.

At the same time, the women also noticed that many political figures—especially those in the Bush administration—were worried about the political backlash from any sort of governmental accounting of how the attacks of September 11 had taken place and why America was caught off guard. Indeed, in that first year, the fear of political finger pointing—even among Democrats—became one of the most potent forces in Washington. Democrats did not want to be seen as trying to turn 9/11 into a political football. What's more, the Democrats also feared that the meandering and often unfocused style of the Clinton Administration—with President Bill Clinton spending his final years trying to fight off a sex scandal—might cast the party as being so out of touch that it ignored a menacing terrorist threat.

Republicans voiced other fears. Among some Republicans, there was a collective nervousness that President Bush, who won election by a narrow margin that had to be decided by a special vote of a deeply divided US Supreme Court, had botched one of the first challenges of his administration. At stake, many Republicans felt, was an opportunity after eight years of Democratic rule in the White House by President Clinton to restore the conservative agenda of the Reagan era.

Another source of anxiety among Republicans was President George Bush himself, who was largely regarded even within the party as a president who was unfamiliar with the nuances and challenges of national security, especially when it came to fighting terrorism. Unlike his father, George H. W. Bush, a World War II pilot who represented his Texas district in Congress, served as ambassador to China, ran the CIA, and was Ronald Reagan's vice president before being elected to the top job where he presided over the US invasion of Iraq in 1991, the younger Bush, whose military experience consisted of five years as a part-time pilot with a National Guard unit, had never worked in Washington before he moved into the White House eight months before 9/11. As the governor of Texas—and the son of a president—George W. Bush had risen to power mostly because of his ability to blend conservative Republican standards into a rising populism that was focused on the basic economic needs of America. In the early months of his administration, he had not even addressed in any meaningful way the growing danger of international terrorism even though the decade before he took office was filled with a long list of attacks—and al-Qaeda had even staged a daring assault only weeks before Bush was elected in 2000 on the USS *Cole*, a Navy destroyer that had stopped in Yemen.

Bush smartly surrounded himself with several key advisors who had a broad grasp of the problems of the world, notably Vice President Dick Cheney, Secretary of State Colin Powell, and White House National Security Advisor Condoleezza Rice. But when it came to foreign policy and the complications of international terrorism, critics viewed Bush as an untested lightweight. It didn't help his reputation that on the morning of September 11, Bush did not immediately leave a second-grade classroom he was visiting in Florida when his chief of staff whispered in his ear that a hijacked jetliner had crashed into the North Tower of the World Trade Center in New York City. Instead, Bush nodded and remained seated for seven excruciating minutes as students read a story called *The Pet Goat*. With staffers nervously standing nearby, Bush finally excused himself. But the image of an out-of-touch leader who did not know how to quickly respond to a crisis continued to shadow him.

As the 9/11 attacks unfolded, Bush flew in Air Force One to a military base in Louisiana, then to another in Nebraska that was considered a secure location for him. And while he made some key decisions—notably giving an order to put the military on a special alert and to shoot down any plane that refused to land—he, nevertheless, did not speak to the nation in a TV address from the Oval Office until later that night. And even then, Bush offered nothing about why his government seemed so unprepared or why the nation's top intelligence agencies appeared to have ignored clear warnings that a terrorist attack could happen.

As the Jersey Girls soon learned, the warnings of an attack were clear for years. And during the months leading up to September 11, 2001, the warnings were especially ominous.

In June 2001, the government's security services issued a series of alerts about a possible terrorist attack that were later described as "the most urgent in decades" and the Federal Aviation Administration urged US airlines to maintain a "high degree of alertness."

In July, the government's top counterterrorism official, Richard Clarke, told a White House meeting that included the FAA, the FBI, the Coast Guard, the

Secret Service, and the Immigration and Naturalization Service that "something really spectacular is going to happen here and it's going to happen soon."

Many other warnings were in the bureaucratic winds of the US government, including the fact that the CIA secretly monitored two al-Qaeda operatives as they slipped into the United States a year before, but then dropped their surveillance and blocked FBI Agent Mark Rossini and other agents assigned as liaisons to the CIA from telling their superiors and mounting a manhunt. Rossini had suggested that the FBI could step in and keep track of the two potential terrorists from al-Qaeda. After all, the FBI, not the CIA, was officially tasked with investigating terrorists inside the US borders. The CIA's job was to watch terrorists when they were outside the US. But the two agencies rarely cooperated. And when Rossini asked to pass on the information about the al Qaeda operatives inside the US, he said the CIA prohibited him from passing the information to his FBI superiors.

It would take a government-sanctioned investigation of 9/11 to uncover what the CIA and other top intelligence agencies knew before the attacks—and what they did or did not do about it. Still, even years later, the CIA has never addressed Rossini's allegations and, in particular, why the FBI was not told for more than a year about the CIA's discovery that had two members of al-Qaeda who had been linked to previous terrorist plots overseas secretly entered the US.

This lack of government transparency and accountability was just what Kristen Breitweiser had in mind on September 18, 2002 when she took her seat at a table in the main hearing room at the Hart Senate Office Building. She wasn't just hoping for a lawsuit filed by a group of private attorneys who represented victims of the attacks. She wanted an official government investigation.

* * *

For weeks she had been weighing not only what she would say, but how she would say it, if she had chance to speak to a congressional committee. Like the other Jersey Girls, Breitweiser felt a strong urge to draw attention to how she felt her country had failed in protecting itself—and her husband, Ron—from a terrorist attack. At the same time, she did not want to make enemies on this committee by appearing to needlessly point fingers of blame.

Breitweiser's goal was for Congress to appoint an independent commission of noteworthy public servants who were not holding elected office, as the members of the Joint Inquiry were. Breitweiser hoped for an examination of 9/11 that left no stone unturned and was unafraid to name the agencies and officials who failed. She did not, as many in Congress were suggesting, merely want to look forward and propose methods to prevent the next attack. Breitweiser desperately wanted her government to look first at the past and examine why America was so vulnerable.

She knew she was stepping into a delicate situation. As co-founder of a group that called itself "September 11 Advocates," she wanted to properly represent the diverse coalitions of 9/11 victims, some of whom felt that Breitweiser's tone became too strident and accusatory at times. On the other hand, she desperately wanted to speak the truth to the committee but not so harshly that she might derail her efforts for an independent investigation by angering too many senators and congressional representatives. She knew she would need the committee's support if the Senate and House ever voted on legislation to establish the kind of commission she wanted.

Breitweiser harbored yet another not-so-small worry. As an attorney, she knew how to present an argument. In appearances already to various groups of 9/11 victims, she realized she had a unique ability to speak passionately. But she wanted to convey something besides passion to the Joint Inquiry. Along with the other Jersey Girls, she had amassed such a large and complex mountain of facts that she worried any presentation by her—no matter how clearly she spoke—might be too overwhelming for the Committee to grasp. She needed to weave these threads of information into a coherent story that was thorough but not to the point of being confusing and hard to follow. Breitweiser knew in her gut she could talk for hours. But she had just thirty minutes or so to make her case. She didn't want to push her luck and her time limit. Another relative of a 9/11 victim, Stephen Push, whose wife, Lisa Raines, perished on American Airlines Flight 77 that crashed into the Pentagon, was also scheduled to testify that morning. So was Eleanor Hill, a former counsel to the Department of Defense, who emerged as an invaluable investigator for the Joint Committee.

The day before the meeting, Breitweiser checked into the Hamilton Crowne Plaza Hotel on 14th Street, near a park dedicated to Benjamin Franklin. Two other Jersey Girls, Lorie Van Auken and Patty Casazza, made the trip with her. After getting settled at the hotel, Breitweiser made her way to Capitol Hill.

With a Senate staffer, she then walked through the choreographed routine in the hearing room. She would enter from a back door to avoid the media. She could not take a bathroom break. A glass of water would be on the table. The hearing would be televised across the nation.

Back at the hotel that night Breitweiser slept fitfully—"frozen in fear" as she later described herself. The next morning, she walked to a nearby Starbucks and telephoned the fourth Jersey Girl, Mindy Kleinberg, who could not make the trip but was always good for a short pep talk, coupled with a dry one-liner such as "Don't worry if you mess up. It's only national television and we'll still love you."

On the phone, Kleinberg's easy-going style calmed Breitweiser a bit. When she returned to the hotel, Van Auken and Casazza reminded her that they would be sitting right behind her in the hearing room.

Breitweiser then found herself thinking of her husband, Ron, and what his last minutes or seconds of life might have been like as he realized he was about to die in his office at the South Tower of the World Trade Center. While painful to think about and certainly graphic to imagine, Breitweiser often returned to that image whenever she felt nervous before a TV interview or when she spoke to a large group about 9/11. She did not want Ron's death—and those of thousands of others on 9/11—to be forgotten or even minimized because she was too nervous or afraid to speak up.

* * *

Breitweiser stepped into the hearing room and walked to her seat on the left side of a long witness table that was covered with a crimson cloth. She set down the 4,000-word statement she planned to read. Across the room, separated by a swarm of news photographers, some two dozen senators and congressional representatives took seats on raised platforms.

They were members of the intelligence committees in their respective Congressional houses. And because Congress was divided at that time—with Republicans controlling the House and Democrats holding a majority of seats in Senate—the two committees decided to combine their efforts to examine 9/11 into what they labeled a Joint Congressional Inquiry.

The Senate contingent included a future Democratic vice presidential candidate, John Edwards of North Carolina, and a future Republican governor,

Mike DeWine of Ohio. The House delegation included a future CIA director, Porter Goss, a Republican from Florida, and Nancy Pelosi, a California Democrat who would become the first woman Speaker of the House of Representatives. Goss and Pelosi posed for a photograph with Joint Inquiry Chairman, Senator Bob Graham, a Florida Democrat, and with the vice chairman, Senator Richard Shelby, a Republican from Alabama.

Graham began by reminding the audience that fifty-three weeks had passed since nearly 3,000 people had been killed in the September 11 attacks. "We are here today," he said, "because so many Americans have been personally touched by those horrific events." He then made a point of saying that he hoped the committee could present a series of recommendations on how America might better defend itself and prevent the next attack. The three other leaders of the Joint Committee—Goss, Pelosi and Shelby—then spoke, each praising Breitweiser and the other victims' relatives for showing up and promising a thorough inquiry.

Breitweiser, in a black jacket and a white blouse, with her curly, blond hair pulled back, placed her left hand atop her right, then her right atop her left. Her eyes darted side to side, scanning the line of officials as she listened to the opening statements.

After thirty minutes, Senator Graham finally invited Breitweiser to speak. The room quieted except for the click of news photographers' cameras. Breitweiser leaned forward slightly. Van Auken and Casazza had taken seats in the row behind her. Nearby, two other women, each holding 8-by-10-inch color photographs of their lost loved ones, also looked on: Sally Regenhard, whose twenty-eight-year-old son, Christian, a former Marine Corps sergeant and a FDNY probationary firefighter for just six weeks, perished in the collapse of the twin towers, and Monica Gabrielle, whose husband, Richard, worked on the 103rd floor of the South Tower.

Breitweiser began by thanking the committee for the "tremendous honor" of being invited to testify. She added that she "will do my best not to disappoint the families or the memories of their loved ones." She described her daughter having to place flowers on an empty grave and her memory of the last words to her from her husband Ron: "Sweets, I'm fine. I don't want you to worry." She told the Committee that she now wears Ron's wedding band that was found with his left hand in the rubble of Ground Zero.

Then Breitweiser returned to the images of Ron "that haunt me at night" when she tries to sleep—and inspire her when she feels nervous about speaking out.

"I don't really know what happened to him," she said, her voice clear and steady, her eyes occasionally looking up at the Committee. "I don't know whether he jumped or he choked to death on smoke. I don't know whether he sat curled up in a corner watching the carpet melt in front of him, knowing that his own death was soon to come or if he was alive long enough to be crushed by the buildings when they collapsed."

Her words were raw and personal, but Breitweiser wanted it that way. It was important, she felt, to remind the Committee that the victims of 9/11 were not abstract numbers on casualty lists. They were real people with real lives and real families left behind.

But then, as she planned, Breitweiser switched gears. She turned from the personal to a factually-passionate, political rallying cry for Congress to sanction an "independent, blue-ribbon panel" that would "not be limited in scope or hindered by time limits."

"The families of the victims of September 11th have waited long enough," she said. "We need to have answers. We need to have accountability. We need to feel safe living and working in this great nation."

She ticked off, one after another, a list of "specific threats" in the years leading up to 9/11 for terrorists to "use planes as weapons." In particular, she drew attention to al-Qaeda's "Bojinka" plot that included the blowing up of commercial jetliners over the Pacific Ocean. She also mentioned a 1999 report prepared by the Library of Congress that described a potential attack of hijacked jetliners into the Pentagon, the CIA, and the White House by "suicide bombers belonging to al-Qaeda's Martyrdom Battalion."

She went on to list how the CIA, the FBI, and a wide-ranging group of other officials in the government had failed to warn the public about the increased number of threats during the summer of 2001. She wondered how airlines could be so lax that they allowed passengers to carry razor-like box cutters and knives with blades up to 4 inches long. She questioned what she saw as an across-the-board failure by numerous federal agencies to share information with each other. She noted that FBI agents in several of the bureau's offices across America, without knowing the full extent of what they were seeing, had already placed several would-be 9/11 hijackers under surveillance. These FBI agents wondered—correctly—why several men from the Middle East were taking lessons to fly commercial jetliners even though they did not seem to have jobs or even a desire to become pilots. Why didn't anyone in the FBI follow up on these suspicions? Why had the reports that raised these suspicions apparently fallen into a bureaucratic hole and remained unnoticed by the FBI's top counterterrorism analysts?

And then, "perhaps even more disturbing," Breitweiser mentioned that two hijackers—Saudi nationals, Khalid al-Mihdhar and Nawaf al-Hazmi—had been monitored by the CIA long before 9/11 and, with the CIA's knowledge, had actually entered the United States on tourist visas in 2000. Why weren't they arrested?

The names of al-Mihdhar and al-Hazmi had already surfaced in news coverage. But few government officials had publicly asked the kind of question that Breitweiser now posed. How did the CIA mishandle this obviously dangerous and suspicious entry by two known al-Qaeda terrorists into the United States? And if the CIA did not mishandle this situation, what then was the agency's excuse or explanation for its lack of attention to what turned out to be national security threat?

Breitweiser did not yet know the full story of al-Mihdhar and al-Hazmi. Nor could she foresee how important those two would become to what became a long-running investigation of the alleged links by Saudi Arabia to the 9/11 plot. But she was one of the first of the advocates for 9/11 victims' relatives to sense that the CIA's handling of al-Mihdhar and al-Hazmi was an indication of widespread incompetence by America's intelligence agencies who had been formed to stop terrorism before it reached inside the US.

"We need people to be held accountable for their failures," she said as she ended her testimony. "We need leaders with the courage to take responsibility for what went wrong."

She then reminded the Committee members that "each of you here today, because you live and work in Washington, DC, must have felt that you were in the bullseye on September 11," but "there was relief at the end of the day, a relief that you and your loved ones were in safe hands."

"You were the lucky ones," Breitweiser said. "In your investigation, please do not forget those of us who did not share in your good fate."

Breitweiser laid her statement on the table and looked up. The room quieted for a few seconds.

Then the audience clapped.

The next day Breitweiser was invited to the White House where two presidential advisors said President Bush was not necessarily opposed to forming a commission to investigate 9/11; the president felt uneasy about the timing, however.

Breitweiser suspected the timing issue was just a way to sidestep the fact that Bush reportedly did not wholeheartedly support the commission, but now had little choice. Congress and the public wanted answers.

Breitweiser walked out of the White House knowing the Jersey Girls had won.

* * *

Ten weeks later, on the day before Thanksgiving, President Bush signed legislation to create the National Commission on Terrorist Attacks Upon the United States. The formal name would soon be shortened in conversations and the news accounts to a far simpler, informal, and more direct name: "The 9/11 Commission."

Bush did his best to cast the event in positive terms. "The Commission will help me and future presidents to understand the methods of America's enemies and the nature of the threats we face," he said. But it had been speculated for months in Washington that Bush and his political advisors wanted no part of a wide-ranging investigation into what had already become a blemish on his presidency and possibly his chances for re-election. The legislation stipulated that the Commission had just eighteen months to finish its work. Which meant that the Commission's findings—good or bad—would be released in May 2004, just as America was gearing up for the 2004 presidential election.

The formal signing, in the White House Roosevelt Room across the hall from the president's Oval Office, took just six minutes. But before it ended, Bush would stir up an unexpected political storm.

He announced that the Commission's chairman would be Henry Kissinger, the former National Security Advisor for President Richard Nixon and Secretary of State for both Nixon and President Gerald Ford. Kissinger had also won a Nobel Peace Prize for his efforts to end the Vietnam War.

Kissinger was a safe choice for Bush. Though seventy-eight years old at the time and out of public life for several decades as he built a lucrative consulting business with many foreign nations, Kissinger was still regarded as a savvy player in Washington. He knew how to package messages and, just as important, how to massage embarrassing news and keep secrets. If anyone could watch Bush's political back, it would be Kissinger.

Kissinger was no match for the Jersey Girls, however.

Almost as soon as he was named chairman of the 9/11 Commission, he was asked to disclose his foreign clients in his consulting business. The request was the kind of routine background ethics inquiry that officials usually face when they leave the business world and enter government. Kissinger, however, seemed caught off guard. For a man who spent much of his public life knowing how to anticipate political landmines and dodge difficult questions, Kissinger suddenly came off as stodgy, unprepared, and almost sinister.

He refused to say which foreign nations—and foreign businesses—he represented. It hardly needed to be said that he was placing himself—and, to some degree, his overseas clients—ahead of the needs of his own country. He continued to ask the American public to trust him. But even asking that question seemed to stoke the public's distrust.

Republicans tried to support him. The ongoing anger and pain of 9/11 was too raw, however. Why should the man running the investigation of the 9/11 attacks not have to explain his business ties to foreign governments—especially when one of Kissinger's suspected clients was Saudi Arabia or some of the kingdom's most prominent business figures and financial institutions?

Kissinger would never confirm or deny that he represented any aspect of political, governmental, or business life in Saudi Arabia. But his refusal to answer the question created a storm that would not easily disappear.

An editorial in *The New York Times* raised questions about "Henry Kissinger's Entangling Ties." Another *Times* editorial was entitled "The Kissinger Dodge." The White House tried to draw a fine line in the political sand, arguing that because Kissinger had been appointed by the president, he was not legally required to abide by the same kinds of disclosure rules as commissioners appointed by Congress. *The Wall Street Journal* added to the debate with an editorial, entitled "Borking Henry Kissinger"—a reference to Republicans' long-festering anger over how they felt Democrats had wrongly questioned conservative judicial scholar Robert Bork in 1987 as a way of upending Bork's nomination to the US Supreme Court.

On Thursday, December 12, the Jersey Girls, joined by a half-dozen or so other women who had been advocating for the 9/11 Commission, sat down with Kissinger at his office on Park Avenue in Manhattan. The day before, former US Senator George Mitchell of Maine, who had been tapped by Congressional Democrats as the commission's vice chairman, resigned, citing the fact that he did not believe he should disclose the name of clients he represented in his post-government consulting business.

Given what had happened with Mitchell, it was not surprising that the women asked if Kissinger would release his client list. He refused and, again, asked them to trust him.

The conversation went back and forth before one of the Jersey Girls, Lorie Van Auken, broke in. Van Auken's husband, Ken, had been an executive at the Cantor Fitzgerald brokerage firm, which occupied the upper floors of the North Tower. And while their families lived only a few dozen miles from each other in New Jersey—Van Auken in East Brunswick; Breitweiser in Middletown—the women did not know each other before their husbands were killed.

Looking at Kissinger as he sat on a couch in his office, Van Auken did not mince words or offer a stream of polite niceties as a verbal walk-up to what she wanted to say. She got right to the point. "The kind of thing that we are worried about," she said, "is whether you might ever have had a member of bin Laden's family as a client."

Kissinger seemed stunned, several witnesses later said. After two weeks of verbal dancing, he now sat in a room with the relatives of 9/11 victims facing a basic question that required just a yes or no answer. There was no escaping. No more promises to "trust me." No more nuanced and diplomatic evasions. That wouldn't cut it. Did Kissinger, who took pride in his role as the foremost American diplomat of the last half-century, ever represent the family of the world's most dangerous terrorist? Yes or no?

In one of those rare moments of his carefully structured diplomatic life, Kissinger was trapped. If he answered "yes," his reputation would be tarnished, opening the door to even more questions about his loyalty to his country. But even a "no" answer would surely raise the concern about why Kissinger had been so evasive about his client list in the first place. Was he hiding something else? Merely answering this single question, it could open the door to more questions. Did Kissinger represent Saudi royalty? Saudi banks? Saudi charities?

In other words, Kissinger was being asked to do something he rarely did as a diplomat—to be completely open. No careful wording. No polite evasions for the sake of protecting America's overall reputation. Van Auken's question cut right to the heart of Kissinger's personal choices. Did he represent a client with ties to the terrorist who orchestrated the 9/11 attacks?

Breitweiser remembers a series of polite and uneasy chuckles by Kissinger. Then one of the women tried to smooth over the request, saying: "It would be our hope that no client like that would be found on your client list. . . . But, nevertheless, we have an obligation to ask."

Kissinger never answered.

The women left his office.

The next day, Kissinger resigned as chairman of the Commission. He explained that, for privacy reasons, he could not disclose his client list. It would be the last time he was asked to serve his country.

Twenty-four hours later—on a Saturday afternoon—the phone rang at the home in Bedminster, New Jersey, of Thomas H. Kean, the former governor of New Jersey and now the president of Drew University, a small liberal arts college just twenty miles away in the small town of Madison, New Jersey. Karl Rove, the chief political advisor for President George W. Bush, was on the line.

Rove wanted to know if Kean could serve on the 9/11 Commission. Kean did not hesitate. He said yes.

The next day—Sunday—Bush's chief of staff, Andrew Card, called with another question: Would Kean take the job as the commission's chairman? Kean again said yes.

On Monday, Kean's phone rang again. It was President Bush himself, formally offering Kean the job.

Thomas H. Kean, former governor of New Jersey and chairman of the National Commission on Terrorist Attacks Upon the United States—the 9/11 Commission—outlining recommendations from the Commission's 567-page report that was released in 2004. Photo by Mark Wilson/Getty Images.

8

The Commission

Nineteen months after taking the chairman's role of the 9/11 Commission, Tom Kean stood at one end of a crowded auditorium in Washington, DC, grasping each side of a wooden lectern as if he were holding the steering wheel of an unwieldy truck on a bumpy road.

It was 11:30 a.m., July 22, 2004, a sweltering day in Washington, DC. The National Commission on Terrorist Attacks Upon the United States that President George Bush had asked Kean to run after the public relations and political debacle with Henry Kissinger nearly 600 days earlier had officially finished its work. In the insular world of Washington, where partisanship, leaks, and name-calling were as common as the summer's humidity, Kean and the Commission's nine other members had done what many thought they could never do.

They created a bipartisan team that did not point fingers or dissolve into the usual divisive talking points and arguments that characterized nearly every policy debate in Washington. And they actually produced a report that was far more comprehensive than the public relations cover-up that many critics feared. Kean's commission not only offered extensive insight into how the 9/11 attacks took place, but it also provided a sobering set of recommendations on what an otherwise slow-moving government intelligence bureaucracy—and even New York City's police and fire departments—needed to do to protect the nation from the growing threat of international terrorism. One of the report's core messages was as simple as it was complex: America's expensive and sophisticated collection of intelligence and law enforcement agencies needed to cooperate better with each other.

The Commission's report did not offer a complete, ironclad assessment of the 9/11 tragedy in which every question was answered. Far from it. For example, the Commission had not been able to fully uncover how the hijacking team—and al-Qaeda, in general—financed the 9/11 plot. Also, rising concerns and nagging questions—many of them cited in Ron Motley's lawsuit—that Saudi financial institutions and even government officials may have assisted the hijackers were certainly raised in the Commission report but not fully answered. Firm resolutions to those explosive allegations were left as a mystery yet to be solved. And, not surprisingly, within the Commission itself staffers and commissioners engaged in all manner of debates over how to pressure the Bush administration for documents and how America, in general, should face the concerns about Saudi links to 9/11. Despite such concerns, however, the Commission had managed to address most issues.

As America prepared for the 2004 presidential election, the Commission's work and especially its bipartisanship also seemed to set a new style of how government could actually work, especially when it came to turning a spotlight on itself and assessing its mistakes and sensitive matters. In public, the Commissioners actually seemed to listen and talk to each other as colleagues, not as political enemies from warring political parties. Indeed, when commissioners appeared in TV interviews, they always came as pairs—one Republican and one Democrat.

Those pairings were one of the first rules that Kean insisted upon. There would be no Democratic or Republican spokespeople who talked separately about the Commission's work and its decisions. Kean wanted the Commission to speak with a bipartisan voice or not at all.

Another of the Commission's unofficial rules followed that same logic. Kean felt that the Commissioners should not sit in meetings with Republicans on one side of a table and Democrats on another—the usual Washington style. Instead, he insisted that they stagger their seating so that a Republican sat next to a Democrat. To underscore how serious Kean was about this kind of bipartisan seating arrangement, he had his staff create place cards that assigned seats for the Commissioners before one of their early gatherings.

As a final guard against accusations of partisanship, Kean also stipulated that both he and his Democratic vice chairman, Lee Hamilton, who Kean barely knew, would have to sign off together in hiring each of the Commission's eighty staffers who ranged from former intelligence analysts to lawyers and investigators.

All these measures by Kean were his way of sending a message: Yes, he had been hired by the Bush administration, but he was no Republican partisan patsy. By setting up a system that forced opposing political parties to cooperate, in a quiet way he was trying to create a new formula for governmental policy discussions. For Kean, who had essentially bowed out of public life a decade before, the moves were considered a natural extension of how he had long felt political discourse ought to be conducted but, in many respects, had been sidelined and often out-shouted by the increasingly rancorous partisanship that had come to dominate American politics in recent years. As the Commission completed its work, many political experts in both parties concluded that Kean's bipartisan methods in unifying the Commission were innovative political masterstrokes.

The Commission conducted twelve nationally televised hearings. It listened to public testimony from 160 people, ranging from terror experts and firefighters who responded to the World Trade Center to the directors of the CIA and FBI. The Commissioners and their staffers studied more than 2.5 million pages of documents. They also interviewed more than 1,200 people in ten countries and even convinced a reluctant, defensive Bush administration and members of the equally reluctant and defensive Clinton administration to cooperate and provide, with a few notable exceptions, most of the documents they needed. In the final weeks, Presidents George W. Bush and Bill Clinton were even persuaded to sit for interviews, though the Commission allowed them to do this in private.

Initially, the Commission's budget was a paltry $3 million and the deadline of May 2004 was ridiculously limiting for all that the Commission had to do. But after begging Congress and the White House, Kean had managed to receive a few million dollars more and extend the deadline by two months.

In the final weeks, working around the clock to meet their deadline, the Commission produced a well-organized, deeply researched report of 567 pages—almost 200,000 words—that traced how a band of Islamic zealots pulled off the deadliest attack in US history. And they wrote the report in a storytelling, narrative style that was deliberately geared to the public, not bureaucrats and lawyers.

It was hardly a surprise that a paperback edition of the report quickly shot to the top of the nation's best-seller lists. Unlike so many government reports, which seemed as if they had been written in complex engineering codes, the Commission's report was structured like a novel. *Time* magazine described it as "meticulous in its reconstruction and unflinching in its conclusions." *The Washington Post* praised it as a "document of historic sweep and almost unprecedented detail." *Publishers Weekly* gave the report perhaps its most notable review: "It reads like a Shakespearean drama" but "without trivializing any of the events or diminishing the people involved."

Each of the report's recommendations had been unanimously endorsed by all five of the Commission's Democrats and its five Republican members. This was another rule that Kean insisted upon. He wanted the Commission to speak in a unified voice. Unlike the US Supreme Court, where the various justices are not reluctant to share their differences in public, Kean felt history would not be served if Commissioners wrote the equivalent of "dissenting opinions." If a commissioner objected to wording or to a conclusion, Kean insisted that the group find ways to compromise. He felt that a growing body of 9/11 conspiracy mongers would have a field day of spreading falsehoods if there was any hint that key information had been withheld from the public or that the Commission disagreed on any substantial conclusions.

"Openness," said Kean later, "was a must."

Kean also made a point of staying in touch with the relatives of victims, in particular the Jersey Girls. In some ways, it was another example of Kean's astute political strategy, typical of the style of politics that he learned back in New Jersey. He knew that his Commission needed the support and trust of the increasing number of victims who were calling for a close examination of why America seemed so defenseless on September 11, 2001. Kean later conceded that when he ran into bureaucratic roadblocks in obtaining documents—particularly from the Bush administration—he would privately ask the Jersey Girls and other victims' relatives such as Mary Fetchet of the "Voices of 9/11" advocacy group to use their increasingly powerful political leverage. By the end, Kean said: "The Commission could not have done its work without the victims' relatives. Whenever I needed something done, I called them."

Perhaps most remarkable, however, the Commission managed to accomplish its massive task as America was not only still mourning the losses of the 9/11 attacks, but also conducting a controversial war in Iraq, stretching US legal standards by imprisoning and torturing suspected terrorists without formal charges at a US Navy base in Cuba, and trying to cope with the already negative cacophony of the 2004 presidential campaign.

By the spring of 2004, some of Bush's supporters worried that the increasing criticism by relatives of 9/11 victims—in particular Kristen Breitweiser of the Jersey Girls, who had become more outspoken—might hurt the president's chances of re-election. Right-wing radio talk-show host Rush Limbaugh even accused Breitweiser of being a Democratic operative, even though she made no secret that she was a registered Republican who voted for Bush in 2000. Another right-wing media star, Bill O'Reilly, said, without evidence, that "some 9/11 families have aligned themselves with the far left."

In fact, the Jersey Girls—indeed, most of the relatives of 9/11 victims—had followed an understanding among themselves to avoid partisan politics. When US Senator Jon Corzine, a Democratic senator from her home state of New Jersey and a prominent player in his party's national strategy and fundraising, reached out to Breitweiser after the criticism from Limbaugh and O'Reilly, Breitweiser told him she wanted to steer clear of any partisan involvement, at least for now. Breitweiser would change her decision in the coming months, however, after the Bush Administration, and the Republican Party in general, appeared reluctant to support some key reforms the Commission proposed with US intelligence agencies.

Much like the Warren Commission that investigated the 1963 assassination of President John F. Kennedy, and another commission that examined the Japanese attack on the US Navy base at Pearl Harbor in Hawaii in 1941, America seemed to collectively sense that the 9/11 Commission represented one of those rare moments when the government actually studied its mistakes and found ways to improve. Before the 9/11 Commission finished its report, a Pew research poll had already found that a staggering 60 percent of the American public had been actively following its work. But would Congress, the White House, and the rest of the Washington bureaucracy take the bold steps needed to embrace the Commission's recommendations for a complete overhaul of the US intelligence services? Like so much of the 9/11 investigation, that question would not be easy to answer. For now, however, Kean and his Commission members and staff took satisfaction in the fact that they had managed to complete their work despite numerous challenges.

* * *

On that muggy July 2004 morning in Washington, Kean was in no mood to gloat. He leaned forward on the wooden lectern that had been set up on a stage at one end of an auditorium named for Andrew Mellon, a former treasury secretary who presided over the unregulated economic boom of the 1920s that led to a massive stock market crash and the Great Depression of the 1930s. The auditorium, ornate and gilded in a way that seemed to reflect Mellon's economic policies favoring America's wealthy, dominated the first floor of the neoclassical headquarters of the Department of Commerce on Constitution Avenue, just a few blocks from the White House. Afterward, Kean would say he felt an almost unwieldy burden in that moment to make sure the nation heard an unfiltered yet hopeful message from him.

Dozens of 9/11 survivors, along with relatives of those who died, showed up. A large media gaggle and a thicket of TV cameras would carry Kean's opening remarks live to the rest of the nation and parts of the world. On the stage, on each side of the lectern, sat the other nine members of the Commission. On a nearby table sat paperback copies of the Commission's report with its distinctive red, white, and blue cover.

All that remained was for Kean, clad in a dark charcoal suit, white shirt, and sky-blue tie, to provide some insight, something that cut across all those pages of the report and offered a concise summary of how a group of Islamist zealots could carry out a scheme as outrageous as the 9/11 attacks against his nation.

"Good morning," he began.

"Today we present this report and these recommendations to the president of the United States, to the United States Congress, and the American people," Kean said as an introduction, adding that "this report represents the unanimous conclusion of the National Commission on Terrorist Attacks Upon the United States."

Then, he turned to the emotional heartbeat and purpose of the Commission's mission.

"On September 11, 2001, nineteen men armed with knives, box cutters, Mace, and pepper spray penetrated the defenses of the most powerful nation in the world," Kean said. "They inflicted unbearable trauma on our people, and at the same time they turned the international order upside down."

He asked the audience "to remember for a moment how you felt that day: the grief, the enormous sense of loss. But remember also how we came together that day as a nation: young and old, rich and poor. It didn't matter whether you were a Republican or a Democrat. We had a deep sense of hurt, but out of that came a deep sense of purpose. We knew what we had to do as a nation to respond, and we did."

Kean spoke of how "it's also fair to say that on that September day we were unprepared." He noted that America "did not grasp the magnitude of a threat that had been gathering over a considerable period of time."

And then, he opened a door on the heart of what had bothered him and the Commission for months: The 9/11 attacks represented a gross failure of government policies and management. Kean said—and the report noted in great detail—the killers laid out their plans ahead of time for Americans to study. But America was too distracted, too arrogant to pay attention. The nation's primary lines of defense—its military financed by a half-a-trillion-dollar budget, along with its widespread intelligence agencies who are able to plant bugs on phones in most corners of the world—could never conceive of such a grandiose terror attack.

It was, said Kean, "a failure of imagination" by almost every corner of American government.

* * *

Tom Kean never imagined he would be in this spot—in Washington, DC, as a national newsmaker, appointed by the president to a prominent government position, playing a role in possibly changing the way his nation conducted business.

Yet here he was.

For Kean, the 9/11 attacks—and many of the deaths—were personal. He knew several victims who worked in brokerage houses at the Trade Center. He also knew many officials at the Port Authority of New York and New Jersey, the octopus-like governmental monolith that built bridges, managed airports, and oversaw docks where the world's container ships unloaded cars, bicycles, clothing—basically a smorgasbord of retail goods for American consumers that were delivered by trucks or trains across the nation. The Port Authority had not only built the World Trade Center but had acted as its landlords until only a few weeks before the attacks when New York real estate developer Larry Silverstein signed a ninety-nine-year lease to run the complex.

On the day of the attacks, Kean left his home in plush Bedminster, New Jersey—and what he thought might be a day of recovering from dental surgery—and drove quickly over the twenty miles of New Jersey's farm country to the Drew University campus.

Classes had emptied as students gathered by television sets to watch the day's chaos. Kean counseled many of them, especially those who thought someone they knew might be missing. He advised others who wanted to drive to the Trade Center as volunteer helpers to hold off for now. He even found himself with a new challenge: How to stem a rising anger toward some of his Muslim students?

It was night when Kean was able to leave the campus and drive home. For much of the trek, he made his way over back roads, passing horse farms and through the small New Jersey commuter towns that were home to many Wall Street executives—and, certainly, more than a few with offices at the World Trade Center. As Kean drove past several railroad stations where commuters caught trains that would deliver them to Manhattan, he noticed that far too many cars were still in the parking lots. He wondered to himself: Were those the cars of men and women who were missing and probably not ever coming home?

Kean pondered the image of the empty cars for much of his drive home, also wondering, as so many did that night: How would America ever recover from such a tragedy?

A few weeks after the attacks, Kean was asked to deliver remarks at a memorial service in New York City for employees of the Fiduciary Trust investment house where he was a member of the board of directors.

As he stepped before a lectern in the century-old Episcopal Cathedral of Saint John the Divine, the world's fourth largest church, which sits atop Morningside Heights on Manhattan's Upper West Side, Kean scanned the crowd. So many of the mourners seemed young, he thought. Indeed, so many of the more than eighty men and women from Fiduciary who had been killed were just beginning their careers.

Then his eyes turned to the front row and a group of widows who were noticeably pregnant. Those children, Kean thought, would never know their fathers.

Since leaving his governorship in New Jersey in 1990, after two popular terms, Kean had been actively recruited by Republicans and Democrats for a variety of federal jobs. Republicans were drawn by Kean's ability to cross party lines while still holding on to his core GOP beliefs in low taxes and reduced government regulation on business. Democrats loved his left-of-center social views on abortion and other cultural issues. Both parties sensed that Kean possessed that rare political gift of being able to bring together people of diverse views.

But Kean turned down all the offers. His wife, Deborah, who relished her privacy, had never been comfortable in the political spotlight. As for Kean, he feared that American politics had tumbled into a deep ravine of partisanship. He wanted no part of any fracas.

When he left his governor's post, he was only fifty-four years old. Friends and admirers figured Kean would take the next step of running for higher office. But Kean privately told friends that he felt his time in the political limelight had passed. He accepted the post of president of Drew University, a small, liberal arts institution about 66 miles from Trenton in Madison, New Jersey. Kean was still running Drew—and doubling its enrollment, increasing its endowment, and teaching a popular course in politics—when President Bush called on him to run the 9/11 Commission.

In the coming months, Kean would remind himself often that he promised to steer clear of national politics. But he believed the Commission could be different—perhaps a chance to infuse politics with his sense of bipartisanship and policy-making. Also, said Kean: "When the president calls and asks you to do something, you don't say no."

What Kean did not realize—or did not want to admit publicly—is that in nearly thirteen years away from the political spotlight, he was still one of the most respected members of the Republican Party. His admirers were not surprised that Bush chose him.

Kean, who was considered a longtime friend of the Bush family, had run the New Jersey Republican campaign for George W. Bush's presidential campaign in 2000. But Kean also had a long family history of his own that seemed to make him a perfect fit for this moment in history.

One of his ancestors, William Livingston, fought in the American Revolutionary War and served as New Jersey's first elected governor. Kean's father represented New Jersey in Congress from 1939 to 1959. His grandfather and great-uncle served in the US Senate. Another relative, Hamilton Fish, served as a governor in New York during the 1800s.

By the 1980s, Tom Kean had attracted attention in New Jersey by promoting a new style for the Republican Party. He wanted to cast off the party's image as a stodgy clan of white businessmen who rubbed shoulders with each other at posh golf clubs and largely promoted their own interests while also railing against such Democratic-inspired programs as Social Security and Medicare. Instead, Kean saw the GOP as capable of a much wider reach across economic and racial lines. His goal: Find ways to compromise through bipartisanship.

As a politician, Kean certainly recognized that elected officials and their parties often disagree on all kinds of policies. No surprise there. But Kean made a point of trying to find common ground, even with small pieces of that elusive political landscape, where enemies could come together and actually accomplish something.

His demeanor could be disarming. Some opponents—even some in his own party—saw Kean's ability to talk to his opponents and negotiate compromises as a weakness. He often came off as low key, sometimes to the point of seeming shy. In conversation, he tended to hold back and let others talk first. In speeches, Kean was not known to chastise or make fun of his opponents. Unlike so many other New Jersey politicians whose stars burned out—no one could remember him getting into a public yelling match with constituents.

Beneath his polite style lay a none-too-subtle toughness, too. Over time, whether it was trying to pass a bill in the state legislature or managing support from wayward members of his party, Kean learned when to use his sharp elbows and when to use a velvet glove as pressure.

As for winning elections, he quickly earned a reputation as a savvy strategist who knew how to navigate New Jersey's often unpredictable political swamps and fissures. After losing the GOP primary in his first attempt at the state's governorship—in 1977—to a conservative Republican, Kean came back four years later with a mixed bag of conservative and moderate positions that were geared to a broader electorate. He said he still supported home rule across the state's 567 towns and cities—a major issue for the more conservative elements of New Jersey's GOP. But he also positioned himself as a progressive defender of the environment and pledged to clean up the growing number of toxic waste sites in New Jersey, many of them linked to cancer.

For the election itself, Kean allowed the controversial Republican National Committee's Ballot Security Task Force to monitor voting, especially in Democratic communities where Republicans had long suspected Democrats of cheating with vote tallies. He also hired Roger Stone, a Republican operative who was widely considered, rightly or wrongly, to be a specialist in subterfuge, deception, and other political chicanery during President Richard Nixon's 1972 presidential campaign. Decades later, Stone would emerge as one of President Donald Trump's most controversial election advisors. As Stone was about to enter a federal prison after being convicted of several crimes linked to Trump's 2016 presidential victory over Hillary Clinton, Trump pardoned him.

But even as Stone was still being roundly criticized years later as one of the dirtiest players in American politics, Kean found ways to praise him. "I like Roger. He's interesting, very bright," said Kean, while also conceding that he knew Stone could be a liability in his campaigns.

"Roger will jump over that limit sometimes," Kean said. "He's unashamed at what he does. You have to keep an eye on him. He wants you to win so badly that he may be capable of doing the thing which will keep you from winning."

That sort of commentary was typical of Kean. Even when criticizing someone, he often found something positive to say.

Kean ended up winning his first gubernatorial election by just 1,797 votes, the narrowest margin of victory ever in a New Jersey governors race. But the victory seemed to energize Kean. He quickly set out to reshape how Republicans viewed their place in the American political landscape. Kean, who was financially well off and could easily fit into just about any country club setting, let it be known that he was not rejecting the party's pro-business stances. He still favored tax cuts. But he recast those tax cuts as part of a strategy of how government could promote economic growth and jobs for the middle class while also calling for a revitalization in New Jersey's poorest cities, long considered Democratic strongholds and off-limits to Republicans.

With that in mind, he surprised his party by promoting several ideas that had long been considered too progressive for Republicans.

The first was rebuilding New Jersey's public schools, especially in poor cities. Another was protecting the state's fragile environment, especially its 100 miles of beaches which typically generated as much as $8 billion in tourism revenue each year.

Finally, and perhaps most controversial of all, Kean stepped away from his party's increasingly rigid ideology and offered much more nuanced positions in support of abortion and women's rights. His 1988 book, *The Politics of Inclusion*, in which Kean laid out his plans for broadening the Republican coalition, became required reading within GOP power circles.

It all seemed as if Kean was laying out a strategy to run for higher office. He wasn't, though. He saw himself as a political change-agent in his home state. And perhaps his most dramatic effort to alter the New Jersey landscape involved race relations.

For decades, New Jersey had stark class and racial divisions. The suburbs—some of the wealthiest in America—were the domain of whites; African Americans were consigned to some of America's poorest cities such as Paterson, Newark, Jersey City, Trenton, and Camden.

Kean didn't seem to care about those old traditions. As governor, he selected Newark as the site of a new state performing arts center.

Once a manufacturing hub, Newark had fallen to a deep hole of joblessness, chronic poverty, and rising crime. The city was still bearing the scars and a dismal reputation from race riots in 1967 that left twenty-six people dead, 700 injured, and caused $10 million in damage, while also setting off a massive exodus to the suburbs of white middle-class families.

To suggest that Newark could now become a cultural hub with a performing arts center that featured ballet and opera seemed preposterous. But Kean took the risk. He pledged that the state would invest $200 million in the new center.

That kind of deft move typified Kean's politics. For him, politics was not just a matter of drawing boxes around towns where his party could amass votes and build power. He saw politics as a way of erasing those invisible boxes and drawing people together. His mantra seemed to be as simple as it was disarming in a state where politics was considered a blood sport: "It's okay if we disagree," Kean often told opponents. "But can we find common ground where we can get things done?"

Yet, another attribute that endeared Kean to wide swaths of voters was his folksy promotion of New Jersey tourism. TV ads featuring Kean proclaiming "New Jersey and You; Perfect Together" became a national hit.

By 1985, Kean, who set the record for the smallest margin of victory four years earlier, won re-election with 70 percent of the vote, the largest margin in state history. More than 60 percent of the state's African American voters supported him.

The GOP wanted him to run for the US Senate against Democrat Bill Bradley, the former basketball star. President Bush and his father, President George H.W. Bush, and reportedly even Democrat Bill Clinton considered Kean for a variety of cabinet posts. Meanwhile, some prominent GOP power brokers thought Kean would be an appealing candidate for vice president.

Kean turned them all down. To him, Washington had become a political boxing ring. And within the rapidly growing world of round-the-clock cable news, politics had become much more a game of one-upmanship, with officials insulting each other with curt and quotable one-liners, many created by public relations specialists and political strategists. The days of substantial policy discussions and the kind of deal making that call for compromise were disappearing. Or so Kean thought.

* * *

As he spoke to the crowd that July morning at the Mellon Auditorium in Washington, Kean did not mention his own journey. Nor did he seem out of place in that moment—a stranger in what he had long believed would be a strange land of Washington politics. To the contrary, Kean seemed right at home. As he said later, he felt his country needed to hear clear voices on how to protect itself.

After citing America's "failure of imagination," Kean ticked off a series of specific mistakes—and underestimations of the enemy the nation faced.

"We recognize, as commissioners, that we have the benefit of hindsight," he said. "And since the plotters were flexible and resourceful, we cannot know whether any single step or series of steps would have defeated them. What we can say with a good deal of confidence is that none of the measures adopted by the United States government before 9/11 disturbed or even delayed the progress of the al-Qaeda plot."

In other words: America was defenseless. In relying on old techniques of diplomacy and long-distance spy satellites to gather information, it had set up the equivalent of France's Maginot Line of concrete forts along its border with Germany before World War II. Just as Germany's army found ways to bypass the Maginot Line with its fast-moving tank divisions, so too had the 9/11 hijackers found ways to take advantage of the all-too-obvious holes in America's own defenses against terrorism.

Kean cited "several unexploited opportunities"—notably the failure of the CIA to monitor two well-known al-Qaeda terrorists—Khalid al-Mihdhar and Nawaf al-Hazmi—who entered the United States on government-approved visas. And even though the FBI arrested a suspicious Islamist, Zacarias Moussaoui, on immigration violations three weeks before the 9/11 attacks, the bureau failed to properly assess and warn the rest of the FBI about Moussaoui's unabashed interest "in flight training for the purpose of using an airplane as a terrorist act" and whether his mysterious desire for flight training was an indication that he might be part of a larger al-Qaeda plot. Nor did US immigration officials discover false statements the hijackers made on visa applications or recognize passports that were manipulated in a fraudulent manner.

Kean called such blatant oversights a part of "a broader national security picture where the government failed to protect the American people."

He pointed out that even though American officials knew the location of Osama bin Laden's base camps in Afghanistan—several American journalists actually visited them—"our military forces and covert action capabilities did not have the options on the table to defeat al-Qaeda or kill or capture either bin Laden or his top lieutenants."

Kean went on to say: "Our intelligence and law enforcement agencies did not manage or share information or effectively follow leads to keep pace with a very nimble enemy. Our border, immigration, and aviation security agencies were not integrated into the counterterrorism effort. Much of our response on the day of 9/11 was improvised and ineffective, even as extraordinary individual acts of heroism saved countless lives."

On the morning of September 11, the US Air Force had fewer than ten fighter jets on the entire Eastern seaboard that were armed and fueled. Even then, the jets couldn't locate the hijacked jetliners. Civilian air traffic controllers, not the military, controlled radar inside the United States. Incredibly, America had no system for the inter-agency communications and sharing radar information.

Kean's remarks were a devastating indictment of the Washington bureaucracy. Almost every agency failed miserably, from the FBI and CIA to the military and other government agencies that monitor immigration.

Such revelations were both tragic and enraging. But as was his custom, Kean figured it would be useless at this point to single out any specific people for blame. "Our failures took place over many years and administrations," he said. "There's no single individual who is responsible for our failures. Yet individuals and institutions cannot be absolved of responsibility. Any person in a senior position within our government during this time bears some element of responsibility for our government's actions. Having said that, it is not our purpose to assign blame. As we said at the outset, we look back so that we can look forward. Our goal is to prevent future attacks."

With that, however, Kean offered what would turn out to be the scariest element of the Commission's findings.

"Every expert with whom we spoke told us an attack of even greater magnitude is now possible and even probable," he said. "We do not have the luxury of time. We must prepare and we must act."

Kean predicted that the al-Qaeda network was already seeking "more ambitious targets" and even more lethal weapons.

Osama bin Laden and al-Qaeda "despise America and its policies," Kean said. "They exploit political grievances and hopelessness within the Arab and Islamic world. They indoctrinate the disaffected and pervert one of the world's great religions. And they seek creative methods to kill Americans in limitless numbers, including if they can do it, with the use of chemical, biological, and nuclear weapons. Put simply, the United States is faced with one of the greatest security challenges in our long history."

"We are not safe," he said, as he ended his speech. "We cannot let our guard down."

* * *

Kristen Breitweiser thumbed through her copy of the report as she sat in the Mellon auditorium listening to Kean's remarks. Dressed in jeans and a black jacket, Breitweiser turned suddenly to fellow Jersey Girl, Lorie Van Auken, who sat next to her with her own copy of the report.

The moment, captured by a news photographer, shows Breitweiser, her eyes widening, pointing to one of the report's footnotes on page 502—what Breitweiser would later describe as "the mystery of footnote 44."

What she had found opened the door a bit wider on one of the most significant controversies of the 9/11 Commission. For the first time, America was learning that an FBI agent serving in the CIA's team called "Alec Station" that monitored bin Laden and his al-Qaeda operatives, tried to sound an alarm that two al-Qaeda terrorists—al-Mihdhar and al-Hazmi—had sneaked into the United States in early 2000. But the CIA had blocked that agent from even telling his own colleagues at the FBI.

That agent was Mark Rossini.

Breitweiser did not know Rossini yet. Indeed, America had no idea who he was at that moment. Not only did Footnote 44 corroborate Rossini's claim that he and at least one other FBI liason at the CIA were prohibited from notifying the FBI about al-Mihdhar and al-Hazmi, but the footnote added a new mystery: The CIA claimed it had drafted its own official "cable" to warn Rossini's FBI superiors about al-Mihdhar and al-Hazmi. The implication was that it was unnecessary for Rossini to worry about telling the FBI about the two al-Qaeda operatives on the loose in America. The CIA says it already passed on that information to the FBI. But the Commission's investigators were unable to "locate anyone who claimed to have shared the information."

The story of al-Mihdhar and al-Hazmi's secret entry into the US in 2000 had already been widely reported by the time the Commission's report was released. But the failure to catch them had been chalked up to outmoded bureaucratic rules that separated much of counterterrorism work by the CIA and FBI. The CIA, citing its mandate to collect intelligence only outside the US and not participate in spy investigations inside the American borders, had explained that it had been barred by law from sharing what it knew about al-Mihdhar and al-Hazmi with the FBI. A series of federal regulations known collectively in the CIA and in the FBI as "the wall," essentially placed a bureaucratic barrier that prohibited the agencies from sharing information with each other.

While seemingly absurd—especially after the 9/11 attacks—the regulations had long been a part of America's intelligence system. The idea was that the CIA would not spy on American citizens within the nation's borders. Such regulations were meant to protect citizens' rights of privacy and prevent America from coming under the thumb of an authoritarian leader.

Such rules seemed to make sense, especially after a Congressional investigation in the 1970s uncovered a string of abuses by the CIA in spying on American citizens. But the practical impact of protocols separating the domestic intelligence investigations by the FBI from the foreign intelligence gathering by the CIA meant that America's two most powerful intelligence agencies rarely cooperated. Over time, each agency saw the other as a rival, not an ally with a common set of enemies, especially when it came to battling international terrorism that was slowly seeping into America.

But while acknowledging how the law blocked the CIA from sharing exclusive spy information it had gleaned on its own with the FBI, the CIA had not mentioned that it had blocked an FBI agent on the CIA's bin Laden team from telling his own bosses. What seemed like a subtle distinction would soon blossom into a major controversy.

The CIA, with the help of other foreign intelligence agencies, had tracked al-Mihdhar and al-Hazmi as they traveled from the Middle East to a series of secret meetings with al-Qaeda leaders in Kuala Lumpur, Malaysia. (If the CIA was alarmed, it did not say so publicly.) After the meetings and with the CIA still trailing them, al-Mihdhar and al-Hazmi left Malaysia for Bangkok, Thailand. Incredibly, al-Mihdhar and al-Hazmi had obtained tourist visas to travel to America. After a day or two in Bangkok, they booked a flight to Los Angeles. Soon after, the CIA reportedly lost track of al-Mihdhar's and al-Hazmi's whereabouts inside the US.

By summer 2001, the CIA's handling of al-Mihdhar and al-Hazmi had become a crisis for the agency. After al-Mihdhar and al-Hazmi could not be located and amid a disturbing array of warnings that a major attack on America might be in the offing, the CIA finally broke down its "wall" of separation from the FBI and asked the bureau to track down the two terrorists. But it was already too late. The CIA's request did not arrive until August 2001—only weeks before the attack. And then, the CIA did not say how dangerous al-Mihdhar and al-Hazmi might be. The FBI ended up initially assigning just one agent who did not have much experience in counterterrorism.

Why did the CIA wait so long? And if the CIA found a reason in the summer of 2001 to bypass the nation's espionage rules about sharing information with the FBI, why didn't it come to that conclusion sooner?

Those questions have never been answered fully.

What the CIA and the FBI did not know until too late during the summer of 2001 is that an ordinary police patrol officer in the tiny borough of South Hackensack, New Jersey, had already stumbled upon al-Mihdhar and al-Hazmi.

It was a Saturday night in June 2001. Officer David Agar had been assigned to swing through the parking lots of a series of cheap motels along the Route 46 highway that ran through his town on the way to the George Washington Bridge. The motels, police had long suspected, were used by drug dealers and prostitutes. If Agar saw anything suspicious, he was to notify his sergeant back at police headquarters.

Agar pulled into the driveway of the Congress Inn and noticed a light blue Toyota Corolla with California license plates parked in front of the motel's room 506. Agar figured the car from California seemed unusual.

Agar typed the license plate number into a computer in his police cruiser that connected him to the FBI's national system that let local cops check on unpaid traffic tickets, arrest warrants, and even reports of terrorism. A name flashed on Agar's screen: Nawaf al-Hazmi. The information on the screen merely said that al-Hazmi had rented the car. It offered no other details about him—certainly not the most important information that he was a suspected terrorist. Only after the CIA formally told the FBI in the middle of the summer of 2001 that al-Hazmi and his colleague Khalid al-Mihdhar were members of al-Qaeda did the FBI update its computer network with a warning. By then, al-Hazmi and al-Mihdhar had disappeared and were hiding as they prepared for 9/11.

On that night in June, Agar understandably figured that Nawaf al-Hazmi was just another traveler with an Arabic name—not uncommon in New Jersey. Agar had no other reason—no "probable cause" in the legal parlance of law enforcement—to confront al-Hazmi and question him along with al-Mihdhar who was with him inside the motel's room 506. Agar put his police cruiser in gear and drove away, not knowing that two of the key figures in the 9/11 plot were only a few feet from his car and behind a door in Room 506.

Here now, as Breitweiser noticed, Footnote 44 of the 9/11 Commission report was even more evidence of how America's counterterrorism network had mishandled the investigation of al-Mihdhar and al-Hazmi, and, in a larger sense, skirted the possibility of stopping the 9/11 attacks before they took place.

How is it possible that something so outrageous could happen? Why would America's intelligence bureaucracy make such a monumental mistake?

Breitweiser found herself getting angry as she asked herself those questions. Her government seemed not only inept but engaged in what she felt might be a cover-up.

During the nearly three years since the attacks, Mark Rossini had continually agonized over those same questions. The footnote did not name him as one of the FBI agents who had been blocked by the CIA from passing the information to his bosses at the FBI's counterterrorism teams. But Rossini knew he was at the center of that footnote. What he did not know is that the story was even worse than he thought.

The 9/11 Commission discovered—along with Congressional investigators before it—that al-Mihdhar and al-Hazmi were met by a group of Saudi citizens living in America when they arrived in Los Angeles in January 2000 on the flight from Bangkok, Thailand. This group included a Muslim cleric with ties to the Saudi government ministry that oversaw religious affairs and a Saudi intelligence operative who reported to the Saudi embassy in Washington, DC. Whether the CIA knew about al-Mihdhar's and al-Hazmi's welcoming party—and its links to the Saudi government—was not immediately clear. For the Commission, however, the presence of a Saudi intelligence operative and a Muslim cleric with ties to the Saudi government understandably raised a series of daunting questions. For example, how had two members of al-Qaeda suddenly been able to connect so easily with the Saudi community in Southern California? And did that Saudi community know beforehand that two al-Qaeda operatives just happened to arrive for a visit?

When al-Mihdhar and al-Hazmi arrived in Los Angeles, the Saudi intelligence operative who met them turned out to be Omar al-Bayoumi. The Muslim cleric was Fahad al-Thumairy. With their links to the Saudi government—and allegedly to the Saudi embassy in Washington and the Saudi consulate in Los Angeles—both would later emerge as mysterious and major factors in the investigation on alleged Saudi links to the 9/11 attacks.

An important question loomed over the revelation of the meeting in Los Angeles between the Saudi intelligence agent (al-Bayoumi), the cleric (al-Thumairy) and the the future hijackers, al-Mihdhar and al-Hazmi: Were al-Mihdhar and al-Hazmi instructed by their al-Qaeda bosses to contact al-Bayoumi and al-Thumairy after arriving in America? If not, how did al-Bayoumi and al-Thumairy know that al-Mihdhar and al-Hazmi would be arriving?

While Rossini and Breitweiser had not met or spoken to each other yet, they separately shared the same suspicions and questions. The meetings between the terrorists and the Saudi-connected officials did not seem accidental. And if they weren't accidental, were al-Bayoumi and al-Thumairy acting on their own as rogue Islamist zealots who just happened to be connected to the Saudi government in some way or were they taking orders from someone in the government?

Finally, and most provocative: Did al-Bayoumi and al-Thumairy know that al-Mihdhar and al-Hazmi were members of al-Qaeda and were about to carry out a major attack within the United States?

The Commission did not answer these questions in a substantial manner. However, it did drop quite a few hints that it had been deeply concerned about the allegations that Saudi Arabia officials had been involved in the attacks.

"Saudi Arabia has been a problematic ally in combating Islamic terrorism," the Commission wrote in an executive summary of its longer report. And in a separate sixteen-page monograph that explored the complexities and mysteries of how Islamist terrorism had been financed, the Commission found that "fundraisers and facilitators throughout Saudi Arabia and the Gulf raised money for al-Qaeda from witting and unwitting donors and diverted funds from Islamic charities and mosques."

The monograph went on to say in careful language that "the Commission staff found no evidence that the Saudi government as an institution or as individual senior officials knowingly support or supported al-Qaeda." But the monograph cautioned that "a lack of awareness of the problem and a failure to conduct oversight over institutions created an environment in which such activity has flourished."

Meanwhile, the Commission found that US officials seemed all too willing to gloss over and not pursue the fact that al-Qaeda financing may be tied to Saudi Arabia. "From the 9/11 attacks through spring 2003," the Commission wrote in its monograph, "most US officials viewed Saudi cooperation on terrorist financing as ambivalent and selective. US efforts to overcome Saudi recalcitrance suffered from our failure to develop a strategy to counter Saudi terrorist financing, present our requests through a single high-level interlocutor, and obtain and release to the Saudis actionable intelligence."

The Commission reported that "by spring 2003, the US government had corrected these deficiencies." But it did not say what Saudi officials or institutions had been at fault in the first place.

For example, the Commission made no reference to a still-secret twenty-eight-page excerpt from the special report in 2003 by the Joint Congressional Intelligence Committee that outlined in great detail a laundry list of alleged connections between Saudi Arabia and the 9/11 attacks—including the mysterious meetings with al-Bayoumi, al-Thumairy, al-Mihdhar, and al-Hazmi in Los Angeles. The twenty-eight pages also detailed a disturbing financial contribution from the wife of the Saudi ambassador to the United States, Prince Bandar bin Sultan al Saud, into an account with alleged al-Qaeda connections and the suspected al Qaeda cell in Southern California that supported al-Mihdhar and al-Hazmi.

In its official report that Kean introduced to the world in July 2004, the Commission offered a cautionary and carefully worded analysis that certainly raised suspicions about Saudi Arabia's connection to the 9/11 attacks but presented no firm answers. In fact, the Commission's conclusion was confusing—so much so that Kristen Breitweiser and Mark Rossini would separately come to believe that it was an appalling oversight in the Commission's report.

"Saudi Arabia has long been considered the primary source of al-Qaeda funding," the Commission wrote, "but we have found no evidence that the Saudi government as an institution or senior Saudi officials individually funded the organization. This conclusion does not excuse the likelihood that charities with significant Saudi government sponsorship diverted funds to al-Qaeda."

Such meandering explanations by the Commission and other US officials—along with a steady stream of denials by Saudi authorities of any links to 9/11—would continue to baffle the team of 9/11 victims' lawyers and investigators for years in their efforts to pin down the truth behind the alleged Saudi connections to the attacks. For the victims themselves and their relatives such as Kristen Breitweiser, the other Jersey Girls, and Terry Strada, the years of not really knowing the truth would leave behind deep and painful scars, as well as agonizing doubts about why their own country seemed so unwilling to investigate such important allegations.

* * *

As she sat through the remainder of presentation at the Mellon Auditorium by Kean and the other commissioners, Kristen Breitweiser tried to keep her skepticism, disappointment, and rising anger in check. This was no time to start a public fight, she figured. When she approached Kean to sign her copy of the report, a news photographer snapped a picture of Breitweiser. She was smiling. So was Kean. The two seemed like kindred spirits who enjoyed working with each other.

Across the Potomac in his new office with the Terrorism Threat Integration Center, which the CIA established to begin the arduous task of coordinating intelligence from across the world and within the United States, Mark Rossini began reading the Commission report. Rossini left the CIA's "Alec Station" bin Laden group in 2003. He needed a break. Plus, he had been deeply frustrated by "Alec Station," not to mention guilt-ridden for not breaking the rules and telling his FBI supervisors that two terrorists had been on the loose in America before the 9/11 attacks.

Rossini was impressed as he began to read the Commission's report. Clearly, the Commission and its staff understood the wide reach of al-Qaeda across the world—as Rossini did. But the more he read, Rossini realized that the Commission had deftly avoided the real problem between the CIA and the FBI. He had been blocked from sharing important information—and he still did not know why. The only evidence that Rossini found of this blockage of important information was Footnote 44 on page 502—not exactly an indication that the Commission wanted this information highlighted and extensively discussed.

Rossini wondered whether the CIA had another secret agenda he did not know about and that the Commission could not reveal. Or was the experience he endured just another old-fashioned bureaucratic cover-up to protect the CIA after it blew its chances to stop the 9/11 attacks?

Each day, when he returned to his job, Rossini remembers feeling overwhelmed with guilt at what he did not do in those months before September 11, 2001.

He was tired of following rules now.

In the coming years, this would be his undoing.

A suspected Islamist terrorist, imprisoned at the US Naval Base in Guantanamo Bay, Cuba, holding prayer beads during a Muslim prayer service. At its peak, the base held more than 700 suspected terrorists from forty-eight countries. Photo by Mark Wilson/AFP via Getty Images.

9

The Chaplain of Gitmo

Eleven days after the 9/11 Commission released its report in Washington, DC, a US Army officer at his base on the other side of America decided to end his military career.

What brought Captain James Yee to turn his back on what his superior officers once predicted would be a promising future in the Army turned out to be one of the most contentious and controversial episodes for America in the years immediately following the 9/11 attacks.

Yee, a West Point graduate and one of only a dozen or so Islamic chaplains in the entire US military at the time, found himself accused of espionage amid the anti-Muslim fervor after the 9/11 attacks. The offenses were so serious that Yee was told he faced the death penalty.

Those claims—and threat of execution—turned out to be baseless, however. Nine months after apprehending him, the Army dropped the spying accusations and restored Yee's status as a chaplain at Fort Lewis, Washington. Additional claims that Yee violated the Army's code of conduct by reportedly carrying on an adulterous affair and storing pornography on a computer were also dismissed, with a four-star general taking the unusual step of overruling a lower ranking general who filed them.

It was a relief-filled, yet deeply painful, turnaround of events for Yee. He had just endured months of nightmarish legal problems in which his loyalty to America and to the US Army—even to his moral calling as a military chaplain—had been questioned. But as unexpectedly as his troubles began, Yee was told that his record had been wiped clean, that all the fuss was really nothing to worry about. He was free to resume his career.

The sudden change in his legal status and the promise of resuming his career hardly mattered to Yee. He felt wounded—permanently—by the military he had vowed to serve. His marriage was fraying, especially in the wake of the Army's adultery accusation. His reputation as a highly regarded West Point-trained officer who had been recommended for a promotion only a few days before his arrest had been shattered. And, he knew how the military worked: Even though he had a diploma from West Point and an otherwise spotless record as an Army officer, his colleagues would now forever wonder if he really was a spy for the terrorists in Osama bin Laden's al-Qaeda network.

Many supporters, notably among America's Muslim communities, felt that Yee had been unfairly harassed—especially with the adultery and pornography charges that were unrelated to the espionage accusation and another claim that he mishandled classified documents that turned out to be baseless. But Yee felt his pride had been scarred, not to mention his heart and soul.

Plus, he felt badly mistreated at the hands of military investigators.

Besides a series of brutal, mind-boggling legal skirmishes with the Army and the ultimate admission by military investigators that evidence of his alleged spying was completely unfounded, he had nevertheless spent seventy-six days in solitary confinement in a military prison where the lights in his cell were never turned off for long periods of time, and he was even forced to wear handcuffs and leg shackles during his one hour of outdoor exercise each day. For several weeks, his wife and daughter—along with his parents and two brothers who were also serving in the US Army—had no idea where he was. To them, Yee had vanished.

When he drafted his formal letter of resignation on August 2, 2004, Yee felt he would never be able to regain the trust from the Army with his "faith and patriotism under fire." Indeed, his own trust and belief in the righteousness of the Army had been broken. How could he ever forget what had happened to him? He had to leave.

* * *

The sequence of events that led to Yee's dramatic decision began with one of the most ordinary and expected elements of life for any member of the military. In the fall of 2002, Yee received orders that he was being deployed to a new assignment from his post as a Muslim chaplain amid the bucolic foothills of the Cascade Mountains at Fort Lewis, Washington.

In the wake of the 9/11 attacks, as America expanded its war on terrorism, more than three million US military personnel would be sent overseas. These ranged from highly trained jet fighter pilots and the Army's elite Green Beret teams to cooks and truck drivers from National Guard units. The first contingents landed a month after the 9/11 attacks in the mountains of Afghanistan to hunt for the suddenly elusive Osama bin Laden and his followers. In the years to follow, thousands more US military personnel would head to the deserts of Iraq in search of what the White House believed were weapons of mass destruction.

None would return, however, branded with the kinds of wounds that Yee came home with: Falsely accused of betraying his country.

Yee's new assignment after Fort Lewis was an aging Cold War outpost: the US Naval Station at Guantanamo Bay, Cuba. As a fluent Arabic speaker, he was told he would be the Muslim chaplain for the hundreds of suspected terrorists who were being brought to a specially constructed base prison, initially known as Camp X-Ray and then renamed Camp Delta. Within weeks after he arrived, however, several of Yee's colleagues felt he was not merely communicating with the alleged terrorists that the Pentagon called "detainees;" they ended up believing—wrongly, it turns out—he had become part of a group of US soldiers and translators who were Muslims and who were secretly helping detainees send messages to their homes. Without Yee knowing, the Army started collecting information on him and several others.

Whether such suspicions were little more than a reflection of the growing distrust of Muslims that swept through America in the wake of the 9/11 attacks or whether it was just a matter of the Army stumbling over its own makeshift security precautions after the attacks, is still a mystery. Many of the Guantanamo prison guards came from National Guard units across America, and had little training in handling prisoners, let alone scores of men from the Middle East who might have ties to terrorism or might have been wrongly apprehended amid the fog of war. What's more, the suspicions about Yee contrasted sharply with the image he tried to nurture after he arrived.

Not only was he enthusiastic about his assignment at Guantanamo, but the Army's brass there felt he would be a welcome addition. Indeed, even before he arrived, Yee had established himself as one of the Army's most articulate and enlightened spokesmen on Islam.

At Guantanamo, however, Yee was entering an environment in which American and largely non-Muslim prison guards faced a difficult time with their Muslim captives. Few guards spoke Arabic or any of the other dialects that were common in Afghanistan and other parts of the Islamic world. Few captives, in turn, spoke English.

Then there was the trust factor. Could a Muslim chaplain remain objective in dealing with devoutly Muslim captives who might be terrorists? Three Muslim chaplains preceded Yee. Each had left under clouds of suspicion, with the Pentagon thinking they had developed all-too-close relationships with the Muslim prisoners.

Yee seemed markedly different. He had a West Point degree. He was also not a lifelong Muslim; he had converted to Islam as an adult after being raised as a Lutheran. Before that conversion, he had served as an officer in an air defense unit, based first in Germany and then in Saudi Arabia.

As a chaplain, Yee already had built a substantial reputation in the months after 9/11 as a positive voice for the US military as it juggled its mission to hunt down a group of Islamist zealots who had embraced terrorism while also trying to assure Muslims (and plenty of others) that it was not targeting all of the Islamic world. He regularly gave instructional lectures at Fort Lewis to large groups of non-Muslim soldiers on Islam and why bin Laden's terrorists had perverted standard Islamic theology as a way of justifying the murders on 9/11. The Army viewed Yee as rational and clear in his thinking. With his West Point bearing, he was becoming something of a poster boy for the Army's efforts to fend off any criticism that it was anti-Muslim. The Army even gave Yee permission to be interviewed on such progressive media outlets as National Public Radio and MSNBC as a way of softening criticism from abroad—especially in the Middle East—that America's military was anti-Muslim and had essentially declared war on the entire Islamic world.

Some of Yee's most noteworthy and unheralded work involved fellow Muslim soldiers, however. Within the Army itself, Yee said that since the attacks of 9/11, he found himself sometimes counseling Muslim soldiers who wondered how they could fight against an enemy who shared their same religious faith.

Yee's answer, framed by a basic interpretation of Islamic theology and yet also addressing a soldier's vow to defend the nation, underscored why the Pentagon brass came to admire him so much. Yee did not speak in complicated terms. Nor did he offer any confusing qualifiers. His message was simple, direct, and straightforward, the kind of language that soldiers respected and expected from their officers. Muslim soldiers, Yee typically said, should realize that their own faith would support their efforts to fight against a Muslim enemy that violated Islam's precepts against killing innocent people. "An act of terrorism, the taking of innocent civilian lives is prohibited by Islam, and whoever has done this needs to be brought to justice, whether he is Muslim or not," Yee told *The New York Times* in summarizing his philosophy in an interview a month after 9/11.

After another year at Fort Lewis, where his reputation as a clear-thinking chaplain grew even more, Yee set out on his trek to Guantanamo. It was November 2, 2002, Election Day across America. By nightfall, when polls across the nation closed, Republicans would regain their majority in the US Congress.

Yee had already said good-bye to his wife and small daughter at Fort Lewis. After several days of travel—first to Fort Benning, Georgia—he made his way to the US Navy's airfield in Jacksonville, Florida. Just after dawn, he stepped on to a chartered commercial jetliner.

Yee remembers that the plane seemed unusually crowded. CIA analysts and translators who would help interrogate prisoners sat with soldiers and construction workers who were sent to Guantanamo to upgrade the Cold War-era buildings or set up the enormous infrastructure of tents and other facilities to house what would become a garrison of nearly 3,000 soldiers and others.

* * *

For decades, the US Naval Station at Guantanamo Bay had been viewed by the Pentagon as little more than a backwater outpost. Few Navy officers wanted to be assigned there. In the acclaimed film and Broadway play, *A Few Good Men*, Guantanamo was depicted as a dangerous place, where Marines stood guard on a "wall" against communism. But that depiction dated back to the early 1960s. By 2001, Guantanamo was hardly a war zone—or even a spot that was vulnerable to a crisis.

The hilly landscape was dry and craggy—more like an Arizona desert than a Caribbean island. Instead of swaying palms, Guantanamo was home to an array of cactus trees and a species of unusually large iguanas who thrived in the harsh climate. Old-fashioned telephones with rotary dialing mechanisms were common in some of the homes. Many base roads that were made of crushed coral had become so riddled with potholes that US Marine Humvees often broke down on patrol. The officers club, with its tiki bar, seemed more like a set for a 1950s movie.

The US seized control of the base in 1903 as part of the spoils of winning the Spanish-American War. In fact, when Captain Yee arrived, Guantanamo still had a monument atop one of its hills to the Navy officer and five Marines who were killed when the US won a battle there against Spanish forces.

For more than a half-century, the base was little more than a refueling stop for US Navy ships patrolling the Caribbean or heading to the South Atlantic. For much of that time, Cuba's government welcomed the base as a source of jobs for local Cubans. Meanwhile, if there was any aspect of life on the base that the American sailors and Marines admired, it was the beaches and, just offshore, some of the best snorkeling reefs in the Caribbean.

That comfortable and quiet relationship changed on New Year's Day 1959 when Fidel Castro seized power in Cuba, upending years of brutal governmental rule by dictator Fulgencia Batista. Within months, Castro demanded that America abandon Guantanamo. The US refused, especially after Castro declared that he planned to install his own communist authoritarian regime in Cuba and become a Caribbean outpost of the Soviet Union.

As a result, Guantanamo achieved a new status. Not only was it one of the oldest US overseas military bases; it was the only US military installation in a communist country.

Guantanamo's garrison of US Marines was enlarged and equipped with tanks and artillery. And the Pentagon built what would become one of the world's largest minefields along the 17-mile perimeter that separated the base from the rest of Castro's Cuba. But the US and Castro's military forces never went to war. Castro's most notable aggression and attempt to punish the US for maintaining its presence at Guantanamo was to cut off the base's water supply. But that tactic failed. The US responded by building special plants that would desalinate sea water.

By the late 1990s, with threats by Castro fewer and fewer and with the collapse of the Soviet Union, the Guantanamo base had the look of a ghost town. The Navy no longer used the base for training. The Marine garrison numbered less than 200.

That strange and weirdly unchanged world transformed dramatically in the months after the September 11 attacks and the US military's incursion into Afghanistan.

As US military and CIA units swept through the Afghan hills, they encountered dozens of suspected al-Qaeda operatives. In some cases, US officials even paid Afghan leaders to point out alleged terrorists. As the US later learned some of the so-called terrorists were not members of al-Qaeda but had merely been caught in some sort of tribal feud, with their punishment consisting of being turned over to the US authorities on false charges that they were hardline members of al-Qaeda.

US officials made little effort to sort the terrorists from ordinary Afghans who just happened to be in the wrong place at the wrong time. The US began arresting hundreds of suspects. But it had no place to put them. Worse, it had not been able to amass the kind of evidence needed to actually transport the alleged al-Qaeda operatives back to the US for a formal indictment and possible trial in American courts.

Yes, US military leaders in Afghanistan had captured what they felt were prisoners of war. But since there was no formal declaration of war against al-Qaeda and these so-called POWs were not identifiable by uniforms, the US legal experts who advised the Bush Administration faced an odd quandary: How would they categorize the prisoners who had been captured? It's not as if al-Qaeda kept lists of its operatives and put them in uniforms that clearly designated them as the enemy.

If the prisoners were allowed to go free, US military authorities in Afghanistan and at the Guantanamo Bay detention center feared that some might resume their places as al-Qaeda terrorists. But did the US military have the legal authority to hold them without clear evidence that they had been involved in any way with al-Qaeda?

Rather than settling such questions, the Bush Administration created the equivalent of a holding pen at the Guantanamo Bay naval base for prisoners that were now designated as "detainees" and "enemy combatants." Such prisoners were not on US soil so they did not fall under the extensive legal umbrella of rights that generally protected anyone arrested in America. By being placed in cells in a prison camp at Guantanamo Bay, however, the "detainees" would still be under the thumb of the US military and the CIA where they could be questioned more extensively and perhaps convinced to cooperate in the large manhunt for Osama bin Laden and other high-ranking al-Qaeda leaders.

With that strategy in mind, the US military, along with the CIA and the White House, decided to assign scores of interrogators to the prison camp at Guantanamo who would try to extract information from the detainees. Soon, those interrogators were given permission to use "enhanced interrogation techniques" that were later compared to torture and were suspected of violating the Geneva Accords standards for caring for prisoners of war. Some of these "enhanced interrogation" methods included placing hoods over prisoners' heads and binding them in ways that forced them to sit in contorted positions. It also involved subjecting prisoners to deafening noises that deprived them of sleep, and "waterboarding" them by forcing so much water down their throats as they lay on their backs that they thought they were drowning.

One of the military's advocates of these so-called interrogation enhancements, Army Major General Geoffrey Miller, arrived at Guantanamo only weeks after Yee. Miller, who would later emerge as one of the figures behind the international controversy involving the mistreatment of prisoners by US soldiers at Iraq's notoriously brutal Abu Ghraib prison, was soon given an order from US Defense Secretary Donald Rumsfeld to carry out the "First Special Interrogation Plan" at Guantanamo which included seventeen "enhanced" methods of questioning detainees. It did not take long for accusations of torture to be raised by human rights groups.

For any military chaplain, especially one like Captain James Yee who was trying to set new Army standards on how it treated Muslims and yet maintain the Army's moral standing to fight against Islamist terrorists, it was probably the worst moment to arrive. Indeed, as Yee stepped off the chartered jetliner at Guantanamo Bay in November 2002, he found himself entering an untested, unstable, and potentially dangerous legal, cultural, and religious terrain. The prisoners had staged at least one hunger strike to protest their treatment. Seven prisoners had already attempted suicide.

* * *

At Guantanamo, Yee was assigned three very different tasks as a chaplain. On one hand, he was asked to offer orientation lectures about Islam to the rapidly growing garrison of nearly 3,000 soldiers, sailors, Marines, CIA staffers, and civilian contractors at Guantanamo. He was also asked to offer religious counseling and conduct prayer services for the several dozen Muslims who were part of that garrison. And, finally and perhaps most difficult, he was supposed to minister to the mostly Muslim population of prisoners from forty countries. These included zealous al-Qaeda fighters who were not shy about wanting to fight the United States and grizzled old men with long beards who aligned themselves with al-Qaeda in Afghanistan only when it suited their need for a job or just protection from other rival tribal warlords. Then there was the most mysterious group: fresh-faced teenagers whose links to al-Qaeda and terrorism were dubious, but nonetheless suspicious enough to cause them to be transported to Guantanamo.

Yee had one advantage that other chaplains—and most guards—did not have. He could speak Arabic, the language common to many of the detainees. Yee soon learned that the relationships between guards and prisoners had grown tense and occasionally confrontational. Prisoners reportedly threw urine and feces at some guards as a way of protesting their confinement. Some guards responded by deluging prisoners with loud music or, in some cases, confiscating an inmate's copy of Islam's holy book, the Quran.

Meanwhile, General Miller had orders to improve intelligence collection from the inmates. As a result, the prisoners were not merely held in their small cells. They were regularly brought to interrogation rooms to be questioned by CIA officers using the controversial "enhanced" methods.

Yee said he had been instructed that he should not get involved with intelligence collection. He was actually relieved that the Pentagon did not ask him to participate in the interrogation sessions. Such a role, he felt, would violate his calling as a chaplain and break whatever bonds of trust he had established in counseling the prisoners and the guards, as well as some of the interrogators.

But Yee found himself trying to navigate a middle ground. On one hand, he was an Army officer so he had to remain loyal to what the Army was doing in its harsh interrogations even though he might disagree with those tactics. On the other, he was a chaplain—not just for soldiers but for their captives who were increasingly complaining to Yee of their treatment. In an interview with a visiting TV crew, Yee was asked how he balanced his Islamic beliefs and care for prisoners with his military status and vow to defend his nation. Yee's answer offers hints at the moral wrestling match he was engaged in as an Army officer and chaplain. "Professionals never allow personal things to affect the way they perform a job," Yee said. "If they do, then they're not professional."

Yee tried to intervene in some disputes between guards and inmates. But in doing that, he risked losing trust from each side. Many prisoners considered him a traitor to Islam and not someone to confide in. Guards wanted him to intervene in inmate disputes while also wondering whether Yee was growing too close to the prisoners during his long talks with some of them.

No matter what he did, Yee knew his ministry would be measured by each side: Was he advocating in favor of prisoners or guards?

Each day, Yee said he wondered how he could remain neutral in a place where neutrality was nearly impossible. He counseled guards on their difficulties in dealing with the Muslim prisoners. At the same time, he also made a special effort to make sure each of the more than 600 Muslim prisoners had copies of the Quran and access to Islamic literature. He instituted Muslim prayer calls over loudspeakers. He made sure the prisoners had prayer rugs to kneel on and prayer beads.

Some segments of Islam prohibit non-Muslims from even touching a copy of the Quran. When Yee helped to institute a series of guidelines for handling an inmate's Quran while searching a cell, some guards felt betrayed and angry, asking why a chaplain—a Muslim, no less—should set rules on how guards can protect themselves from their Muslim prisoners who might be planning an uprising or violating rules.

What seemed to emerge was a growing distrust among some guards over Yee's role. As a spiritual minister, he tried to spend as much time as possible on the prisoner cell blocks, sometimes listening to complaints of those behind bars. But guards questioned whether Yee's spiritual guidance and closeness to the prisoners had tipped the balance and turned him into an advocate.

Writing in the Guantanamo base newspaper, Yee seemed to be trying to address what he perceived as the latent distrust between the American guards who were still angry about the 9/11 attacks and the Muslim prisoners. "Why has it been so difficult for most in our society to distinguish between millions of peaceful Islamic worshippers from the extreme fanatical minority?" Yee wrote. "Why are we still afraid of Islam, the religion?"

Such sentiments drew praise. One of the Army colonels at the detention center was said to have recommended that Yee "be promoted at the first opportunity." Others had become more wary of Yee and a group of Muslim soldiers and interpreters who seemed to spend quite a bit of personal time together. Soon, the group became known as the "Muslim clique," and Guantanamo counter-intelligence specialists quietly launched an investigation.

* * *

Yee was not raised as a Muslim. Nor was he raised to be anything but loyal to the United States.

Yee's father, who grew up in Pittsburgh, was drafted into the US Army just three days after graduating high school in 1945. World War II was winding down. Germany had already surrendered in May 1945; Japan surrendered three months later. Yee's father ended up serving most of his Army stint near Seattle, not far from Fort Lewis. After the war, Yee's father worked for years as an engineer at Bell Laboratories. After marrying, Yee's father and mother, also a Bell Labs staffer, settled in the New Jersey suburb of Springfield, where they raised their five children—three boys and two girls—as Lutherans.

The Yees also made no secret of their patriotism. A family photo from 1976 shows Yee's parents and his brothers and sisters dressed up in Revolutionary-era garb to commemorate the 200th anniversary of American independence.

In high school, Yee was named captain of the varsity wrestling team. By the time he was a senior, Yee had narrowed his college choice to just one institution—the US Military Academy at West Point, the Army's premier training ground for its officers.

At West Point, Yee won a spot on the wrestling team. He also found himself interested in learning more about Islam. After graduating in 1990 as a second lieutenant, he studied Islam more deeply after his air defense unit was deployed to Saudi Arabia in the wake of the first Persian Gulf War in 1991. After leaving the Army a few years later during military cutbacks by the Clinton administration, Yee worked in Tennessee for a pharmaceutical company. But he never lost his interest in Islam—or the Army. He felt called to be a Muslim imam, the equivalent of a Christian pastor or a Jewish rabbi. In his spare time, he began searching for an Islamic school where he might learn to become an imam.

First, he tried the University of Medina in Saudi Arabia, one of the top Islamic centers in the world. Yee even participated in the Hajj, the Islamic pilgrimage to the holy city of Mecca in Saudi Arabia that Muslims try to complete at least once in their lifetime. But the University of Medina rejected Yee, telling him that he was too old. At the time, Yee was only twenty-six.

Yee did not give up. He participated in a summer seminar at another top Islamic seminary at Abu Noor University in Damascus, Syria. After the summer, the university accepted Yee as a full-time student.

Yee spent most of the next four years in Damascus where he learned to speak Arabic. He also met his wife, Huda, a Palestinian-Syrian woman who returned to America with him.

It was now 1999. Yee brought his new wife back to New Jersey and moved in with his parents as he tried to figure out what sort of job he could find as a newly minted imam who also happened to be a US citizen and West Point graduate.

Around that time, an old military friend who happened to be a Muslim invited Yee to a Ramadan banquet at the Pentagon. Not long afterward, the friend called again and said that the Pentagon was looking to expand its corps of chaplains to include Muslims. Was Yee interested?

In 2000, Yee returned to the Army—this time as a captain and wearing the Army's black beret with an Islamic crescent pinned to it to signify his new status as a chaplain.

* * *

After several months at the base that came to be known as "Gitmo," Yee felt it was time for him to take a vacation. He was tired. He needed a rest. Plus he wanted to see his wife and daughter. The chaplain's job had become far more complicated than just counseling fellow Muslim soldiers, conducting prayer services, and making sure the prisoners had copies of the Quran. But amid the growing tension between guards and prisoners—and his own concerns about whether the so-called "enhanced interrogations" of the prisoners amounted to torture—Yee felt he couldn't get away.

General Miller and the other top officers looked to Yee often to speak with journalists who passed through. He was even asked to greet visiting congressional representatives and other government officials. To the Army, Yee was "on message"—meaning that he had a knack for assuring visitors that Muslim prisoners were being treated well. In February 2003 and again in July 2003, the Army gave him Joint Service Achievement medals.

By the end of the summer of 2003, Yee passed his most important test. He received top grades in his Officer Evaluation Report, the so-called OER which the Pentagon sees as one of its measures of whether an officer should be nurtured for a career and perhaps promotion to a top rank. As Yee noted years later, "These evaluations are like job reviews in civilian life, and they carry tremendous weight in the military. A good one can make an officer's career and a bad one will destroy it."

When Yee read his OER in early September 2003, he was elated. "It was the best evaluation I had yet received" in all his years in the Army, he remembers thinking. Each of the high-ranking officers who evaluated him praised Yee as a key asset to the Guantanamo mission. One lieutenant colonel said that Yee had been invaluable in developing "culturally sensitive, yet force protection focused, Standard Operating Procedures" and recommended that Yee be promoted to handle chaplaincies for an Army brigade or even an entire division of 15,000 soldiers. Another colonel, citing Yee's leadership in conducting religious and cultural awareness briefings on Islam for non-Muslim soldiers, said that Yee should be promoted as soon as possible to a higher rank.

As he read the OER, Yee felt he was well on his way to a long Army career. "I wanted to be the first army Muslim chaplain to make lieutenant colonel," he wrote afterwards.

The date of his stellar OER was September 8, 2003.

Two days later Yee was arrested.

* * *

Finally, after ten months at Guantanamo, Yee received permission to take a short furlough away from the base.

Early on the morning of September 10, 2003—the day before the second anniversary of the 9/11 attacks—Yee made his way to the Guantanamo airstrip and took a seat on the chartered commercial jetliner that was flying to Jacksonville, Florida. From there, he planned to catch another flight to Seattle, Washington, where he would reunite with his wife and daughter.

He never made it.

Before Yee even left Guantanamo, military investigators, working with the FBI and US Customs officials, devised a secret plan to take Yee into custody. Only they faced a significant problem: They had yet to gain approval from a judge to file formal charges against Yee. Nor had these investigators given any hint of their investigation to the other officers who gave Yee such high marks in his Officer Evaluation Report. It was as if two wildly different views of Yee's work had emerged at Guantanamo.

To some, he was an asset who deserved a promotion. To others, a traitor.

When law enforcement officer detained him at the Jacksonville airport, he was not told for hours why he was being arrested. Nor was he told that he had the Constitutional right to remain silent—the standard instruction given to anyone arrested in America. And he was not offered the opportunity to contact an attorney—another standard Constitutional provision generally extended to most people who are arrested in America.

Adding to the confusion, an FBI agent warned US Customs officials at the Jacksonville airport that Yee was likely carrying classified documents. He wasn't.

Yee had a security clearance at Guantanamo. But he rarely read any classified reports or other documents. He didn't see the need. The one exception was his decision to study the hurricane evacuation plan for the base as a storm approached. But after the weather cleared, Yee shredded the document.

Investigators also believed Yee had copied sensitive information about the prisoners or the base in personal notebooks. What they found in his backpack were background reports on Syria that he had downloaded from the internet for an online graduate course he was taking. Back at the base, he had left a chaplain's notebook in which he had listed prisoners' complaints that he passed on to higher ranking officials who could act on them if they chose to.

Perhaps most ludicrous of all was the belief by investigators that a drawing found in Yee's papers was a diagram of the Guantanamo base that could be passed on to terrorists who might want to stage an attack. In fact, Yee said, diagram was a drawing of the human body that he had made during a lecture on how combat stress affects the body.

Within hours, it appeared that the case against Yee was flimsy. But it did not matter. Yee was placed in a cell. It seemed as if his investigators were determined to hold him—and then find evidence that he broke the law.

At some point that evening, Yee remembers a guard banging on his cell door and asking if Yee knew why he had been arrested.

"No," Yee said.

The guard, said Yee, read five charges—Article 92, 94, 104, 106, and 106a.

To Yee, they were just numbers. The Uniform Code of Military Justice, the set of laws and regulations that govern behavior in all branches of the US military, consisted of 134 punitive articles. Yee had not memorized any of them.

The guard at the cell door, apparently sensing Yee's confusion, then read one of the charges. "Article 92 is failure to obey a lawful general order," Yee remembers the guard saying. "That's all you need to know."

The guard walked away, saying nothing more.

Yee was dumbfounded. He had no idea what order he had violated—if, in fact, he violated any orders. And if he had violated orders, why had he been evaluated so highly by the Guantanamo brass only two days before his arrest?

Yee spent the next four days in the cell at the Jacksonville naval prison. On the fifth day, he was brought to a pretrial confinement hearing. Yee hoped that by now, the FBI would have contacted his superiors back at Guantanamo, especially the base commander, Major General Geoffrey Miller.

Once Miller got involved, Yee figured the confinement hearing officer would at least set him free from the prison and he could then contact an attorney and have the charges against him dismissed. Yee considered Miller a supporter of his work at the Guantanamo prison. It turns out that Miller was one of his most ardent accusers.

As the officer presiding at the hearing read Yee's request for release, Yee was handed several documents that outlined a case against him, including a memorandum signed by General Miller and dated the day after Yee was arrested.

"Yee is known to have associated with known terrorist sympathizers," the memo said, without mentioning who these alleged terrorist sympathizers were.

The memo went on to accuse Yee of carrying classified documents at the airport and that airline tickets for a trip to London had been found in his room, implying that Yee may have been planning to bring the classified documents to an overseas contact. None of that, Yee said, was true.

Yee had not bought any airline tickets to London. He wrote afterward that he "didn't know any terrorists or anyone who associated with terrorists" and that he wasn't carrying any classified information. "Yet these accusations," Yee said, "were made under the signature of a major general in the US Army"—Geoffrey Miller.

As if that wasn't ominous enough, the memo went on to state that Yee was now also being accused of mutiny, sedition, aiding the enemy, spying, and espionage. Yee did not have to be reminded of the seriousness of the charges, but General Miller made a point of stating the potential consequences anyway. "Captain Yee is suspected of several extremely serious crimes, including espionage, which potentially carries the death penalty," the general wrote, adding that he believed Yee to be a "flight risk" and that keeping him in jail until his trial was "an absolute necessity."

As he studied the memo and its litany of charges and lack of evidence, Yee felt he had fallen into a nightmarish trap. He was confused and angry, and he believed he would not see his wife and daughter anytime soon. "In fact, I stopped believing in many things," he later wrote.

The next day, Yee was strip searched, handcuffed, and shackled, then led outside and ordered to get into the back seat of a truck. An armed guard sat beside him. Another guard slipped into the driver's seat, another into the passenger's side.

No one told Yee where he was going. He had still not been allowed to speak with an attorney. And while he had some idea of the accusations against him, he still had not been formally charged yet. The memorandum that had been signed by General Miller only listed charges that the military intended to bring. Yee learned later that military prosecutors hoped the threat of charges might be enough to persuade him to confess.

Yee wondered whether the military was bluffing—accusing him of spying without having enough evidence but believing Yee would then be scared enough to offer more details that would then lead to formal charges.

After being driven for five hours along highways, the guard next to him placed special black goggles on his eyes to prevent him from seeing and soundproof headphones over his ears.

It seemed to Yee that the truck drove for another hour before finally stopping. Still wearing the goggles and headphones, Yee remembers feeling as if he might be inside a large hangar. He was then marched through a maze of corridors.

The goggles and headphones were removed. But no one said where he was. It wasn't until the next day, when he was handed a prison handbook, that he realized he had been brought to the Navy's brig in Charleston, South Carolina, a military prison of roughly 400 cells where the military's most violent criminals were housed and where several suspected terrorists were also being held.

On September 20—ten days after his arrest—*The Washington Times* broke the story of his arrest and possible charges. But the story had not been officially released by the Pentagon. *The Times* found out about Yee's predicament from its military sources. The story said Yee's arrest had been ordered by an official "at the highest levels" of government but it didn't say who. It also said Yee was under surveillance for some time, but it didn't say how long or why. Nor did it address why Yee's superior officers would recommend him for a promotion in his laudatory Officer Evaluation Report if he was being investigated for espionage.

Yee wasn't allowed to speak to his wife until September 25—fifteen days after his arrest. As news of his arrest spread, other media reported that Yee had been in touch with Syrian government officials (not true), that he was affiliated with al-Qaeda and the Taliban (not true) and that investigators found maps of the Guantanamo prison and lists of detainees when he was arrested. (Also not true).

For Yee, the world suddenly seemed like a bad dream where almost every aspect of his life had been misinterpreted or even falsified.

Yee finally met with two military defense lawyers who were assigned to his case. Already, one of the attorneys had been told by military prosecutors that he ought to find a civilian attorney who was experienced in defending prisoners facing the death penalty. Was this yet another bluff by prosecutors to force Yee into a confession that would save them the trouble of actually collecting evidence? Yee did not know. But given his predicament, Yee certainly suspected something nefarious was in the works.

Yee had still not been charged with any crimes. That formality did not occur until October 10—thirty days after he had been arrested and jailed. Yee was handed a paper listing only two charges—that he had taken classified information to his apartment at Guantanamo and that he transported classified documents without placing them in a proper container.

On November 25, two days before Thanksgiving, Yee was released from jail. An Army legal officer took him to dinner, then drove him to Fort Benning, Georgia. Yee was, after all, still on active duty. His new assignment would be with the chaplain's office at Fort Benning.

A new set of troubles emerged, however. Yee learned the Pentagon had sent investigators to interview his parents in New Jersey and that the FBI sent an agent to talk to his wife in Washington State. The Army also added four more charges to go along with the two counts of mishandling classified documents. One charge accused Yee of adultery, a serious violation in the military. Two other charges claimed he had downloaded pornography on his government computer. The final charge accused him of making a false statement.

The Army's case against Yee no longer involved charges of treason, sedition, or even spying—with the possibility of the death penalty as punishment. But the case against him still carried serious penalties. Yee knew that if he was convicted of these new charges, the Army could sentence him to a maximum of fourteen years in jail. Meanwhile, his marriage had become so tense, especially with the adultery accusation, that Yee said his wife called him one evening and said she wanted to take her own life. Yee desperately wanted to take a break from Fort Benning to visit with his wife in Washington State. But he was not allowed to leave.

Media reports spread additional falsehoods. *The Washington Post* quoted an unnamed "military official" as saying that Yee was "in a quagmire" about whether he was loyal to the US or to the Muslim detainees at Guantanamo. *The Post* reported that the official said that Yee had been "disappointed" that he was not asked to participate in interrogations of the prisoners at Guantanamo. Once again, the story was false. Likewise, a report in *The New York Times* that Yee kept maps of the Guantanamo prison and notes on which detainees were questioned and on what subjects was also false.

It wasn't until December 8—three months after his arrest—that Yee finally was allowed to attend a formal court session, an Article 32 hearing in which military prosecutors were required to present evidence against him to back up their charges.

The first prosecution witness was a female US Navy lieutenant, who had been granted immunity to testify. She claimed that Yee carried on an adulterous affair with her. The prosecution offered no other witnesses to corroborate the woman's story.

The next witness, a US Customs agent who spoke by telephone to the court because he was based more than 100 miles from Fort Benning, testified that he was ordered to search Yee's bags for classified documents. But the Customs agent was not allowed to describe what he found because the telephone line he spoke on was not secure.

Next came another US Customs agent whose task was to testify that she had checked Yee's ID on the plane and could confirm Yee's identity—a fact that was not in dispute.

Two US Army investigators who specialized in computer forensics then took the witness stand. Yee and his attorneys expected them to testify that they had found documents on his computer that they would consider to be classified. Instead, they only testified that Yee had kept alleged pornographic images on his laptop.

That was the extent of the prosecution's case. No evidence of a spy ring. No secret lists of detainees. No names of interrogators and the questions they asked. No secret drawings of maps of the Guantanamo prison. And no evidence that Yee was in touch with anyone from al-Qaeda, the Taliban, or any other terrorist group.

The next day, Yee's attorneys asked prosecutors to produce a copy of their supposed classification review of the documents Yee was said to be carrying. Prosecutors said such a review had still not been completed. Incredibly, the military, while hardly shy about leaking false information about Yee carrying classified documents, was now admitting that it had never bothered to categorize the documents found in Yee's bags to determine whether they were classified or not.

Yee was dumbfounded. Hadn't prosecutors bothered to examine the handful of items in Yee's backpack and luggage, as well as go through his papers in his room at Guantanamo? And, if the military had not conducted such a review, why was it still leaking stories that Yee had illegally transported classified documents? Indeed, why had General Miller signed a memorandum that essentially accused Yee of violating the military's rules on classified information?

Yee never got a clear answer.

General Miller postponed the case for forty-five days.

After several weeks, prosecutors said they wanted to quietly settle Yee's case and asked if they could arrange some sort of plea bargain.

Yee was interested—and why not? He was tired, confused, and angry. But Yee insisted all six charges against him be dropped and that he be allowed to resign with an honorable discharge.

Several weeks later, prosecutors agreed to Yee's requests—with two exceptions. General Miller insisted on keeping the adultery and pornography charges. But they would be handled administratively—meaning that the worst punishment Yee would receive was a reprimand. Since the deal also included the stipulation that Yee would receive an honorable discharge, any administrative reprimand—if it came—would be meaningless. Or so Yee thought.

General Miller insisted on a public hearing. On March 19, 2004, Yee faced General Miller again, this time in a conference room at the headquarters of the US Southern Command in Florida. Miller announced that all the charges against Yee would be dismissed. But Yee would be given "nonjudicial punishment"—a reprimand for his alleged adulterous affair and for reportedly storing pornographic images on his Army computer.

Dropping all the charges and clumsily seeming to try to save face by reprimanding Yee over allegations that had nothing to do with treason, spying, or aiding the enemy was an embarrassing set back for the Army and General Miller. But Miller seemed desperate to have the final word and perhaps temper what had evolved into a public relations disaster for him and for the Army. In a statement from his office at the Southern Command, General Miller said he dismissed the charges "related to the alleged mishandling of classified information" because of "national security concerns that could arise from the release of the evidence." Miller did not specifically cite what those "concerns" might be. Nor did he offer any hints.

It was, at best, a murky ending to a confusing investigation of treason and spying. General Miller and his investigators at Guantanamo came off as reckless. Yee had won—that much was clear. He would not face a trial with a possible death penalty. But the Army had humiliated him—unjustly he felt. And now, General Miller's imprecise statement seemed like a cheap shot that humiliated him even more by unjustly planting doubts about Yee's loyalty as an Army officer and what otherwise was a distinguished career.

The New York Times, with an editorial entitled "Military Injustice," wrote that the flimsy reprimand for adultery and pornography by General Miller "appears to be the military's feeble attempt to make Captain Yee look bad." The New York City Council passed a resolution calling on the federal government "to initiate an immediate inquiry" into Yee's ordeal. US Senator Jon Corzine, a Democrat from Yee's home state of New Jersey, not only called on the Army to reverse General Miller's administrative reprimand of Yee but also called on Congress to launch an investigation of how the case even started in the first place. Even one of the Army's lieutenant colonels went public with a letter he wrote to the military in which he claimed that the investigation of Yee was "based on prejudices and petty jealousies."

Finally, on April 14, 2004—seven months after Yee's arrest—the four-star general in charge of the US Southern Command, James Hill, granted Yee's appeal to erase all charges from his record, including the reprimand from General Miller.

It was unusual for a general to overrule another general. But General Hill stopped short of criticizing General Miller or the Army for making so many false allegations against Yee. General Hill's reasoning seemed an attempt to please both sides—and thereby did not please anyone.

Countermanding General Miller's harsh reprimand was clearly a victory for Yee. But General Hill made a point of noting that he did not condone what he described as Yee's "misconduct." Hill felt that continuing the legal case would amount to "further stigmatizing Captain Yee" and "would not serve a just and fair purpose."

Nonetheless, General Hill said he supported General Miller's decision to investigate Yee. As General Hill noted: "Major General Miller would have been derelict in his duties" if he did not pursue a case against Yee.

* * *

Yee returned to his chaplain's post at Fort Lewis, Washington. His marriage had been badly scarred. He feared that his reputation was also tattered. An Army friend telephoned him one day from a base in Hawaii to say that he had just attended an Army briefing on espionage in which Yee's case was mentioned—with the false accusation that Yee had maps of the Guantanamo prison and information about the alleged terrorists in custody there. In other words, the Army may have cleared Yee from charges, but Yee felt the Army was still circulating false and defamatory information about him.

Another friend called Yee to say he heard the same falsehoods repeated at an Army briefing at a base near Washington, DC. Even an Army colonel reached out to Yee from Afghanistan to say that the military's espionage lectures to its officers still included the inaccurate story about Yee's alleged spying.

By summer, Yee reached a difficult conclusion: The Army was setting him up to fail if he tried to continue his career as a Muslim chaplain.

On September 13, 2004, the Army approved Yee's request to resign and receive an honorable discharge.

Four months later, on January 7, 2005—a Friday—Yee loaded a box at his chaplain's office with family photos, books, and other personal mementoes. He then stepped into a nearby room where he once conducted Islamic prayer services. It was empty. He pulled a metal folding chair from a closet and sat alone in silence for a few minutes.

Then Yee took the box to his car and made his way to the main gate of Fort Lewis. He remembered how he drove the opposite way through the same gate on the morning of September 11, 2001, knowing that he needed to be at Fort Lewis to counsel and advise soldiers.

"There was no other place I wanted to be," Yee remembered thinking that day as he wondered how the terrorist attacks of 9/11 would impact the Army.

But now, more than three years later, he knew he had to drive away. James Yee needed to find another place to practice his faith.

Part Three

The Remnants of Reckoning

"We did a great job taking care of the dead but a terrible job taking care of the living"

PHIL MCARDLE, FIREFIGHTER, HAZMAT 1, FDNY

A Port Authority police officer rings a bell at the annual 9/11 memorial service at Ground Zero. The bell ringing corresponds to the precise times that jetliners hijacked by terrorists crashed into the Twin Towers of the World Trade Center, the Pentagon, and a field in Shanksville, Pennsylvania, as well as the times when the Twin Towers collapsed. The ceremony also includes the reading of names of the nearly 3,000 people killed at the Twin Towers, at the Pentagon, and in the crash at Shanksville. Photo by Michael M. Santiago/Getty Images.

10

The Pit

. . . Five Years after 9/11

The broken cement and twisted steel had been cleaned up. The fires were extinguished. The smells of death, wet concrete, and burned plastic were gone.

By the fifth anniversary of the attacks, Ground Zero had become a construction site. And the platoons of architects, urban consultants, and landscape designers assigned to rebuild it were envisioning a vastly transformed sixteen acres that had once been the site of the World Trade Center.

A massive hole the size of three football fields and 30-feet deep had already been excavated in the spot where the twin towers once stood. On the western side of the hole, workers were busy fortifying the Trade Center's underground retaining wall that had miraculously survived the collapse of the towers and the more than 1.5 million tons of rubble that crashed to the ground on September 11, 2001. If the wall had fallen, engineers said the Hudson River might have flooded the area. Now dozens of steel rods had been drilled horizontally like long screws into the wall to fasten it more securely to the surrounding bedrock.

On the north side of the site, workers riveted foundational steel beams in place for a new 1,776-foot-tall skyscraper, already nicknamed "The Freedom Tower." Nearby, a river of concrete was being poured for an underground museum to memorialize the victims and first responders and to display artifacts from the attacks such as fire helmets, crushed police cruisers, and some of the steel beams that crashed to the ground with the towers. Also in the works was a new subway station, a performing arts center, and two acre-sized pools of water with waterfalls that would commemorate the footprints of the North and South Towers and would be surrounded by bronze parapets with the names of the victims. When all that was finished, landscapers would plant more than 400 swamp oak trees on a ground-level plaza in what they were already describing as symbols of "hope and renewal" and a "green roof" of shade.

With so much work being done, it was difficult to imagine on the fifth anniversary what the site would finally look like. It was not inconceivable, however, to understand why it was still a place of mourning. Many considered the site a graveyard and still referred to it as Ground Zero.

As another golden morning sun climbed into another cloudless blue sky, more than 2,000 relatives of victims, survivors, and others returned for a simple ceremony that in just five years had already become a solemn tradition on each 9/11 anniversary.

At precisely 8:46 a.m., when the first hijacked jetliner had struck the Trade Center's North Tower, a New York City firefighter pulled a cord that rang a silver bell. The crowd fell silent for a minute. Then, as a quartet of cellists and violinists played slow and mournful tunes in the background over the next four hours, victims' relatives or close friends read the names of the dead. In future years, children and even grandchildren would read the names. But on the fifth anniversary that task was turned over to victims' spouses and significant others.

The readers paused just five more times that morning: At 9:03 a.m., when the second hijacked jetliner struck the South Tower; at 9:37 a.m., when the third hijacked plane hit the Pentagon; at 9:59 a.m., when the South Tower collapsed; at 10:03 a.m., when the fourth hijacked plane plowed into the field in Pennsylvania; at 10:28 a.m., when the North Tower fell.

After each reader finished reciting a dozen or so names, each was allowed to offer a short message about the person who was lost.

One woman invoked the "gentle soul" of a boyfriend who died. A husband pledged that his wife's thoughts would be his thoughts "till the end of time." A widow promised to be "together one day" with her husband. A young gay man praised "my beloved partner."

* * *

After five years, and especially amid the solemn and simple symmetry of the 9/11 anniversary ceremonies, just thinking about the victims opened doors to the deep pain of loss. In the personal tales and memories, people sometimes found a small piece of solace. But all too often they were reminded of the persistent trauma that continued to shadow their lives—an emotional rubble that seemed impossible to move away.

Firefighters and police officers wore the brass-buttoned uniforms they usually put on for parades and funerals. Soldiers donned their service uniforms as did pilots and flight attendants from the airlines that had been hijacked. Many knew and even worked with the flight crews of the hijacked jetliners who had been the first to be murdered on 9/11.

Wives who lost husbands held the hands of small children. Teenagers who lost fathers and mothers linked arms and leaned on each other. Grandparents pushed walkers.

"There is a journey, and today is not the same as yesterday," said Diane Horning who lost her son at the Trade Center. "But many of us are stuck."

On this fifth anniversary, Horning—like many others who lost a loved one—found herself recalling almost every minute of September 11, 2001.

First, there was the news about the planes striking the twin towers. Then, the worry for her son, Matthew, a twenty-six-year-old data processing administrator with the Marsh and McLennan management firm on the ninety-fifth floor of the North Tower.

Diane Horning remembered how she turned on her computer that day and checked her email, then a few social media platforms on the internet—and found hope. Someone had posted a note that Matthew was safe. Moments later, she learned the information was incorrect.

Then the phone rang.

And a voice.

"Hi, Mom."

"Oh, Matt, where are you?" Horning remembered asking—only to have her hopes dashed again.

It was her brother-in-law on the line, thinking he had called his own mother-in-law whom he routinely called "Mom." He had dialed the wrong number.

The day continued as a series of emotional boomerangs. Still, Horning refused to give up hope. "I had great expectations that Matthew would make it out," she remembered. "He was young. He could run down those stairs. I was just cheering him out."

Then, hours later, Horning had to confront the grim realization that she had dreaded all day: Matthew never made it to safety.

By October 2001, Matt's remains had still not been found, but the Hornings held a memorial service anyway at a Catholic Church.

Five more months passed. The Horning's phone rang again with news of Matthew. This time, it was the New York City Medical Examiner's Office with the type of call more and more relatives of victims were now receiving. A small piece of Matt's body had been identified.

The Hornings were not yet ready for a formal funeral. Suppose more pieces of Matthew's body were found? They asked a local funeral director to keep the fragment of Matthew's body.

During the next three years, the Hornings received three more small pieces of Matt's body—or so they thought. In 2004, the Medical Examiner's Office called again. One of the pieces had been mistakenly identified. Could the Hornings return it?

They did.

In May 2005, a week after Mother's Day and nearly four years after 9/11, Diane Horning and her husband Kurt finally felt ready for Matt's funeral.

"His remains fit in a small box," Horning said. "I held it on my lap."

* * *

Neal Auricchio did not lose any friends or relatives on 9/11. He did not have to plan a funeral as Diane and Kurt Horning did. But he came anyway to Ground Zero for the fifth anniversary.

Standing erect in the middle of the crowd of mourners and listening to the litany of names being read, Auricchio recalled how his volunteer work in cleaning up Ground Zero inspired him to enlist in the Marine Corps. Back then, the nation seemed united, with a common purpose. Auricchio wanted to do his part.

He was now twenty-five years old, home from a combat tour in the sands of Iraq where nearly 3,000 Americans had already been killed. What was supposed to be an invasion by the US military to find weapons of mass destruction had descended into a war of roadside bombs, ambushes, and snipers.

On this day to honor the victims of 9/11, Auricchio wore his Marine dress uniform. On each sleeve, he sported lance corporal's stripes. On his chest: a Purple Heart medal.

Auricchio pointed to his right calf.

"On April 14, I took a sniper's bullet in Fallujah," he said. "It's OK now. I'm happy I can stand on it."

Across the plaza, Brian Faustina, a Port Authority police officer, guarded one of the chain-link gates on the fence surrounding the Ground Zero construction site.

On September 11, 2001, Faustina was supposed to join a special police unit that was assigned to patrol the Trade Center's buildings and underground mall. But that day, his sergeant ordered him to go to traffic court in Newark.

Weeks earlier, Faustina had slapped a ticket on an illegally parked taxi when he was on patrol at Newark International Airport, which, like the Trade Center, was patrolled by the Port Authority's police force. Faustina figured the taxi driver would just pay the ticket.

Not this time, however. The taxi driver decided to fight the ticket in a local courtroom in downtown Newark and subpoenaed Faustina. The hearing was scheduled for the morning of September 11, 2001. If Faustina did not show up, a judge would hold him in contempt of court.

Faustina was making his way that morning to Newark when the first hijacked jetliner struck the Trade Center's North Tower. He turned around and headed to the Trade Center. But he arrived late and was a safe distance from the towers when they collapsed and killed thirty-seven of his Port Authority police colleagues.

"If I didn't have that ticket, I would probably have been inside the buildings," Faustina said.

He paused as he silently pondered the consequences. Then his eyes turned to a group of victims' relatives walking by. Many of them carried single roses.

The group headed down a ramp that construction workers had erected for trucks to carry steel and concrete to the bottom of the excavation pit at Ground Zero. At the bottom, the mourners left the roses in two small pools of water workers had built for the ceremony.

The idea was to allow the mourners—especially those whose loved ones had not been identified—to honor what many considered to be the unmarked graves of Trade Center victims who had yet to be identified.

"None of those families have closure," Faustina said.

As for himself, he said he keeps a small bit of closure and a reminder of his luck.

"That traffic subpoena," he said. "I keep it in a shoebox."

* * *

On the edge of the crowd, Jessica Correa-Gutierrez waited for the name of her brother to be read. She had just started her senior year of high school in New Jersey when the 9/11 attacks took place. Two months before those attacks, her brother, Danny Correa-Gutierrez, then twenty-five years old, started working as an intern with the management consulting firm, Marsh and McLennan, on the ninety-eighth floor of the North Tower

"I drove him to the interview," Jessica said.

Jessica was now twenty-two years old. For the fifth anniversary commemoration, she wore a white T-shirt emblazoned with her brother's photograph. After hearing her brother's name, she left the section of West Street where the crowd had gathered. She walked south for a block, then turned east on Liberty Street, the southern perimeter of the Trade Center site, and made her way to a temporary "Wall of Remembrance" that listed all the victims' names.

In the background, she could still hear the steady litany of the dead. *Catherine "Cat" MacRae, just twenty-three years old and a year into her job as a research analyst. Richard Madden, who left behind a nineteen-month-old daughter. Simon Maddison, a British citizen and father of three children. Noell Maerz, whose wife, Jennifer, was pregnant and would give birth to a daughter seven weeks later.*

Jessica placed her fingers on the name of her brother on the memorial wall. Then she bowed her head for a few silent seconds in her own moment of silence.

"I remember his smile and his sense of humor," Jessica said, looking up.

Her thoughts then drifted back to what she remembered of September 11, 2001. Just after 9:00 a.m., she walked into a classroom at her high school. A TV was on. On the screen, she noticed smoke pouring from the North Tower and instantly knew her brother was in trouble.

As she stood now at the Wall of Remembrance, she thought of her brother's personality. His laugh. His smile. How vibrant and alive he always seemed. But then she conceded that even trying to recall the best memories exacts a toll.

"It doesn't make this day any easier," she said.

* * *

In Maspeth, Queens, Phil McArdle had decided to create a memorial to the nineteen firefighters from his firehouse who died on 9/11. The death toll, which devastated the two elite units, Hazmat 1 and Squad 288, who made their home at the firehouse, was the highest of any firehouse in New York City's fire department. The nineteen men who perished left behind fifty-one children who would grow up without fathers.

McArdle already found the money for the memorial. A longtime admirer of the FDNY who lived in California gave McArdle $50,000 for a permanent monument that listed the names of the dead at the Maspeth firehouse.

McArdle figured a series of brass plaques—one for each of the nineteen firefighters—would be best. The firehouse certainly had the space.

A wall just to the left of the large garage doors to the firehouse was already home to a plaque that honored just one firefighter from the firehouse who had died in the line of duty—William Walding, who had been killed in 1947 fighting a blaze in which deadly anhydrous ammonia gas had been released. Next to the plaque memorializing Walding, McArdle decided to add plaques for the nineteen who died on 9/11.

Then he decided to add one more.

As the emotional toll mounted after the attacks during that first year after so much time poking through Ground Zero's rubble in search of bodies and so many funerals, McArdle and his surviving colleagues found themselves facing a new kind of casualty of 9/11. One of Maspeth's firefighters had become so stricken with grief after the attacks and the loss of so many friends that he had taken his own life. It was the first suicide after 9/11 by a FDNY firefighter.

The FDNY and the Maspeth house did not try to hide why Firefighter Gary Celentani died. Even his family openly discussed why he took his own life.

Celentani, who was thirty-three years old and a member of Maspeth's Squad 288, had sunk into a deep depression at the loss of so many friends and colleagues. Then his mother died and his girlfriend broke up with him.

Around 6:40 p.m. on a Wednesday in September 2002, a few weeks after the first anniversary of the attacks, Celentani stood before a makeshift shrine he had built in the living room of his apartment in Queens to memorialize friends who perished on 9/11. He placed a shotgun to his chest and pulled the trigger.

Days later, eulogizing Celentani at his funeral in a Catholic Church, the FDNY's highest ranking chief, Dan Nigro, who would become New York's fire commissioner a decade later, said, "Gary may be our first casualty of September 11 that did not die that day."

"His heart overflowed with compassion and kindness," Celentani's sister, Christine, added. "I know there were so many things he never told us about."

In Celentani's death, firefighters like Phil McArdle and others saw a chance to convey a message to the world—that the impact of 9/11 and terrorism in general had created all kinds of other painful wounds in people's lives. In the case of Celentani, it resulted in suicide. But McArdle noticed that far too many firefighters were drinking more alcohol. Some marriages had begun to fray. And as the years started to roll on, more firefighters complained that the occasional gagging they felt in their throats that they initially dismissed as "a Ground Zero cough," had morphed into serious respiratory ailments and worse.

McArdle and the other firefighters considered Gary Celentani as another victim of 9/11. So when the wall at the Maspeth firehouse was dedicated, with its heading "Brothers in Battle," it would be home to twenty new plaques. There were nineteen—one for each of the firefighters from Hazmat 1 and Squad 288 who perished on 9/11 and another for Gary Celentani.

"It was the right thing to do," McArdle said. "Gary was one of us. He suffered like us."

* * *

Nearly 100 blocks—about five miles—north of the former Trade Center, another kind of Ground Zero was slowly taking shape.

In a suite of offices and exam rooms on the third floor of Mount Sinai Medical Center, a sprawling complex that occupied nearly two blocks between New York City's Fifth and Madison Avenues, a steady stream of men and women who had been among the first responders to the 9/11 attacks were showing up for medical check-ups.

Many complained of coughing too much or not being able to catch their breath when they walked fast or tried to run up a flight of stairs.

What would take place in that suite of offices at Mount Sinai would turn out to be one of the most devastating legacies of the 9/11 attacks.

Thousands not only died on September 11, 2001, in the collapse of the Trade Center's twin towers, but tens of thousands more who rushed to the scene to help with rescues would suffer from a long list of ailments caused by the toxins released in the rubble and fires.

The death toll from health problems would eventually surpass those killed on September 11, 2001.

* * *

Frank Silecchia, the construction worker who found the "Ground Zero Cross," was one of the first to sign up for the medical tests.

In the first year, doctors said he was fine. Silecchia, they said, seemed unharmed by the Ground Zero toxins that had invaded the lungs and bloodstreams of so many police officers, firefighters, and construction workers.

But by 2002, Silecchia felt that he just couldn't catch his breath. Even walking was difficult.

Doctors performed more medical tests and found that Silecchia had lost 20 percent of his lung capacity. By 2004, after more medical tests, the doctors told Silecchia he had lost another 20 percent.

By the fifth anniversary of the attacks, Silecchia found he was unable to work anymore on construction sites around New York City. He had to move out of his apartment in New Jersey and was now living in a small trailer on a friend's lawn not far from the Belt Parkway in Brooklyn.

"My main goal in life is to keep that cross," he said just before the fifth anniversary.

"My cross," as Silecchia now called it, was still fixed to a concrete pillar on the edge of the Ground Zero construction site. But Silecchia wanted a permanent home for it.

Silecchia said the cross took away "my despair and my hardships" from what he had seen at Ground Zero and his work in recovering victims' remains.

"It rejuvenated me," he said.

* * *

NYPD Detective Marty Davin figured he might have asthma. He would try to draw a breath, then find he couldn't. He wasn't worried though—at least, not at first.

Like many members of the NYPD, Davin, a plain-clothes detective, wasted no time in heading to the Twin Towers on September 11, 2001. He left his undercover wardrobe of T-shirt and jeans at the building about ten blocks away where he served with federal and state detectives in a special anti-drug task force.

Davin put on his blue NYPD uniform that he kept in a locker and quickly made his way to the corner of West and Murray Streets.

The towers had already fallen. His job was just to guard the area to prevent looting or to take care of any injured firefighters or police officers who happened to stumble by.

In the following months, Davin volunteered to help with the teams of police and firefighters who searched for the dead—or their remains—in Trade Center's rubble pile.

The air smelled bad. And instinctively Davin sensed that it wasn't healthy. But like so many other first responders, he also felt the need to lend a hand.

By the fifth anniversary, Davin not only felt his breath shorten—as if he was fighting asthma—but that he had begun to suffer from a near-constant feeling of indigestion.

He chewed gum. He popped antacids and hoped for the best.

But he also knew something was not right. Too many police officers were complaining they had trouble breathing. The most devastating—and scariest—story the officers heard involved another detective, James Zadroga, who had been fighting for his life in the year before the fifth anniversary of 9/11.

On January 5, 2006, Zadroga died, only a month before his thirty-fifth birthday. An autopsy, conducted by a county medical examiner in New Jersey where Zadroga died, concluded that his death was "directly related" to 9/11 toxins in his body. It was the first time that the death of any first responder to the 9/11 attacks was linked to the dangerous substances released at Ground Zero when the twin towers fell.

New York officials rejected that conclusion. Mayor Michael Bloomberg even said that Zadroga did not die as a hero. And, the New York City Medical Examiner went so far as to suggest "with certainty beyond doubt" that the dust, glass, and fibers found in Zadroga's lungs "did not get there as the result of inhaling dust at the World Trade Center or elsewhere" but that Zadroga had damaged his lungs by grinding up drugs and injecting them directly into his bloodstream. The Medical Examiner's conclusion was incorrect, doctors later said, and Mayor Bloomberg's comment came off as unnecessarily cruel. Nevertheless, the bitter debate over the cause of Zadroga's death hung over the police force as a none-too-subtle message that officials were not all that willing to recognize that increasing numbers first responders were now suffering severe health problems connected to the 9/11 attacks. For now, the officers, like Marty Davin, who found themselves trying to cope with breathing problems and other ailments, ranging from skin cancer to blood disorders, would not be considered official casualties of the 9/11 attacks.

Zadroga had been placed on disability status. And when he died, the NYPD declined to offer him a funeral with full honors that included a color guard and the department's bagpipe band and recognized the fact that his death had been caused by his service at Ground Zero.

Zadroga's funeral ended up taking place in a Catholic Church in North Arlington, New Jersey, where he had grown up and his father was the police chief.

A US flag hung from the extended ladders of two trucks from volunteer fire departments in New Jersey. A bagpipe band comprised of New Jersey police officers showed up.

Not a single official from New York City came. There was no long row of New York City police officers lining the street and offering Zadroga a "white glove" salute as they did with the funerals of officers who died as a result of their police work. The NYPD brass told officers they could attend Zadroga's funeral but only if they were off duty.

It was as if James Zadroga just happened to have retired as a police officer and had now died as a civilian.

But Zadroga would not be forgotten. In the coming years, as his ailments were conclusively linked to Ground Zero's toxins, a federal law granting special health benefits to first responders who became sick from Ground Zero's poisons would be named after him.

Zadroga's death was yet another piece of the emotional rubble, latent anger, and uncertainty that persisted after the 9/11 attacks. In the years to come, this new kind of rubble would be far harder to remove than the steel and concrete of Ground Zero.

Construction worker Frank Silecchia (left), who discovered the "Ground Zero Cross" in the rubble of the World Trade Center, stands with Father Brian Jordan, a Franciscan priest who blessed the cross and ministered to search teams at Ground Zero after his colleague, Father Mychal Judge, was killed in the 9/11 attacks. Silecchia and Jordan led a successful campaign to preserve the cross at the 9/11 Museum at Ground Zero. Photo by Graham Morrison/Getty Images.

11

The Crucible of Memory

. . . 10 years after 9/11

On an oven-baked Texas evening, two men who once worked at the World Trade Center slipped into a booth at a steakhouse restaurant on the outskirts of Dallas.

It was mid-August 2011. The prairie and rolling hills that encompassed what city planners had dubbed the Dallas-Fort Worth "metroplex" had already experienced forty consecutive days of the temperature exceeding 100 degrees. By summer's end, there would be seventy 100-degree days.

But on this night, the men did not speak of the hyper-heated weather or even the welcome air conditioning of the restaurant.

As old friends often do when they haven't seen each other in a while, they first told a few jokes and traded tales about new jobs and how their families and former colleagues were doing. Then they turned their thoughts back to that September Tuesday a decade before in New York City when they almost lost their lives.

"It doesn't seem like ten years," Doug Brown said as he wrapped his fingers around a coffee cup.

"No, it doesn't," said Stan Kapica, shaking his head as the two friends slowly began to recall what took place that day.

On September 11, 2001, Brown and Kapica arrived on the seventieth floor of the World Trade Center's South Tower for an 8:30 a.m. meeting of the small marketing staff at the Morgan Stanley investment firm. Sixteen minutes later, the Trade Center's North Tower, less than 200 feet across the plaza, was struck by the first of the commercial jetliners hijacked by terrorists. Seventeen minutes after that, their own South Tower was hit by another hijacked plane. Over the next hour, through a combination of luck, spunk, and their own plucky courageousness, Brown, Kapica, and several other close colleagues who were the last Morgan Stanley staff members to leave the seventieth floor barely escaped with their lives.

"It was dark," Brown recalled. "And smoke was curling along the floor like a snake."

The fires set off by the hijacked jetliner that had crashed into the South Tower only eight floors above their meeting were spreading ominously along the walls, ceilings, and carpets. Instinctively, the group headed for a stairway—the one they used for fire drills. But there was a problem: The stairway was blocked.

The group stopped in the dark hallway. Brown remembered a wave of fear rising in him. Then the group saw the beam of a flashlight in the gray dust and heard a voice with a command none would forget all these years later: "If you hear me, follow me."

It was a security guard, Dereck Lovell, who was substituting for just that day because the floor's regular guard had a dentist appointment.

Lovell had already found a clear stairway. After dashing down seventy floors, and with Kapica and Brown carrying a badly injured worker from an upper floor who they met halfway down, the group ran to safety. Thirty minutes later, the South Tower collapsed.

Kapica and Brown had since moved on—Kapica to Dallas and a job with an investment firm; Brown to San Francisco as a financial consultant who traveled often to Texas. But like so many others who experienced the trauma of the 9/11 attacks, they often found themselves in the intervening years inexorably drawn back by the memories of their brush with death and their fortunate path to life. And even though ten years had passed, they were still trying to make sense of what had taken place and how they survived and so many others did not.

They found that what they experienced—the feeling of being trapped, then the exuberance of running into the security guard who guided them to safety—was not necessarily typical of everyone's experience at the World Trade Center that tragic day. But as they retold their story ten years later in the Dallas restaurant, they both conceded that their unique experience was emblematic of the physical and emotional trauma of the day and its aftermath: In particular, how ordinary people performed extraordinary feats and how the intervening years have been a slow rebuilding of broken hearts, wounded souls, and scarred memories.

And they also discovered something else: None of their Morgan Stanley colleagues whose lives became so deeply connected by their escape from death on 9/11 worked in New York City anymore. None even remained with Morgan Stanley. It was as if everyone just needed to move on. Or as Doug Brown explained: "We all fell off as leaves and got blown in different directions."

* * *

By the tenth anniversary of the terrorist attacks of September 11, 2001, roughly 6,200 American soldiers had been killed in combat in Afghanistan and Iraq. Osama bin Laden had also been killed in May 2011 by an elite team of US Navy SEALs. But the US government was still trying to figure out what to do with bin Laden's al-Qaeda top henchmen who had been captured and imprisoned at the Naval Base in Guantanamo Bay, Cuba.

At the sixteen-acre piece of New York City that many still called "Ground Zero," the steel skeleton for the new Freedom Tower had already reached almost eighty of the 100 floors that would eventually be constructed. At the tower's base, workers were busy with the final installations of walkways and benches for a memorial plaza with its canopy of more than 400 swamp oak trees.

But the opening of the plaza on the tenth anniversary was not as welcome as organizers had hoped. A substantial number of victims' families were still urging the memorial's designers to build a special monument on the plaza to hold the remains of the more than 1,000 victims who were still not identified. The designers held firm, however; they wanted the unidentified remains to be placed underground, in a special vault, on the bottom floor of the 9/11 museum that would not open for another three years. For many victims' relatives, the decision to keep the remains underground once again raised fears harbored by many of them that their loved ones would eventually be forgotten.

* * *

As the dinner that night at the Dallas restaurant wound down, Kapica spoke of another kind of emotional rubble he was trying to sort through—in particular, the horrific images that remain entombed in his own memory vault.

"Our understanding of reality changed," he said. "For me, the most horrendous memory of that day is seeing people forced to jump to their deaths. I still see those people jumping."

Brown mentioned the deafening roar of the plane. "It's a sound I'll probably never hear again," he said.

Both men conceded they still have trouble stitching together the meaning of the day and its place in their lives—in particular, why they survived and others did not.

"I had this feeling instantly that I was going to be okay, that I was going to survive," Kapica said, recalling his mindset in the midst of his escape down the South Tower stairs. "But I never thought the buildings would collapse. That was unfathomable."

Brown nodded. Like Kapica, he conceded that he will never forget what happened on 9/11. How could he really? But Brown noted that he tries not to talk about it all that much outside of his family and circle of close friends and colleagues. "I make a conscious decision not to bring it up," he said. "It doesn't seem relevant, and I don't want the discussion to become about me."

What Brown and Kapica did on 9/11 was not so much escape and save themselves, however. They rescued a badly wounded man who might otherwise not have survived. All these years later, Brown and Kapica still vividly recall their decision to stop and help Silvion Ramsundar, an assistant vice president for the Mizuho Capital Markets investment firm.

Ramsundar happened to be standing outside an elevator bank on the seventy-eighth floor when the hijacked jetliner struck the South Tower. Flaming jet fuel poured like lava across the floor, burning Ramsundar's hair and face. A fist-size chunk of metal cut into his chest, barely missing his heart. Blood soaked his white shirt.

Somehow Ramsundar could walk. He made his way to an escape stairwell and had descended to the sixty-fifth floor when Brown, Kapica, and the other Morgan Stanley colleagues—all of them lucky, like him, to find the same debris-free stairwell—came upon him.

"He was burned and he was dirty," Brown said, remembering his impression when he saw Ramsundar. "His head looked like a charcoal briquette when it gets hot. It was gray."

Brown and Kapica also noticed something else about Ramsundar—the steady flow of blood from the deep gash just above his heart.

Kapica pressed tissues to the wound. Brown reached in his pocket for a handkerchief.

Then Brown and Kapica each took hold of Ramsundar's arms and walked him down the stairs, eventually reaching the bottom and placing him in an ambulance.

A photographer for *The New York Daily News*, Susan Watts, happened to be nearby. Her photograph showed Ramsundar, his eyes blank and his white shirt now red with blood, trying to sit up. Next to him, Brown, in a crouch with his briefcase strapped across his chest, was pleading with a firefighter: "You've got to get him out of here. He's fading fast."

The ambulance pulled away. But before it left, Ramsundar gave Brown and Kapica his phone number, which allowed them to keep in touch. In the ensuing weeks, Ramsundar would learn that he was one of only sixteen people above the seventy-eighth floor of the South Tower to survive.

As they finished dinner at the Dallas restaurant and thought back to that scene, neither Kapica nor Brown wanted to be called a hero. The label seemed embarrassing in a way, they said. "We were just Good Samaritans," Brown explained. "The real heroes were the firefighters going up the stairs that morning."

As the tenth anniversary neared, Ramsundar, who was now 41 and healed, described the experience another way: "Stan and Doug saved my life."

He recovered from his wounds at his home in Queens. Doctors removed the piece of metal that had lodged near his heart. He tried to return to the fast-paced work as a Wall Street investor. But he quit after a few years and turned his attention to commercial real estate.

"I really don't like to talk about 9/11," Ramsundar said as the tenth anniversary neared. "To me, it's in the past. Some people like to say I'm a 9/11 survivor. Don't get me wrong, I'm lucky to be alive. But it's been hard, too."

* * *

For the other Morgan Stanley workers on the South Tower's seventieth floor, the memory of what happened to them on September 11, 2001, often meandered between the desire to forget and the realization that forgetting is impossible. Like

Silvion Ramsundar, they said they often reminded themselves that the memory of surviving a trauma was actually a nurturing gift. They were, as Ramsundar noted, along with Brown and Kapica, not just lucky to be alive. But their escapes were made possible because other people stepped forward to help. In Ramsundar's case, it was Brown and Kapica. For Brown and Kapica, it was Dereck Lovell.

But after ten years, a painful question remained like a scar that would not disappear. Why did some people find their way to safety and others did not?

* * *

A few weeks before the tenth anniversary, Nancy Kennedy stopped at a coffee shop in her hometown of Ridgewood, New Jersey. She spoke of how she thought often of her Morgan Stanley colleagues. The memories were clear and not disappearing—especially of Doug Brown and Stan Kapica helping Silvion Ramsundar; of the group's leader, Jack Kemp, encouraging everyone to keep going down the stairs as cracks opened in the walls; of her childhood friend and coworker, Alison Greeley, grasping Nancy's hand as they skipped from one stair to another and Alison later telling Nancy that she had planned to announce to the rest of the staff that she was expecting a baby; of another colleague, Kevin Perry, feeling traumatized as he watched workers jump to their deaths from the upper floors of the nearby North Tower before he escaped.

Kennedy also smiled as she reminisced about her life with the group before the 9/11 attacks—the hilarity of their jokes, the teamwork they shared, the deep bond of friendship that was often rare in the high-stakes world of Wall Street finance.

But then she conceded that even by the tenth anniversary, she still found herself sometimes trying to come to grips with the fact that she and her colleagues had survived and others from other floors—and even one from her staff—had not.

"Why did some mothers and fathers not make it to safety and I did?" she said.

Jack Kemp had moved to Vero Beach, Florida, where he worked part time for a small investment firm. In the summer leading up to the tenth anniversary, he rented a beach house with his wife, Kathy, in the New Jersey shore town of Mantoloking.

Kemp agreed to retell the story of his escape for a documentary about 9/11 that the *History Channel* was producing. "It was cathartic," Kemp said, as he sat with

Kathy one morning in an airy room of the beach house. "I actually found it good to talk about it. It got it out of my system. But I didn't talk about the bad parts."

Kevin Perry, who also worked on the South Tower's seventieth floor and was one of the first to see victims jumping to their deaths from the neighboring North Tower, was now the father of a son and daughter, and working for a global financial firm in Singapore, 9,500 miles and twelve time zones away from Ground Zero. But despite his distance from New York and the passage of ten years, Perry said he was unable to leave behind the memory of what he saw on the morning of the 9/11 attacks as he gazed out his office window on the seventieth floor of the South Tower. "I saw people falling or jumping out of windows," he said. "It was a terrible experience. I never understood what post-traumatic stress was until after that event."

Alison Greeley was now the mother of two sons and had moved with her husband to Ridgefield, Connecticut. She remained with Morgan Stanley until 2008, then left.

She found, however, that she could not leave behind the memories of the fire and smoke and jet fuel. "I could taste it and smell it," she remembered in the weeks before the tenth anniversary.

In her new hometown, Greeley, at first, told few neighbors about her escape from the South Tower. Sharing those feelings with strangers seemed awkward and cumbersome. "Socially and gracefully, I didn't know how to put it out there," she said.

She finally told her story after she volunteered for a committee to build a 9/11 memorial in her new town.

With her young sons, however, Greeley faced an even more difficult struggle on how and when to explain what happened to her on 9/11. The son she was carrying in her womb that day had just celebrated his ninth birthday. Her other son was now only seven.

Would they be old enough to understand? Greeley didn't know. In particular, Greeley did not know how to explain to her oldest son that his middle name, Thomas, was a tribute to Tom Swift, the only member of the team who never made it to safety.

Greeley and Swift seemed as different as their hometowns: Ridgewood and Jersey City, respectively. But they shared a common bond: Both were intense

Yankees fans. Along with Doug Brown, they also loved a good joke. And on September 11, 2001, as she and the other Morgan Stanley staffers tried to escape, Greeley felt that the colleague everyone called "Swifty" would certainly escape, too. After all, Swift had been one of the first on the seventieth floor to head for the stairs.

As the tenth anniversary approached, the memories of Swift and how he was the only one from the seventieth floor to perish were difficult to forget—especially the clear evidence now that he had probably been burned to death when jet fuel poured into the South Tower's elevator shaft just after he stepped onto an escape elevator.

Swift's wife, Jill, still kept the wedding ring that Swift left behind on the morning of September 11 when he wore a college ring his mother had just purchased for him as a reward for receiving his MBA degree.

Jill had since remarried and was now the mother of an eighteen-month-old daughter. She moved to Freehold, New Jersey, where her husband ran a firm that installed solar panels.

"It's always a part of me," Jill said of 9/11 in the weeks before the tenth anniversary. "That's never going to change. It's always there because of what I lost."

Her struggle to come to grips with her first husband's death and figure out how to shape her own future was not easy, she said. A major emotional obstacle was the fact that Swift's remains were never recovered. Nor were any of his belongings. No briefcase. No identification card. Not the college ring he wore for the first time that day to the office.

"It's weird," she said. "We're so used to what happens when someone dies. You have a wake, a funeral. Even though Tom is gone, there was no finality to it."

In the ten years, she had reconciled with herself that she could not change the past—or escape the pain of memory. "I have a new life," she said. "But my old life is still a part of my life. The memories never go away."

* * *

Like the Morgan Stanley staffers from the seventieth floor—and, indeed, thousands of others touched by 9/11 and its aftermath, James Egan wrestled with his own conflicted memories.

Two years before the tenth anniversary, Egan, a captain in charge of a National Guard unit that included a grandmother, a man in his fifties who served in the Vietnam conflict, a police officer, a bus driver, and a young woman who had given birth to a son only a year earlier, was standing in the center of a dusty US Army outpost in the southern desert of Iraq that had been named after Ronald Bucca, a FDNY fire marshall who died in the South Tower after climbing all the way to the 78th floor to rescue office workers.

It was December 2008—a few days before Christmas.

"Good morning," Egan said, as he walked from a line of steel boxes resembling cargo ship containers that the Army had converted into housing for Camp Bucca's garrison. He stopped near a bomb shelter constructed from concrete slabs.

"Good morning," I answered.

The morning sun was still trying to fight through the orange haze that hovered over southern Iraq like a permanent cloud that would not blow away. Egan's eyes traced across the flat desert southward—to a series of bright lights and guard towers.

The prison camp.

I had followed Egan for nearly two years as part of a series of newspaper articles I had been writing in which I chronicled how the members of his National Guard unit known as "Foxtrot Company," moved from their civilian lives—and their families—into the roles of full-time soldiers.

Based in a National Guard armory in New Jersey, Foxtrot had been considered a low-risk unit that specialized in coordinating supplies and trucking them to the front-line combat soldiers. Hence, its acceptance of older soldiers and others who were not as physically fit as those who served in combat units.

Here, in Iraq, however, Foxtrot had a far different mission: Its soldiers spent their days and nights as guards at a massive detention center that housed more than 10,000 Iraqi fighters who had been captured during battles with US troops in Baghdad or other hot spots.

"We're meeting some captured Iraqis today," Egan said. "I want to show you a new program we are trying to set up to establish a dialogue."

Egan was no stranger to Iraq—or difficult missions. But as part of his mission in 2008, he was still wrestling with the memories of what he saw on his first deployment four years earlier and what he did.

In 2004, he arrived in Baghdad as a second lieutenant with the famed First Cavalry Division, one of the US Army's most decorated combat units. On a

Sunday morning during that first deployment, a platoon-sized patrol of about twenty soldiers from the First Cavalry in several lightly protected Humvees was assigned to escort a convoy of sewage trucks through the Sadr City neighborhood of Baghdad, a tight enclave of narrow streets that was home to the city's two million Shiite Muslims.

The First Cavalry's commanders had been told that Sadr City had been quiet. There were few skirmishes. But the patrols were necessary, if only to check on the neighborhood and remind the residents that the US Army was in charge.

The patrol on that Sunday was considered just another routine assignment.

It wasn't.

The patrol drove into an ambush of more than 1,000 Iraqi militia fighters. Within a few minutes, eight US soldiers had been killed. Another fifty were wounded over the course of the day as other First Cavalry soldiers rushed to the scene to reinforce the trapped patrol.

Egan, who was assigned to an intelligence unit, spent part of that day issuing commands over a radio at a base, trying to coordinate the rescue patrols.

The memory of what he saw over the next few hours would not leave him. A truck carrying wounded soldiers drove into a makeshift medical station that the Army had set up behind the walls of a compound. The truck's tires had been flattened from bullets and grenade fragments. As a soldier popped open the truck's rear gate, blood poured into the sand.

"I'd never seen so much blood," Egan recalled later when he spoke about the incident at a spiritual retreat for Catholic men in New Jersey.

The battle, which was named "Black Sunday" by the troops and was later vividly documented in the book, *The Long Road Home* by TV correspondent Martha Raddatz, was the beginning of an intense period of fighting in Baghdad that was considered a defining moment in the war. Instead of a victory—and the toppling of Iraq's authoritarian leader, Saddam Hussein—Iraq had become an intense battleground in which guerrilla fighters tried to kill American soldiers with close-quarter skirmishes in crowded cities or with booby trap bombs planted on roadsides.

Egan was angry. Several friends died. And for years, he would wear a silver bracelet engraved with their names.

Days after the Sadr City "Black Sunday" battle, however, Egan was told that the First Cavalry had captured a Muslim sheik who was also a leader of a militia group in Sadr City. The sheik, Egan learned, might have been involved in the ambush—or had at least played a role in it or other attacks on American soldiers.

Several years later, feeling ashamed at himself, Egan wrote down what took place in the following hours so he could accurately speak about it before the Catholic men's retreat. But in recounting that day, he had another purpose: He wanted to remember what he was capable of doing.

The sheik was brought into a dimly lit room, Egan said. Cracks ran down the walls. Water dripped from the ceiling.

"I remember at the time thinking it was a perfect place for the purpose it served," Egan said. "The moldy smell, the small, concrete cells with just a blanket and a mattress. I thought it was very fitting for men who probably shot at us or even killed some of our soldiers. I remember getting excited about the chance to interrogate this guy, this militia leader who, without a doubt, had a hand in planning the ambush that forever changed our lives, and ended others. I was *angry* with him. I had never met him, never spoken with him, yet I had a rage inside me that I had never felt before... dare I say, a *hatred* towards him."

Egan yelled at the sheik—so much and in such a threatening way that the sheik started crying and screaming. "The look of fear in his eyes was something that I had never seen before," Egan said.

Egan stopped and left the room.

He felt nauseated and disgusted with himself. "What had I just done to this man? Who was I becoming?" he remembers asking himself. "My mother and father didn't raise me to be this kind of person."

Hours later, Egan returned to the sheik's cell. He opened the door, walked inside and handed him a bottle of water and some food.

Then Egan apologized.

"I told him that I was just angry because I had just lost friends of mine and I took it out on him," Egan said.

With that the two began to talk. The sheik pulled up his pants leg, revealing a set of scars from torture he received at the hands of Saddam Hussein's secret police who had shackled him, suspended him upside down, whipped him, and seared his skin with electric prods.

Egan then let the sheik walk outside his cell to pray. And in the following days, the sheik opened up about his role in the militia. The two conversed easily and readily—the Army officer and the sheik.

"You can't seriously like this guy?" Egan remembers asking himself. "He is your *enemy.* He probably killed some of your friends. But I couldn't ignore the obvious feelings I was having and the simple fact that if I had met this man on the street in America, I would have gotten along with him."

In the end, Egan felt he was able to learn valuable information that would help protect other US patrols in Sadr City. He also learned something about himself. Even in a war zone, he needed to remind himself to find ways to preserve his humanity. And, at the heart of his humanity, was kindness.

In 2008, as he stood in the desert at Camp Bucca, Egan planned to try to use the same friendly technique in dealing with the prisoners that his National Guard company was assigned to guard.

He was four years removed from "Black Sunday" and the behavior he came to regret. Now, on a new mission in the Iraqi desert, Egan walked along the chain-link fence with me that surrounded the perimeter of a compound that held hundreds of prisoners.

Several wandered from a tent. Others knelt on a set of Muslim prayer rugs to recite prayers. Overhead, one of Egan's Foxtrot soldiers climbed the steel walkway to a guard tower.

Egan watched the guard move into place. Then as he gazed across the yard. A prisoner named "Zak" approached the fence.

"Are you enjoying it here?" Egan asked Zak.

Zak, who spoke English, nodded and smiled.

"This place is good," he said. "There is no punishment."

The two men fell silent, each seeming to search for something else to speak about.

Zak spoke first. He mentioned that he feels he has all he needs—salt, a place to pray, shampoo, water.

Egan nodded. Then Zak wondered whether he might be set free soon.

"Oh, you'll get your 'Happy Papers," Egan said, using the nickname for release paperwork.

"We appreciate all you do for us," Zak said. "We are trying for a new start."

Zak turned and walked away. Another prisoner approached Egan.

"I know it's your duty to keep me here," the man told Egan. "I respect you because you respect me."

Egan knew the situation—the Iraqis being held captive; the Americans guarding them—was not a situation that breeds friendships. But Egan wasn't looking for rosy miracles either, he said.

He just wanted people to respect each other—not so much as enemies but as fellow human beings.

* * *

Back in New York City Father Brian Jordan and Frank Silecchia were also looking for respect for the Ground Zero cross. And as the tenth anniversary of the 9/11 attacks approached, they felt they had finally found it. Father Jordan and Silecchia had managed to convince the designers of the new museum to include the cross of steel beams that had become so meaningful to the police, firefighters, and other volunteers who searched the rubble pile for bodies.

Several months before the tenth anniversary, Father Jordan called together nearly 300 veterans of the cleanup for an inter-faith service as the cross was delivered to the museum. He blessed the cross as he did a decade before when it was pulled from the rubble and a crew of construction workers placed it on a concrete pedestal near the still-smoking rubble.

With the cross now officially accepted as a relic of the 9/11 museum, Father Jordan decided to read a series of "commitments" as part of the service, many of them inspired by St. Francis of Assisi, the patron saint of his Catholic order of priests, the Franciscans. Father Jordan began by proclaiming "our firm conviction that violence and terrorism are incompatible with the authentic spirit of religions" and that "we commit ourselves to doing everything possible to eliminate the root causes of terrorism." He read nine more, with the final commitment pledging to "commit ourselves to urging leaders of nations to make every effort to create and consolidate, on the national and international levels, a world of solidarity and peace based on justice."

Jordan figured his words might help to smooth over what he now perceived as a return to the divisivness that was prevalent across US culture and politics before 9/11, but had disappeared for a few months afterward as America came together in ways it had not done for decades.

Jordan viewed the cross as the kind of unifying symbol that might inspire America to overcome any renewed discord. His hopes were quickly dashed, however. Two days after he blessed the cross as it was brought to the museum, lawyers for the American Atheists Association filed a lawsuit in federal court only a few blocks from Ground Zero. The atheists said the cross's presence in the museum was a "clear violation of church and state" and should be removed. A federal judge said the cross could stay until a decision was reached.

It wasn't the first battle over religion at Ground Zero. It would not be the last. A year earlier, a group calling itself Cordoba House proposed to build a thirteen-story Islamic community center on the site of a building constructed in the 1850s just two blocks north of Ground Zero. The initial design included a 500-seat auditorium, a swimming pool, a basketball court, a childcare area, a bookstore, an art studio, a food court, a memorial to the victims of the September 11 attacks, and a mosque that would accommodate more than 1,000 worshippers.

The project stalled after the proposal became politicized, with critics claiming that the center—and especially its mosque—would be insulting to the victims of the 9/11 attacks. Another problem was the imam, Feisal Rauf, who was a key force in promoting the Islamic Center. A newspaper investigation uncovered records that Rauf operated several substandard apartment buildings in Union City, New Jersey, where tenants complained he had delayed making repairs. Union City's mayor called Rauf a slum lord.

* * *

In Washington, Mark Rossini's FBI career had come to a crashing halt. By 2008, Rossini had risen through the FBI's ranks to become supervisory agent in the bureau's counterterrorism division. He had also gained a great deal of respect for his work with the CIA in organizing the Terrorist Threat Integration Center, which became known as the National Counterterrorism Center.

But the FBI forced Rossini to resign when it discovered he illegally gained access to classified reports containing details of a federal investigation of Anthony Pellicano, a controversial private investigator in Hollywood. Rossini had nothing to do with the Pellicano investigation by the FBI. Rossini's girlfriend at the time, Linda Fiorentino, an actress who starred in such films as "The Last Seduction" and "Men in Black" and who knew Pellicano, reportedly asked Rossini to look into the files. Federal prosecutors said that Fiorentino told Rossini she was researching a screenplay on Pellicano. Rossini went ahead and opened the FBI's Pellicano files. When one of the classified records Rossini accessed was later used in a court filing by Pellicano's attorneys, FBI investigators confronted Rossini.

Besides giving up his FBI career, Rossini ended up pleading guilty to five felony violations of illegally breaking into an FBI database for personal reasons. In 2009, a federal judge in Washington, DC, ordered Rossini to pay a $5,000 fine and sentenced him to a year's probation and 250 hours of community service.

As he reflected years later on the incident, Rossini conceded he had made a terrible mistake that derailed his otherwise stellar law enforcement career. After the 9/11 attacks, he felt bitter and ashamed. He could not escape the nagging feeling that he had a chance to stop the attacks if only he had ignored his CIA supervisor's orders and told the FBI that two al-Qaeda operatives were on the loose in America. Deep in depression and guilt Rossini said he told himself that he did not care about following rules anymore.

"I was reckless," he said.

* * *

Rossini was not alone in trying to sort through the psychological scars he carried from 9/11. Ten years after the attacks, at his office not far from the Passaic River in Little Falls, New Jersey, psychotherapist Peter Killeen was still trying to counsel hundreds of officers with the Port Authority's police department who wrestled with an entirely different set of unhealed wounds over the guilt they felt in the wake of the 9/11 attacks.

None were in the kind of position that Rossini was in—and feeling they might have stopped the attacks. The Port Authority police were in charge of security at the World Trade Center. Simply put: they were the first of the first responders.

Which meant they were on the front lines—ahead of the FDNY and NYPD—when the terrorists crashed their hijacked jetliners.

Killeen discovered that even after a decade many officers felt guilty that they survived while their buddies did not. Others carried the guilt of ordering subordinates to remain at dangerous—and fatal—places at the World Trade Center to help guide escaping office workers. Still others simply did not know how to handle the sadness of so much loss of life in their close-knit department.

"The cops stepped up to the plate. They did what they had to do and went above and beyond their work," Killeen said. "But ten years later, it's had a negative impact on a lot of people emotionally."

Trying to sort through so many emotional thickets inevitably impacted Killeen. He was the only therapist available for the agency's 1,500 cops. "My workload increased 60 to 70 percent," he said. "I never felt at the end of a day that I did enough because there was so much to do."

For the tenth anniversary of the attacks, Killeen figured he had to find a way to close the emotional doors on the steady stream of regret and negativity that handcuffed many officers—and himself. He decided to throw a party at a Manhattan bar known as "Hogs and Heifers," which was a popular hangout of rough and tumble motorcycle riders including a Port Authority officer who was one of the thirty-seven officers in the department who died on September 11, 2001.

Killeen called the event a "celebration of life."

On the afternoon of the tenth anniversary—a Sunday—officers gathered with Killeen at the bar. They toasted the dead and praised the living, in particular a group of retired Port Authority officers known as "Team Romeo" who volunteered at Ground Zero in the search for bodies.

When they labored at Ground Zero in the months after 9/11, Team Romeo seemed to take on a legendary status—a none-too-subtle reminder that even retired police still felt a connection to their calling and to their fellow officers. But when one of their most popular members, Jimmy O'Hanlon, later committed suicide by jumping off the George Washington Bridge, Killeen was again reminded of the kinds of psychological hardships some cops face even after they retire.

Killeen deliberately included this painful reminder of death and the fragility of officers' emotional lives as part of his "celebration of life" at the Hogs and Heifers biker bar.

"I can't change the past," Killeen said. "I can only look at the present and impact the future."

* * *

A few hours before the Port Authority police gathered at the biker bar with Peter Killeen, thousands of mourners flocked to the newly opened 9/11 memorial plaza at the site of the World Trade Center.

The site no longer resembled a construction pit. There was no ramp descending from the street to the bottom. At 8 acres, the plaza, with its cobblestone walkways, benches, and kiosks that sold coffee cups and T-shirts, took up almost half the space of the former Trade Center complex. The plaza featured two recessed reflecting pools, each tracing the perimeter of the North and South towers and featuring 30-foot-deep waterfalls that were meant to invoke serenity. Around the edge of each pool and shaded by the 400 swamp oak trees, the names of the dead were etched into bronze parapets.

For this anniversary, James Taylor, with just his guitar in hand and no band, sang a mournful rendition of his iconic song, "You Can Close Your Eyes." Paul Simon, also with his guitar, added an equally mournful solo version of his classic hit, "The Sound of Silence."

There were no speeches, no ceremonial dedications of the plaza. After the moment of silence at 8:46 a.m. that commemorated the first hijacked jetliner striking the North Tower, President Barack Obama stepped forward to a podium with the presidential seal that had been set up behind bulletproof glass.

Obama was not formally introduced. There was no musical flourish. Clad in a black suit and black tie as if to signify the solemnity of the day, Obama stepped forward and gazed at the crowd for a second or two. Then in a measured cadence, he read the forty-sixth psalm, one of the Bible's most famous declarations of the need to trust in God in times of chaos.

"God is our refuge and strength, a very present help in trouble. Therefore, we will not fear," Obama began. One minute and forty seconds later, he ended with the psalm's last lines: "Be still, and know that I am God; I will be exalted among the nations. I will be exalted in the earth. The Lord Almighty is with us. The God of Jacob is our fortress."

Former President George W. Bush followed, reading a letter that President Abraham Lincoln wrote on November 21, 1864—five months before the end of the Civil War and Lincoln's assassination—to a mother who lost five sons in battle. As with Obama, there was no formal announcement that Bush was speaking.

"President Lincoln not only understood the heartbreak of his country," Bush said. "He also understood the cost of sacrifice and reached out to console those in sorrow as best he could."

Bush paused, then continued with Lincoln's letter to Lydia Bixby: "I feel how weak and fruitless must be any words of mine which should attempt to beguile you from the grief of a loss so overwhelming. But I cannot refrain from tendering to you the consolation that may be found in the thanks of the Republic they died to save. I pray that our Heavenly Father may assuage the anguish of your bereavement, and leave you only the cherished memory of the loved and lost, and the solemn pride that must be yours, to have laid so costly a sacrifice upon the altar of Freedom."

With that, victims' relatives stepped forward to read the names of the dead.

When it was Peter Negron's turn to read, he paused after reciting the name of his father, Peter Sr., a Port Authority environmental coordinator who was seen going back into the towers to help others after leading colleagues to safety. Peter Jr. was only eleven years old when he lost his father. Now twenty-one and studying to become a forensic scientist, he summed up what a decade of hurt had done to him. "I stopped crying, but I haven't stopped missing my dad," he said. "I wish my dad had been there to teach me how to drive, ask a girl out on a date, and see me graduate from high school. And a hundred other things I can't even begin to name."

In the crowd, a woman waved a handmade sign that said: "We will never forget you." It was a common feeling, for sure. As with other anniversaries, mourners carried photos of their lost loved ones or wore T-shirts or held a sign. But after ten years, it was also clear that mourning for some had taken on even more pain.

On the edge of the crowd, Richard Tipaldi listened for the name of his son, Robert, to be read. "Empty is empty," Richard said, thinking of how his son was only twenty-five when he was killed. "You lose a lot of feelings."

* * *

Dereck Lovell did not attend the tenth anniversary commemoration at the new memorial plaza in New York where he had been so heroic in helping the Morgan Stanley marketing team find a clear escape stairway.

A few weeks before the ceremony, Lovell walked across the main concourse of Union Station in Washington, DC. He looked for a table at one of the station's restaurants and settled into a chair for lunch.

A steady stream of tourists and workers passed by, either coming to DC or leaving on one of the Amtrak trains or even on the subway system known as the DC Metro.

Outside, the sun beat down on the sidewalks. The summer's thick humidity cast the US Capitol a few blocks away in a ghostly haze.

Lovell sighed as he thought of the tenth anniversary ceremonies that would take place nearly 300 miles away in New York City. He needed no reminding of the horror he saw, along with his own heroism, not only in helping the Morgan Stanley staffers find the clear stairway but then turning back and looking for others who needed help—including two elderly men he guided to safety just minutes before the tower collapsed.

Lovell said he rarely talks about his exploits now. It's not that he wasn't proud of what he did. He insisted he would take the same risks all over again. And he was grateful for the two medals and the $15,000 bonus he received.

But the pain of that day still lingered in Lovell's heart. And he did not know how to make it disappear.

Not long after the attacks, Lovell moved to Maryland and found a job as an overnight security guard at the headquarters of the World Bank in downtown Washington.

Few of his World Bank coworkers knew of his 9/11 experience. Even when he applied for US citizenship and was accepted, he did not say anything about his heroism.

"I did not want to be singled out for praise," he said. "I felt what I did on that day, it was done already. Who I saved and who I helped—they are thankful, and I'm glad we are here. That's good enough for me. Anyway, it was not in my nature to run and leave those people. I couldn't live with myself if I did that."

He shifted in his seat and turned to watch the tourists pass through the rail station on their way into the sunlight and heat outside.

"I will never forget the morning," Lovell said. "But I'm trying to move on, like everyone else."

Terry Strada, center with hands folded, lost her husband, Thomas, in the collapse of the Twin Towers during the 9/11 attacks only four days after giving birth to the couple's son, Justin. She later emerged as a key voice in convincing Congress to pass legislation that allowed relatives of 9/11 victims to file a lawsuit against Saudi Arabia. Photo by Brendan Smialowski/AFP via Getty Images.

12

A Law Called "JASTA"

. . . Fifteen years after the 9/11 attacks

It had already been a busy day on Capitol Hill when the United States Senate quietly agreed on a Wednesday afternoon in September 2015 to consider a new law to battle terrorism.

On that day, few could predict that the legislation that would be shaped over the next twelve months would become one of the most powerful and controversial legal tools in the effort to uncover the truth behind the 9/11 attacks. Likewise, few could predict that the process to enact this law would also set off a contentious political, legal, and diplomatic battle that would leave behind a trail of mistrust and pitted President Barack Obama against some of his closest Democratic allies in Congress.

But one issue was not in doubt: The target of this new law was Saudi Arabia and the persistent and troubling mystery of whether any of the kingdom's officials played a role in the deadliest terror attack in US history. In fact, this new law would be written specifically to address what many had now informally dubbed "the Saudi question." But Saudi Arabia was not mentioned in any line of the bill's text.

As if those issues were not concerning enough, the new battle over this legislation was taking place in Congress against the backdrop of an increasingly bitter and divisive presidential election that began with a dozen Republican and six Democratic candidates and eventually was reduced to two of the nation's most polarizing figures, Hillary Clinton and Donald Trump.

As America approached another 9/11 anniversary—the fifteenth—it was clear that the nation that seemed so unified in the months after the attacks was now riven with a wide range of political and cultural fissures.

In the midst of such unpredictable and unstable discord, John Cornyn, a United States senator from Texas, introduced a 1,500-word piece of legislation that a diverse group of his colleagues felt might inspire some measure of unity in the Senate—and perhaps the nation. The proposed law Cornyn set before the Senate that day was given a number—S2040—and a lofty, if somewhat ambitious title, "The Justice Against Sponsors of Terrorism Act."

This was not the first time that the US Senate was asked to consider the law that had come to be known by its acronym, "JASTA." In 2009—just two days before Christmas—Senator Arlen Specter of Pennsylvania, who had switched his political allegiance a few months earlier from the Republican to the Democratic Party, introduced his version of the "Justice Against Sponsors of Terrorism Act."

Specter's bill sat in limbo in the Senate Judiciary Committee for months. In July 2010, he finally was able to schedule a public hearing on the bill before the Subcommittee on Crime and Drugs, which he chaired.

The subcommittee—and, in particular its name—seemed an odd place to discuss a law dealing with terrorism. Not surprisingly, Specter's version of JASTA never found the political traction it needed for the full Senate to consider it.

By the fall of 2015, however, JASTA had its second wind and was revived. Instead of a maverick senator like Arlen Specter, who was disliked by Republicans for deserting their party and not yet fully trusted by Democrats who viewed him as a convenient convert, JASTA had a new set of champions.

John Cornyn, a tall, white-haired, taciturn Republican, seemed an unlikely chief sponsor of a law that could potentially cause so much political friction. Cornyn did not seem to covet the political limelight as his fellow Texas Republican senator, Ted Cruz, often appeared to do. Instead, Cornyn was known for his methodical and sometimes low-key style of working with his fellow senators—more in keeping with the style he set during the six years he spent as a district judge in San Antonio and another seven years on the Texas Supreme Court. Finally, and perhaps most significant, his political base—Texas—was far from the scene of the 9/11 attacks. By sponsoring JASTA, Cornyn signaled to the rest of the Senate and House—and America—that the aftermath of the 9/11 attacks was not just a matter of concern for Northern Virginia, New York, and the other communities in the eastern United States where most of the victims lived. As a result, and in the midst of an increasingly divided Senate and highly charged political atmosphere across the nation, Cornyn and his co-sponsor, Chuck Schumer, the New York liberal Democrat, had managed to pull together an unusual group of Republican and Democrat senators as co-sponsors. These ranged from liberals such as Al Franken of Minnesota and Dianne Feinstein of California to conservatives like Orrin Hatch of Utah and Ted Cruz.

* * *

Before introducing his new bill, Cornyn did not call a press conference. Nor did he try to draw attention to the bipartisan alliance of senators who were supporting the new version of JASTA. On the afternoon of September 16, 2015, Cornyn simply strode into Senate chambers and asked for permission to speak.

It had already been a long day for senators. The proceedings began at precisely at 10:00 a.m. with the Senate's chaplain, the Reverend Barry C. Black, a Seventh-day Adventist pastor who had retired as an admiral after serving as a US Navy chaplain for more than twenty-seven years, offering a short prayer. "God of grace and love: You guard our lives with Your peace," Black said, before asking the Almighty to "energize" senators "to dare more boldly" and to "accomplish great things for your glory" and while also granting "that their childlike trust in you will free them to serve others."

Senators devoted most of the morning to a debate over the merits of the Joint Comprehensive Plan of Action, a controversial treaty-like proposal by President Barack Obama to ease economic sanctions and offer financial relief to Iran if the Islamic nation dismantled its nuclear weapons program and submitted to international inspections.

Before Cornyn could speak, senators offered a variety of proposals on their own. There was an amendment to the Securities and Exchange Act. Another suggestion to build a "Wall of Remembrance" at the National Korean War Veterans Memorial in Washington, DC. A resolution commemorating the Greek-American philanthropy known as the Daughters of Penelope. A law to block efforts to change the name of the 1,200-foot rock formation in Wyoming known as the Devils Tower to one of several names favored by the Native American tribes who once lived nearby.

Finally, it was Cornyn's turn. JASTA was introduced as "S2040. A bill to deter terrorism, provide justice for victims, and for other purposes." Then Cornyn asked for "unanimous consent that the text be printed in the record"—a parliamentary short-cut that dispenses with a full reading of the bill and a full vote by all senators on whether to formally consider it. The bill was automatically assigned to the Senate Judiciary Committee. But no date was set on when the Committee would debate the merits of the bill or even vote to approve it.

And that was that.

What may have seemed like an uneventful, perhaps even unenthusiastic beginning for JASTA quickly changed, however. Two weeks after Cornyn introduced the bill, a federal judge in New York abruptly dismissed the lawsuit that had first been filed thirteen years before by Ron Motley and a squad of other attorneys seeking to link several powerful institutions and influential people in Saudi Arabia to the 9/11 attacks.

In his ruling, US District Judge George B. Daniels pointed out that a long-standing US law, the Foreign Sovereign Immunities Act, exempted Saudi Arabia's government from the lawsuit.

The judge's decision was hardly a surprise. Legal experts had claimed for years that the diplomatic principle cited in the Foreign Sovereign Immunities Act that prohibited US citizens from suing the government of another nation would turn out to be the most formidable obstacle to any legal effort by relatives of 9/11 victims to hold Saudi Arabia accountable for reportedly helping the 9/11 terrorists in some way. Another important consideration was the fact that the 9/11 Commission had concluded in 2004 that while "Saudi Arabia has long been considered the primary source" of funding for bin Laden's al-Qaeda terrorist network "we have found no evidence that the Saudi government as an institution or senior Saudi officials individually funded the organization."

Yet another factor was the unfortunate death of Ron Motley in 2013 from what his law firm described as respiratory complications related to a long but unspecified illness. Other attorneys stepped forward to take up Motley's leadership role—notably James Kreindler, whose New York-based firm had played a key role in shaping a legal settlement that required Libya to pay nearly $3 billion to the families of victims of the 1988 bombing of Pan Am 103 over Lockerbie, Scotland. But Motley's death was clearly a setback in the legal fight by families who had now spent more than a decade trying to draw attention to their claim that Saudi Arabia played a role in the 9/11 attacks.

Still, another troublesome complication was evidence. The original lawsuit focused on alleged sources of terrorist financing in Saudi Arabia, which included banks, charities, businesses, and members of the royal family. Over time, however, the lawsuit expanded to include the Saudi Arabian government itself. But, as some critics pointed out, the lawsuit's claims, while certainly shocking, were not backed up yet by the kind of rock-solid proof that would be needed to hold a foreign government—a key US ally, no less—responsible for the deadliest terrorist attack ever on American soil. Nonetheless, the evidence the families had already assembled could not be ignored. While largely circumstantial, the evidence pointed toward a disturbing set of links with Saudi Arabia, in particular the kingdom's spy agency and the government ministry that seeks to promote Islam around the world.

It would take several more years for much clearer evidence about Saudi Arabia to begin to surface from classified files kept in secret by the FBI and other government investigative bodies. For now, the lawsuit was essentially placed in legal limbo.

Without the passage of JASTA, only nations named by the US State Department as "state sponsors of terrorism" could be sued by American citizens for terrorist attacks. By 2015, that list included just three nations: Iran, Syria, and Sudan. Cuba had been on the list but US State Department officials removed it after President Obama reopened diplomatic relations with the communist nation. A year later, North Korea would be added to the list.

JASTA was meant to change the legal criteria for holding another nation that was not generally considered a state sponsor of terrorism to be accountable for terrorist acts. Instead of limiting lawsuits to just the small number of state sponsors of terrorism, JASTA would allow lawsuits in US courts against any foreign nation for terrorism-related injuries or deaths to Americans.

But the most important changes that JASTA would deliver—and the clauses in the law that Saudi Arabia appeared to fear most—were how JASTA broadened the definition of what constituted "material support" of terrorists beyond the terrorists themselves. In this way, JASTA was not unlike the federal law known as the Racketeer Influenced and Corrupt Organizations Act—RICO—which was designed to combat organized crime. Instead of limiting prosecutions only to those who actually committed a crime—murder or drug dealing, for example—RICO laws allowed federal prosecutors to target a wide range of organized crime bosses who were involved in a large criminal conspiracy.

With JASTA, the relatives of 9/11 victims could supposedly sue any nation, institution, or person who offered some sort of "material support"—even indirectly—to the gang of al-Qaeda operatives who hijacked the jetliners and crashed them into the World Trade Center, the Pentagon, and the Pennsylvania field on September 11, 2001. At the top of the list of targets was not just a variety of Saudi financial institutions and wealthy Saudi citizens, but the Saudi government itself.

Saudi Arabia, meanwhile, stepped up a none-too-subtle campaign against the bill, reportedly spending millions of dollars on US lobbyists, lawyers, and various public relations experts. In early 2016, not long after the Senate Judiciary Committee approved JASTA and sent it to the full Senate for a debate and vote, Saudi Foreign Minister Adel al-Jubeir flew to America to deliver a stern warning to lawmakers: If JASTA became law, Saudi Arabia would sell up to $750 billion in US Treasury Securities and other financial assets in America. While economists predicted that such a sale could severely sabotage financial markets in the US and elsewhere, the Saudis indicated that they feared a court judgment against them would freeze their assets in the same way that the US government withheld Iranian government finances after Islamic revolutionaries in Iran in 1979 stormed the US embassy and held fifty-two Americans as hostages for the next 444 days before releasing them.

The 9/11 victims' families needed to overcome a far more fundamental problem: JASTA needed to be approved by the US Senate and the House of Representatives and signed into law by President Obama before it could be cited in any lawsuit.

None of that much-needed support was guaranteed. Congress had shown no great desire to pass a law that targeted one of America's most crucial Middle East allies, which also happened to be one of the world's largest oil producers and a major investor in US Treasury bonds. Meanwhile, the White House, with the backing of the US State Department, warned that the passage of such a law could set off a series of legal retributions against American diplomats in foreign nations. The White House even predicted that some diplomats could be placed at "significant risk."

And finally, the White House issued its own threat against JASTA. If Congress passed the law, President Obama would veto it.

For Congress to adopt JASTA, its members would have to ignore the overtures of numerous Saudi lobbyists and then pull together the support of two-thirds of members of the Senate and House to overcome a veto by Obama. So far in Obama's two presidential terms, Congress had never been able to unite enough to override any of the eleven vetoes of legislation by Obama.

By the spring of 2016—and with the fifteenth anniversary of the 9/11 attacks only four months away—the legal pursuit of Saudi Arabia that had been initiated more than a decade earlier by Terry Strada, Kristen Breitweiser, and a growing number of relatives of 9/11 victims seemed stalled.

It would soon have new life, however.

* * *

Tom Kean was worried. His concern was not the political, legal, or diplomatic implications of JASTA—if such a law was ever passed. Nor was he concerned about the lingering claims that Saudi officials were linked to the 9/11 attacks. For years, Kean had said that he felt the accusations of a Saudi involvement were unfounded.

"We looked closely at the evidence," Kean said, describing his own study of the Saudi allegations as well as the wider investigation by the 9/11 Commission. "It just wasn't there."

By 2016—a dozen years after the 9/11 Commission's report and nearly fifteen years after the attacks themselves—Kean decided to raise his voice again, however. He was concerned that America had grown lazy and would soon become the victim of another massive terrorist attack.

Kean was not alone in his fears. For years, US security experts had been pointing to a growing number of terrorist plots that had been orchestrated within America by Islamist extremists and were meant to kill large numbers of people.

In Boston three years earlier, two brothers who were reportedly upset over the US involvement in Iraq and Afghanistan, set off two homemade bombs in pressure cookers at the finish line of the Boston Marathon. Three people were killed and more than 100 were injured—with a dozen victims losing limbs. In the manhunt, the brothers shot and killed a police officer.

Much like the attack on the seemingly impregnable Twin Towers in New York City on September 11, 2001, the bombing at the finish line of the venerable

Boston Marathon on Patriots Day, a holiday when the city celebrated its roots in the American Revolution, inflicted more than just physical wounds. Like New York City after 9/11, Boston suffered a blow to its confidence and sense of peace.

Kean now worried that all of America would soon fall into the kind of emotional abyss that New York and Boston endured if more attacks were staged.

By the fifteenth anniversary of the 9/11 attacks, the FBI and police around the nation, from communities as diverse as Dallas, Toledo, Little Rock, and Seattle—not to mention New York City and Washington—had compiled a list of nearly thirty terrorist plots. Some schemes were foiled by the FBI and local police, such as a plan in 2006 by a self-professed follower of Osama bin Laden to blow up tunnels under the Hudson River that linked New Jersey and New York City. Others were planned so haphazardly that they did not materialize—for example, a car bomb in New York's Times Square that mercifully did not explode.

As Kean studied the ongoing news of foiled terrorist plots, he became concerned that America needed to refocus its attention on defending itself from terrorism.

A week before the fifteenth anniversary, Kean sat in an office in Far Hills, New Jersey, about forty miles from the site of the World Trade Center in New York City. Foot-high stacks of reports sat on his desk. A bookcase was home to a dozen framed photographs of Kean in various stages of his career.

Five months earlier, Kean celebrated his eighty-first birthday. But he had no intention of stepping away from work, especially if it concerned the 9/11 Commission. And, especially now that he felt the threat of another attack could take place.

"We're in danger. No question about it," Kean said. "What we're doing now is not working in many degrees."

By 2016, the US invasions of Iraq and Afghanistan had turned into unpopular stalemates. America's counterterrorism defenses on the home front, while much more unified than before 9/11, were still a jigsaw puzzle of local police fiefdoms that were not always trusted by the FBI.

Kean talked of how he felt that America was "spending enormous amounts of money to make this country a fortress" but that he found too many holes in the nation's anti-terror safety net. He described a new effort involving him and the

9/11 Commission's Vice Chairman Lee Hamilton to work with the Bipartisan Policy Center, a non-profit think tank in Washington, DC, to examine the wide range of how America had been fighting the war on terror since 9/11.

Kean's real goal, he said, was to grab the attention of the 2016 presidential election. He hoped that a report card that he would oversee for the Bipartisan Policy Center would be finished by early 2017—just in time for a new president to be taking over.

But Kean was not hopeful at what he was seeing in America's politics. He felt the 2016 presidential election, with Democrat Hillary Clinton against the Republican nominee, Donald Trump, had reopened the old partisan fissures that Kean had long feared would destroy American politics and, in particular, the fight against terrorism.

Kean had grown so upset over the increasingly rancorous presidential campaigns that he declined to endorse Trump. For a lifelong Republican like Kean, who had been taken as a young boy by his father to the GOP's presidential conventions, his decision to stay on the sidelines of the 2016 election was momentous.

Kean refused to say who he might vote for. He was friendly with both Clinton and Trump, he said. But his message was clear: He did not approve of his party's choice of Trump and he certainly did not like the sharp tone of the campaign. At the same time, he said he did not feel that Clinton had proved that she could be a competent president.

"I'm disappointed in the policy directions that Trump has taken," Kean said, citing, in particular, Trump's stances on immigration. "I'm also disappointed in the lapses in Hillary's judgment, which seem to come out every week now."

That afternoon in his office in Far Hills, he said he hoped he would still remain a prominent political voice—especially when it came to America's strategic planning to fight terrorism. But he also knew the political landscape had shifted dramatically. Suddenly, Kean, a trusted fixture of the Republican Party and a key moderate voice in policy making for nearly a half-century, was not even being solicited for advice on election strategy by his own party.

He wistfully said he hoped a new terrorism study, based on the work of the 9/11 Commission and organized with a bipartisan framework, could become a comfortable space that attracted diverse voices in a balanced discussion. He felt that even the US involvement in Iraq and Afghanistan—and how to resolve those conflicts—might even be addressed. But he was not hopeful. "We need unity," said Kean. "We need to look broadly at policy and not just be reactive. I think it's time to ask ourselves: Is what we're doing working? Politics in both parties has become name-calling. People say things that just don't stand up to rational examination."

Kean said it was especially distracting that summer when Obama, Clinton, and Trump fought over whether it was appropriate to mention an Islamic link to foreign terrorism. Kean said he prefers to use "Islamist extremism," a term coined by the 9/11 Commission and widely accepted by Muslim scholars to describe the influence of radical politics in twisting mainstream Islamic theology to promote such ideas as suicide martyrdom.

Kean also said intelligence experts now believe that America's network of computers that control almost every aspect of life represents one of the nation's most vulnerable terrorist targets. "We don't have a proper defense," Kean said, citing a variety of scenarios described to him by US counterterrorism officials, including attacks on computer systems that control nuclear power stations and Wall Street financial transactions.

"That's not science fiction," Kean said. "It's in the realm of the possible. We're fighting an idea. This is an ideology. You can't beat an ideology simply by military means. We've got to use everything in our arsenal."

As the afternoon wore on, Kean wondered whether it was possible fifteen years after the 9/11 attacks to catch the attention of Congress and the White House in the same way that the 9/11 Commission did. After the release of the Commission report, Kean and his fellow commissioners—Republicans and Democrats alike—spent a year trying to reform US terror policy and intelligence gathering. They made some headway but never fully succeeded.

He said he wanted to start again and call for reforms. But amid the sharply partisan political climate of the summer of 2016, Kean's voice seemed out of place. He seemed to sense that.

America, in some respects, had sadly moved on.

* * *

Kristen Breitweiser had moved on too—or, at least, she tried to.

By the fifteenth anniversary of 9/11, she conceded she was tired of pushing for reforms. She was also tired of being attacked for her views and her determined efforts to expose how the US government failed to protect the nation on September 11, 2001.

The criticism of her by conservative radio host Rush Limbaugh and TV personality Bill O'Reilly in 2004 had been an early sign of what she might expect if she continued pushing for reforms—and also pointing fingers of blame at the Bush administration.

Breitweiser was hardly a political novice. Her father, John Wintestella, had been the mayor for twenty years of the New Jersey shore town of Manasquan. When she took on the role of advocating for the 9/11 Commission, with the 9/11 widows known as the "Jersey Girls," Breitweiser made no secret of her political preference. She was a loyal Republican.

But the experience of lobbying for the 9/11 Commission—and continually prodding the Bush administration to release documents on the 9/11 attacks—soured her. A month after the Commission's report was released in July 2004, Breitweiser, distraught by what she viewed as a lack of forthright support by the Bush administration for the report's recommendations, announced that she was supporting Democratic Presidential Candidate John Kerry in the upcoming election against the Republican incumbent, George W. Bush.

Breitweiser's decision to support Kerry and his vice presidential running mate, US Senator John Edwards of North Carolina, was denounced by Republicans and more than a few relatives of 9/11 victims. But the worst attacks against Breitweiser and the other Jersey Girls were still to come.

Two years after Bush's reelection, conservative activist and author Ann Coulter targeted Jersey Girls for a series of especially caustic barbs.

In a best-selling book, *Godless: The Church of Liberalism,* Coulter, a lawyer and popular fixture on the FOX cable TV's provocative evening lineup of news-talk shows, called the Jersey Girls "The Witches of East Brunswick," a reference to the New Jersey town where two of them lived.

"These broads are millionaires, lionized on TV and in articles about them, reveling in their status as celebrities," Coulter wrote. "These self-obsessed women seemed genuinely unaware that 9/11 was an attack on our nation and acted as if the terrorist attacks happened only to them."

Coulter did not stop there. She went on to claim that she has "never seen people enjoying their husbands' deaths so much" and, without offering any evidence, wondered: "How do we know their husbands weren't planning to divorce these harpies? Now that their shelf life is dwindling, they'd better hurry up and appear in *Playboy*."

Coulter was roundly criticized. Hillary Clinton called Coulter's remarks "a vicious, mean-spirited attack on people whom I've known over the last four and a half years to be concerned deeply about the safety and security of our country."

What seemed to wound the Jersey Girls the most was Coulter's suggestion that their marriages were failing, and that they were "enjoying" their husbands' deaths.

Lorie Van Auken said she was "stunned by the vitriol" from Coulter. "Having my husband burn alive in a building brought me no joy," Van Auken said. "Watching it unfold on national TV and seeing it repeated endlessly was beyond what I could describe. Telling my children that they would never see their father again was not fun. And we had no plans to divorce."

Breitweiser also felt deeply wounded by Coulter. Breitweiser had been criticized before for her positions on how the US should fight terrorism and her zeal in blaming Saudi Arabia. But Coulter's criticism was personal. Asked about Coulter by the media, Breitweiser said: "I'd like her to meet my daughter and tell her how anyone could enjoy their father's death."

Breitweiser's response echoed the same strength that she brought to her statements in testimony before Congress and in her criticism that the 9/11 Commission report was "utterly hollow" in not focusing more attention on Saudi Arabia. But by the summer of 2016, Breitweiser's lingering grief from the death of her husband, Ron, along with the pressure of trying to raise her daughter alone while also traveling the country advocating for more attention to the threat of terrorism had taken its toll. The barbs from Coulter made those wounds more painful.

Months before the fifteenth anniversary of 9/11, Breitweiser had deliberately isolated herself in a house in one of the most remote corners of Long Island, more than 100 miles from Ground Zero and almost 150 miles from the home in Middletown, New Jersey, that she shared with her husband until his death in the 9/11 attacks.

Breitweiser said she just wanted to get away, to spend more time alone and out of the limelight and focus on her daughter's needs. She was still angry at her government. She still wanted to pressure Congress and the White House to delve into the 9/11 attacks more deeply. In particular, she continually called on the federal government to declassify a secret twenty-eight-page section of the 2002 report by Congress into the 9/11 attacks. Breitweiser had also emerged as a key force in supporting JASTA, which was still making its way through the labyrinth of Congress—and still faced opposition from President Obama.

But Breitweiser was worn out. She was also tired of being attacked. She would meet with visitors only if they promised not to reveal the town where she was living.

On a muggy August 2016 morning, I drove more than two hours to speak with her. As we talked that day, it was clear that Breitweiser had not backed down from her strong opinions about the Bush administration and what she saw as a flawed investigation of the attacks.

"It's been fifteen years and not one person has been held accountable," she said. "I want justice, too. I've waited fifteen years. My husband was murdered with 3,000 people and not one person has been held accountable. How is that possible? This is the United States of America."

Breitweiser opened a drawer filled with reports. She still meticulously studied almost every new document about the 9/11 attacks that she could find. "This is the 9/11 drawer," she said, pulling out a thick sheaf of papers, with pages marked by multicolored tabs.

She leaned against a doorpost for a second or two, looking at the papers, then returning them to the drawer.

Time had moved on, Breitweiser said. She said she knew that her country did not seem to want to focus its attention on 9/11 as much as it once did—and certainly not with the same fervor she still had. "It's been fifteen years of frustration," she said. "It's really hard. It's soul crushing."

She spoke of how she still thinks often of her husband. But the memories eventually prompted her to leave New Jersey.

"I just couldn't live there anymore," she said. "I couldn't go past the market where we got our egg sandwiches. And I couldn't go near the woods where we walked every night. I didn't want to be near Spring Lake Beach, where we used to walk on the boardwalk. I didn't want the reminders. Maybe some people would say that's not coming to terms with it. To me it's like not opening the raw wound every single hour of every single day."

Her voice trailed off. Breitweiser's daughter, Caroline, walked into the room. Breitweiser said hello and the two engaged in a few seconds of mother-daughter small talk.

Caroline headed for the kitchen for a snack. Breitweiser turned and gazed out a window.

"I still believe America is the best place in the world," she said. "But I think sometimes America herself forgets that."

* * *

One day in June 2016, a 30-year-old bank executive happened to stop at his mother's home in Middletown, Connecticut. Brett Eagleson did not realize at the time, but that casual visit with his mother would be the first step in his decision to become one of the most vocal advocates in the effort to document Saudi Arabia's alleged ties to the 9/11 attacks.

For years, Eagleson tried to ignore how the 9/11 attacks had changed his life. He was just fifteen and a high school sophomore when his father, John Bruce Eagleson, a shopping mall executive, was killed while attending a meeting at the World Trade Center on September 11, 2001.

As he described it, Eagleson spent much of the next decade "trying to bury" the memory of his father's death.

First, he finished high school. Then he focused on his studies at the University of Connecticut.

"I tried to live as normal a life as I could," he said.

After graduating from the University of Connecticut in 2008, Eagleson said he found another way to ignore the memories of 9/11. He poured himself into his career, first at a small commercial real estate and property management firm, then a job with a larger bank with a $700 million real estate portfolio, and then his plans to be married.

But in moments when he thought about 9/11, he remembers feeling uneasy. "The official narrative never sat well with me," Eagleson said. Or as he continually asked himself when he pondered the attacks and what they did to his own life: How did nineteen Islamist terrorists—most of them unable to speak English—sneak into America and pull off a massive terrorist attack without someone else helping them? How did the killers locate apartments to rent? Or open bank accounts? Or rent cars?

"These guys couldn't figure out how to get out of the airport in Los Angeles because they didn't know what an exit sign meant," Eagleson said.

Once on a college break, Eagleson noticed a letter to his mother from James Kreindler, one of the chief attorneys in the lawsuit against Saudi Arabia. The letter summarized where the case stood. Kreindler regularly sent those sorts of letters, updating his clients in the case.

Eagleson skimmed the letter, then set it aside. He knew his mother had signed on to the lawsuit. He saw no need to get involved, too.

That changed, however, on that day in June 2016 when he visited his mother.

Eagleson walked into his mother's home and saw another letter from Kreindler. This one noted that Congress was debating the proposed JASTA law. If passed, the law would not only help to resurrect the lawsuit that a judge had dismissed nine months earlier, but it would likely re-energize the effort to persuade the FBI, US intelligence agencies, and other parts of the federal government to turn over their secret investigative reports on the alleged Saudi connection to 9/11. Later that summer, Congress would finally declassify the twenty-eight-page secret report on the Saudi connection.

When Kreindler's letter arrived, the US Senate had already approved JASTA—with a unanimous voice vote. The next step was for the House of Representatives to pass it.

But such a step would not be easy. The House was deeply divided. And while Republicans controlled the majority, they did not have enough votes to override a threatened veto of JASTA by President Obama. In order to succeed, JASTA would need the support of a substantial number of Democratic members of the House of Representatives.

In his letter, Kreindler urged his clients to call their local House representatives and ask them to sign their names as co-sponsors to JASTA.

"I can do that," Eagleson remembers thinking.

Representative Rose DeLauro, a staunch Democratic progressive, had represented Eagleson's district since 1991. After 9/11, DeLauro even reached out to Eagleson's mother, not just as a token message of condolence, but to offer help and left a number to contact her legislative aide.

Eagleson asked his mother for the number, then picked up the phone.

Days later, DeLauro signed up as a co-sponsor.

Eagleson then decided to reach out to the four other House members who represented Connecticut in Congress. Like DeLauro, the other four were also Democrats.

Within a week, Eagleson had signed up every one of them.

A local newspaper heard about Eagleson's sudden grassroots political success. Then an aide to Senator Richard Blumenthal called.

Blumenthal, a Connecticut Democrat who was not afraid to speak his mind even if it angered the Obama administration, had emerged as a staunch proponent for JASTA. He asked Brett to stay involved.

"This was ripe for me," Eagleson said.

He was tired of ignoring the 9/11 attacks.

Later that summer, Eagleson emerged as one of the leading advocates in convincing Congress to release the secret twenty-eight-page report, which did not show a direct and official link to 9/11 by the Saudi government but clearly indicated that several Saudi officials had been involved.

Just how directly those Saudi officials were connected to 9/11 was still a bit of a mystery. And another question is whether they were acting on their own or with the tacit approval from higher ups.

Those mysteries would linger for years.

With the twenty-eight-page report now in the hands of the public, however, the momentum started to build substantially to turn JASTA into a federal law. The twenty-eight pages revealed what many had suspected: Several of the 9/11 al-Qaeda hijackers were clearly welcomed into America by Saudis with ties to the Saudi intelligence services and the kingdom's Ministry of Islamic Affairs who helped the hijackers find apartments and meet a network of Saudi friends.

With the Senate approval already in hand, JASTA was presented to the House for a vote. On September 9, 2016—two days before the fifteenth anniversary of 9/11—the House adopted JASTA with a voice vote.

Congress sent the bill to the White House where it sat for two weeks. It was election season and, normally, Congress would adjourn just after Labor Day so its members could return to their home states and congressional districts to campaign for re-election. But the Republican majorities in both the House and Senate held back on adjourning until Obama decided on whether to approve or veto JASTA.

On September 23, 2016, Obama vetoed the bill, issuing a nearly 1,300-word statement explaining his reasoning.

"I have deep sympathy for the families of the victims of the terrorist attacks of September 11, 2001, who have suffered grievously," Obama said. "I also have a deep appreciation of these families' desire to pursue justice and am strongly committed to assisting them in their efforts."

As often was the case with Obama's official pronouncements, his explanation of why he vetoed JASTA was logical and articulate—from his point of view, anyway. Obama did not hold back on his concern about how the new law would also impact many levels of diplomacy and even the basic safety precautions needed for US citizens traveling overseas.

After expressing his sympathy for the victims of 9/11, Obama went on to say that JASTA—the law thousands of victims said was needed to punish the perpetrators of 9/11—"would be detrimental to US national interests."

He claimed it "would reduce the effectiveness of our response to indications that a foreign government has taken steps outside our borders to provide support for terrorism, by taking such matters out of the hands of national security and foreign policy professionals and placing them in the hands of private litigants and courts."

He also said JASTA "would upset longstanding international principles regarding sovereign immunity, putting in place rules that, if applied globally, could have serious implications for the US."

And, finally, he said JASTA "threatens to create complications in our relationships with even our closest partners."

None of Obama's warnings caused Congress to back away from its support of JASTA.

Five days later, the House and Senate voted overwhelmingly to override Obama's veto. In the end, the vote tally wasn't even close. Ninety-seven senators supported the override. Two senators abstained. Only one senator, Harry Reid of Nevada, supported Obama.

In the House, 348 members including more than 100 Democrats rejected Obama's veto.

It would be the only time in Obama's eight years as president that Congress had mustered enough votes to override a veto.

Suddenly, the effort to take Saudi Arabia to court had new life.

Brett Eagleson's job was just beginning.

Juliette Scauso was only four years old when her father, FDNY Firefighter Dennis Scauso, was killed at the World Trade Center in the 9/11 attacks. Two decades later, a medical student, she became a major proponent of a federal lawsuit claiming that several Saudi Arabian government officials based in the US provided logistical and financial help to the al-Qaeda terrorists before they carried out the 9/11 attacks. Photo by Liam McBurney/PA Images via Getty Images.

13

Unfinished Business

. . . *Twenty years after the 9/11 attacks*

Each day several thousand letters pour into the mailroom at the White House in Washington, DC. Some are from people criticizing the president for a speech or a proposed law. Some are filled with suggestions to lower taxes. Some are just simple requests to send a birthday card to a grandmother who turned 100 years old or an encouraging note to an elementary school class studying US history.

Some are ultimatums, however. And a month before the twentieth anniversary of the 9/11 attacks, President Joe Biden received a none-too-subtle ultimatum from relatives of 9/11 victims.

In a letter signed by Brett Eagleson and some 4,000 others, Biden was told he would not be welcomed in New York City at the ceremonies commemorating 9/11 victims unless he ordered the FBI to declassify its secret files on the alleged Saudi connection to the attacks.

In some ways, such a strident demand from the victims' relatives and their vague threat to embarrass Biden by telling him to stay away from the memorial ceremonies on the twentieth anniversary of the attacks was empty. The 9/11 victims' relatives do not control the guest lists at the annual anniversary ceremonies in New York, at the Pentagon, or in Shanksville, Pennsylvania. The 9/11 Museum staff, along with the US Secret Service, police and fire departments, and even the military all play major roles in planning the annual memorial commemorations. Not surprisingly, a sitting president would not be told to stay away from such an important and historical event. And, in any case, several key voices for the victims' relatives such as Terry Strada and Kristen Breitweiser did not support such threatening tactics against Biden.

But Biden and his staff smartly sensed they faced a potential public relations disaster. The large, increasingly vocal, and well-organized coalitions of relatives of 9/11 victims and survivors of the attacks were fed up. After all, it had been nearly twenty years since the attacks. Key questions remained unanswered, especially with the role Saudi Arabia may have played—or may not have.

Biden had only taken office seven months before. And so far, his approval ratings hovered in the mid-50 percent range—five-to-ten points below the ratings that many presidents enjoy during the so-called "honeymoon" of their first six months in office.

By early July, amid a surge in coronavirus cases and rising gasoline prices, a Gallup poll found that Biden's approval rating had dropped by six points in a month to 50 percent. He seemed to be on a downward slide. A survey by the Pew Research Center found that only 35 percent of Americans felt that Biden could unite America, a 13-percent decrease since March.

It was clear that Biden did not need any more setbacks—certainly not an entanglement with the still-grieving and politically active families of 9/11 victims. Plus, Biden had already promised a year earlier during his successful presidential campaign against the incumbent president, Donald Trump, that he would order the release of the FBI files if he was elected.

Indeed, Biden's promise to the 9/11 relatives' families came just weeks before Election Day. Understandably, the families assumed that not only was Biden serious about releasing the documents, but that he would make it a priority.

Writing on October 7, 2020, to James Kreindler, one of the lawyers representing the families in their lawsuit against Saudi Arabia, Biden drew attention to Trump's refusal to honor his own promise to release the files. "I understand that, despite pledges to assist the families in their search for the truth, the Trump Administration has continued to prevent it from emerging," Biden wrote.

It was a bitter reminder to the families of how they felt betrayed by Trump. They were determined that Biden would not do the same thing.

What Biden referred to was a meeting at the White House between the families and Trump on another anniversary of the attacks—September 11, 2019. Amid the solemnity of the day itself and the added dignity of the White House setting, several family members—including Brett Eagleson—approached Trump and asked him to release the FBI files on the Saudis.

Trump agreed. Eagleson remembers him saying, "It's done."

But that promise quickly fell flat. The next day—September 12, 2019—the Trump administration blocked the release of any FBI files on the Saudis. In a statement Attorney General William Barr invoked what he described as a "formal claim of the state secrets privilege in order to protect the national security interests of the United States."

Trump said nothing else in public about the files. He did not explain to the families why he would make a promise on one day to them, then allow his attorney general to revoke that promise the next day. Nor is there any record that Trump attempted to intervene and possibly reject the decision by his attorney general to cite national security as a reason to block the release of important information might link a foreign nation—in this case Saudi Arabia—to a terrorist attack on US soil.

The families—many of whom had voted for Trump—were furious. They felt they had been used as props by Trump for a White House 9/11 ceremony—and were then victims of a bait-and-switch lie, with a photo-op thrown in.

"He looked us in the eye on 9/11. He shook our hands in the White House and said, 'I'm going to help you—it's done'," recalled Brett Eagleson. "I think the 9/11 families have lost all hope that the president is going to step up and do the right thing. He's too beholden to the Saudis."

During his own presidential campaign against Trump, Biden clearly sensed an opportunity to drive a wedge between Trump and the relatives of victims and survivors who often referred to themselves collectively as the "9/11 families." In his 2020 letter to Kreindler, Biden promised that if he was elected, he would order his Department of Justice to "err on the side of disclosure" in releasing secret FBI files especially "in cases where, as here, the events in question occurred two decades or longer ago." As the families saw it, Biden was promising to release as many documents as he could, as quickly as he could.

"The loss endured by the 9/11 families on that horrible day in 2001 is incalculable," Biden said. "Nothing I can say can compensate for their loss."

Then, as a personal message to James Kreindler, who also happened to be a Biden supporter, the president added: "I hope that your work in pursuit of justice and accountability can help bring them some small degree of closure."

Biden was clearly taking sides in favor of the families and their desire to pursue the so-called Saudi connection—or so it appeared.

Since making that promise, however, and defeating Trump and moving into the White House, Biden had not ordered the Justice Department to review the files, much less release them. And now, ten months after the promise and seven months after taking office as president, Biden was being confronted by a threat in which the families would stage a public protest if he came to the upcoming 9/11 memorial ceremonies without carrying through on that promise. He was trapped in a web of his own making.

With another 9/11 anniversary approaching, the families left little doubt at how disappointed they had become. In a statement, issued August 6, 2021, the families said: "Twenty years later, there is simply no reason—unmerited claims of 'national security' or otherwise—to keep this information secret. But if President Biden reneges on his commitment and sides with the Saudi government, we would be compelled to publicly stand in objection to any participation by his administration in any memorial ceremony of 9/11."

To underscore the families' determination to review the secret files and blame Biden if they could not, Brett Eagleson added: "The buck stops with the president."

* * *

By Monday, August 9, 2021, the Biden administration said it would begin the process of turning over files. In a stiffly worded letter to the US district judge and the federal magistrate in New York City who were overseeing the families' lawsuit against Saudi Arabia, the Justice Department wrote that the FBI had "recently" completed a portion of its investigation of the alleged links between Saudi Arabia and the 9/11 attacks. As a result, the Justice Department said the FBI would now examine documents it had labeled secret and had previously not been released because of concerns that their disclosure might compromise America's national security.

But the letter did not say how many documents the FBI was reviewing or how long it might take to decide on whether to release them—or even why they might not be released at all. The letter only promised that the FBI "will disclose such information on a rolling basis as expeditiously as possible."

The families, which had now coalesced into two main bodies—one run by Eagleson; the other run by Terry Strada—were not pleased.

Eagleson was skeptical. "It sounds promising," he said. "But let's see what they actually produce."

Terry Strada was even more forthright. She described the overture as a "half-hearted, insufficient commitment to transparency, accountability, and, above all, justice," adding that the FBI's promise applied to only a limited number of documents from a specific piece of the bureau's 9/11 investigation.

The families wanted a much broader promise to review all the files relating to the FBI's investigation of possible Saudi involvement in the attacks, no matter how small it might be. They also wanted a far more specific process and timetable for reviewing the documents. Simply claiming that the FBI would study the documents and possibly release them on a "rolling basis" seemed like an excuse for more delays.

Twenty-five days later, Biden relented again.

On September 3, 2021—eight days before the twentieth anniversary of the attacks—he issued an executive order calling on the FBI and the Justice Department to release its files on the Saudis.

"When I ran for president, I made a commitment to ensuring transparency regarding the declassification of documents on the September 11, 2001, terrorist attacks on America," Biden said in a statement. "As we approach the twentieth anniversary of that tragic day, I am honoring that commitment."

The FBI, in turn, responded that it "will continue to work in coordination with the Department of Justice and other agencies to declassify and release documents related to the 9/11 investigation."

But what did that really mean? Biden's order, while welcoming, set no firm timetable for the release of the documents. Nor did the order specify what exactly was in the FBI's files or those of other US investigative agencies. The families had no idea of the entire extent of the US investigation of the Saudis.

But Biden's order offered a clue to what might be coming.

At the top of the list of documents to be released was a controversial sixteen-page report by an FBI analyst who outlined what the bureau had learned five years earlier about the alleged Saudi links to 9/11, which included information that several low-level Saudi officials not only met with members of the 9/11 terrorist team but may have known something about what was to take place. The FBI code-named their investigation "Operation Encore." And in his executive order, Biden specifically ordered the FBI and Justice Department to begin the extensive declassification of its 9/11 investigative reports with that sixteen-page summary of what "Operation Encore" found.

Biden's executive order was enough to rescind the threat by families to protest his attendance at the ceremonies commemorating the twentieth anniversary of the attacks. And on the evening of September 11, 2021, after Biden visited the site of the former Twin Towers in New York City, the Pentagon, and in Shanksville, Pennsylvania, the FBI released the sixteen-page "Operation Encore" report.

Many of the sentences—and, in particular, names—were blackened out. The extensive redactions were a sign of what would come. The FBI files would trickle out in the coming months. But the bureau—indeed, the US government—was still not in a mood to fully disclose everything it knew about the alleged Saudi link to 9/11. Many of the documents were riddled with redactions.

On a positive note, however, the sixteen pages offered new insight into how two key 9/11 terrorists, Khalid al-Mihdhar and Nawaf al-Hazmi, were welcomed to America by two Saudis, one of whom, Omar al-Bayoumi, was a Saudi intelligence operative and the other, Fahad al-Thumairy, a cleric at a Saudi-financed mosque in Los Angeles. As the FBI learned, al-Bayoumi and al-Thumairy funneled money to the two al-Qaeda terrorists, helped them find apartments and arranged for them to take English classes in Southern California.

The revelations still did not contain the kind of proof needed to conclusively link the Saudi government to the planning of the 9/11 attacks. Too many questions remained about whether al-Bayoumi and al-Thumairy were acting on their own or on orders from higher-ups in their government. But release of the report was considered a crack in the wall of secrecy that the families had been attempting to penetrate.

"This validates what we have been saying," said attorney James Kreindler. "The FBI agents working this case detailed a Saudi government support network that was working in 1999, 2000, and 2001 to provide the hijackers with everything they needed to mount the attacks—apartments, money, English lessons, flight school."

* * *

Just what was the case at this point against Saudi Arabia anyway?

In 2021, it was still mostly circumstantial. Even the most ardent believers in the complicity of Saudi Arabia conceded that the evidence was murky, filled with reports of strange financial transactions and all-too-convenient chance meetings between al-Bayoumi and al-Thumairy with al-Mihdhar and al-Hazmi who were the first of the nineteen terrorists to arrive in the US.

From those meetings, which took place in Los Angeles and other parts of southern California, the FBI was able to pull together a broad outline of how al-Bayoumi and al-Thumairy helped to link al-Mihdhar and al-Hazmi with a wider network of other Saudis in the US. In the end, this network helped the 9/11 terrorists with a variety of logistical needs, including finding apartments.

Even by 2021, the FBI was still struggling to assemble all the pieces of this network. But the sheer number of possible links between Saudi government-connected players and the 9/11 hijacking that began to emerge, circumstantial or not, was too strong to ignore. As more evidence trickled from the newly declassified FBI's files, it became clear to lawyers representing the 9/11 relatives in their lawsuit—and to many of those relatives, too—that the FBI seemed to have held back on fully investigating all of the possible Saudi connections in the years immediately following the 9/11 attacks. Far too many interesting leads were not properly followed up by agents, including a disturbing video and set of notes by al-Bayoumi which appeared to show possible flight plans for the al-Qaeda terrorists to fly one of the hijacked jetliners into the US Capitol on 9/11. Not long after the attacks, British investigators found the video and notes in a raid of an apartment in Birmingham, England, where al-Bayoumi moved after he left Southern California. The British turned the video and notes over to the FBI but the FBI did not appear to fully examine their significance. In fact, the FBI did not even turn over the video and notes to the 9/11 Commission. Only after President Biden ordered the FBI to review the files it classified during its 9/11 investigation did the video and notes become known.

As more documents emerged from FBI files, it seemed that top officials in the bureau either overlooked various pieces of evidence from agents across the country or missed their significance altogether. Such was one of the painful root causes of the immense frustration that engulfed many families as they attempted to push their government to deepen the investigation of 9/11 even two decades after the attacks.

As Brett Eagleson, Terry Strada, and other leaders of the 9/11 families studied this evidence, they continually asked a basic question: Why didn't the FBI make its Saudi investigation its top priority? The same question could be asked of the CIA. Incredibly, CIA officials were never formally ordered to explain why they blocked the FBI's Mark Rossini from telling his superiors that al-Mihdhar and al-Hazmi entered the United States in early 2000, only months after al-Qaeda bombed the USS *Cole*, a Navy warship that had docked in Yemen, and seventeen months after it attacked two US embassies in Africa. Also, the FBI had never explained why it did not fully investigate the potential implications of the video and notes found in al-Bayoumi's apartment.

A key factor behind the suspicions by the 9/11 families and their team of attorneys was basic common sense: How could nineteen al-Qaeda operatives—fifteen of them from Saudi Arabia—manage to slip into America and settle into comfortable lives for most of a year before the attacks?

It didn't make sense that the nineteen terrorists managed to do so much on their own.

Most could not speak or read English. Most had never traveled anywhere outside the Middle East. Yet, they figured out how to traverse long distances in a nation where they had never driven a car before. They rented rooms in motels and navigated unfamiliar roads and highways. Indeed, at least two are believed to have driven from California to Virginia, then to Paterson, New Jersey.

Eventually eleven of the nineteen 9/11 terrorists lived in northern New Jersey. Not only did they manage to find apartments, but they rented cars, opened bank accounts, used ATM machines, joined gyms for workouts, set up cell phone accounts, located mosques that catered to Saudis, and even took flying lessons.

At one point, the 9/11 plot leader, Mohamed Atta, flew to Newark International Airport in New Jersey and somehow managed to find a motel room twenty-seven miles away in suburban Wayne, New Jersey.

Did anyone help Atta? And what about the other members of the plot? Was it just coincidental that they found their way so easily around the nation and settled so seamlessly into a life that allowed them to be hidden in plain sight?

Put another way: How did this group of terrorists pull off a plot as complicated and deadly as the 9/11 attacks without some sort of on-the-ground network that was set up already in America and waiting for them?

Such were the questions that some FBI agents and even a smattering of local police officers investigating the 9/11 attacks continually asked themselves. Those questions sat for two decades as the murky centerpieces of the accusations against Saudi Arabia. But those questions never seemed to be taken seriously by the FBI's top officials—or those at the CIA.

In the first years after the attacks, FBI agents and analysts, mostly working with computer records of credit cards usage, ATM withdrawals, and other financial transactions, assembled an exhaustive record of how the nineteen terrorists moved around America. But it appears that the FBI did not take the next step to determine whether the nineteen operatives were guided by anyone else.

Despite such holes in the investigation, the FBI had assembled plenty of evidence to raise concerns about a possible network that provided help to the nineteen terrorists.

The most significant and potentially explosive evidence centered on Los Angeles. It was January 2000, almost twenty months before the 9/11 attacks when Khalid al-Mihdhar and Nawaf al-Hazmi arrived in Los Angeles.

The CIA, as well as other western intelligence agencies, were already familiar with al-Mihdhar and al-Hazmi. Both were considered loyal and dangerous members of the al-Qaeda terrorist network. Yet somehow they were able to obtain visas to fly from Thailand to America—this after the CIA tracked them to a meeting of other terrorists in Malaysia.

In Los Angeles, al-Mihdhar and al-Hazmi managed to find their way from the airport to a restaurant where they just happened to meet the Saudi intelligence operative, Omar al-Bayoumi, who helped them find housing in San Diego. Al-Mihdhar and al-Hazmi also were able to meet the Islamic cleric, Fahad al-Thumairy, who presided over a Saudi-financed mosque in Los Angeles and was affiliated with the Saudi Ministry of Islamic Affairs. Investigators also came to believe that al-Thumairy also reportedly worked in some sort of undefined role with the Saudi consulate in Los Angeles.

Al-Bayoumi initially denied he worked for Saudi intelligence when questioned by the FBI. But by 2021, the FBI not only proved he was an agent but that he may have known ahead of time about the 9/11 attacks. What became striking and deeply disturbing, beginning in 2021 as the FBI released more of its previously classified investigative files, was how nonchalant the FBI appeared to have been about its suspicions of al-Bayoumi in the years immediately following the 9/11 attacks. When the previously secret video by al-Bayoumi of the US Capitol and his alleged notes on possible flight plans to strike the building were released, more and more relatives of 9/11 victims understandably began to ask whether the FBI was inept or engaged in some dastardly cover-up.

Incredibly, as if the video and notes were not bad enough, more evidence emerged that indicated that the 9/11 hijackers relied on a support system in America.

Al-Bayoumi reportedly linked al-Mihdhar and al-Hazmi with the radical cleric, Anwar al-Awlaki—first in San Diego, then in Northern Virginia. After the 9/11 attacks, the FBI determined that al-Awlaki had been a member of al-Qaeda. He was targeted and killed in a US drone strike in Yemen in 2011.

In Virginia, a representative of al-Awlaki's mosque who reportedly was also in touch with at least one official at the Saudi embassy across the Potomac River in Washington, DC, helped al-Mihdhar, al-Hazmi, and several other 9/11 plotters to find apartments in Virginia. That same representative then linked al-Mihdhar and al-Hazmi with a gas station worker in Paterson, New Jersey, who not only made his way to Northern Virginia but then helped al-Mihdhar and al-Hazmi relocate to northern New Jersey. In the months leading up to the 9/11 attacks, each of the eleven hijackers who are believed to have lived in Paterson and several other communities in northern New Jersey, were helped or advised in some way by the mysterious gas station worker and his contact in Virginia.

The most explosive accusations centered on the Saudi embassy in Washington, DC and the kingdom's diplomatic consulate in Los Angeles. The declassified FBI documents indicated that al-Bayoumi had been in contact with the Saudi embassy and the Los Angeles consulate. It's not known who al-Bayoumi contacted at the embassay or consulate or whether he passed on information about the al-Qaeda operatives he had met in Los Angeles—or even other 9/11 terrorists as they arrived in the US. But the concerns and questions about al-Bayoumi's connections to the 9/11 hijackers and his alleged links to

Saudi officials deepened and became more persistent over time, especially after information emerged that financial donations by the wife of the Saudi ambassador, Prince Bandar bin Sultan, ended up in a California bank account possibly linked to al-Bayoumi.

It was, for sure, a complicated and unproven web—but nevertheless a web that sparked a great deal of suspicion—and, as the 9/11 families continually said, should have prompted a major investigation by the FBI years earlier.

Saudi Arabia continually denied any connection to the 9/11 attacks. But as the 9/11 Commission and other US investigators learned, Saudi Arabia was not all that cooperative in helping to examine the whole story—and mystery—behind the attacks. At the same time, the FBI, the CIA, and other US investigative agencies were notably reluctant to open their files to oversight investigators even after twenty years. The CIA, for example, never explained why it was not alarmed when al-Mihdhar and al-Hazmi entered the US. Nor did the CIA explain why it prevented the FBI's liaison to the CIA, Mark Rossini, from notifying his FBI colleagues that al-Mihdhar and al-Hazmi were on the loose in America months before the 9/11 when the bureau might have been able to mount an investigation and stop the attacks.

The 9/11 families were determined to keep pushing for answers, however. One of their motivating factors was an explosive report in 2017 by Stephen Moore, a former FBI agent who investigated the Saudi links to 9/11 and was one of the few who would talk about what he found.

Moore concluded that al-Qaeda would not have dispatched al-Mihdhar and al-Hazmi to the US as the first 9/11 terrorists unless "a support structure" had been set up to help them. Also, Moore determined that al-Bayoumi was a "clandestine agent" and that al-Thumairy knew the hijackers "were on a complex pre-planned mission." Finally, Moore concluded that "diplomatic and intelligence personnel of the Kingdom of Saudi Arabia knowingly provided material support to the two 9/11 hijackers."

* * *

Those concerns did not come up on the morning of September 11, 2021, when mourners gathered in Lower Manhattan to mark the twentieth anniversary of the attacks.

The day was eerily similar to September 11, 2001, with a cloudless blue sky, a golden sun, and cool breezes that hinted autumn was coming soon.

As usual, the bagpipers played "Amazing Grace." Children who were not born on that bloody day twenty years earlier read names of relatives they never had a chance to meet. Firefighters pinged a silver bell to mark the precise times when planes crashed and skyscrapers fell, and smoke smudged a perfect azure sky.

But the pain seemed deeper now. A generation had been born since the 9/11 attacks. Five presidential elections had taken place. America had fought its longest war in history. And now, the nation was battling its worst health pandemic in more than a century. Amid all this, there was a sense that Americans were more divided and disdainful of each other than any other time since the Civil War.

George Packer, a highway maintenance worker from Long Island, did not lose any relatives on 9/11. But he returned for the twentieth anniversary at the memorial plaza in Lower Manhattan.

On September 11, 2001, Packer rushed to the smoldering ruins of the World Trade Center. His goal: Help any way he could. And, in the following weeks, he kept coming back, often just to distribute water and meals to firefighters, police, and construction workers who scrambled over the twisted steel and crumbled concrete, trying to find survivors or recover bodies.

What Packer found back then was a sense of unity that he had never felt before in his nation. And now, in 2021, Packer felt that unity had disappeared.

"It's twenty years later and I need to be here to remember and never forget," he said as he listened to the names being read.

He was silent for a moment or two. Then he looked around. He said he felt proud and humble to return—if only to remember the small role he played in helping others.

But America, he said, had changed in ways that worried him. "We're dealing with mass shootings," Packer said. "We're dealing with a pandemic, and people are not getting along."

That sense of disunity—and its shocking contrast to the united spirit of America in the weeks after the 9/11 attacks—emerged again and again on the twentieth anniversary.

Speaking at the memorial in Shanksville, Pennsylvania, Vice President Kamala Harris called on Americans to come together. "If we do the hard work of working together as Americans, if we remain united in purpose, we will be prepared for whatever comes next," she said.

In New York, President Biden did not face any protests from the families as he arrived. His decision to order the release of the FBI's secret 9/11 investigative files was enough to mollify the families for now. On the 9/11 Memorial Plaza in Lower Manhattan, Biden stood with former presidents Barack Obama and Bill Clinton. Later that day, after flying to Shanksville, Biden also pleaded for unity, along with former President George W. Bush who said he "was proud to lead an amazing, resilient, united people" in the wake of the 9/11 attacks. "When it comes to the unity of America," Bush said, "those days seem distant from our own."

Noticeably missing from any of the anniversary ceremonies was former President Donald Trump.

In New York, tears brimmed in the eyes of Tony-winning Broadway actress Kelli O'Hara as she sang an emotional rendition of "You'll Never Walk Alone" between readings of names of the dead at the 9/11 Memorial Plaza in Lower Manhattan. Bruce Springsteen, accompanying himself with just an acoustic guitar, seemed to choke slightly as he began his own anthem of sorrow and death, "I'll See You in My Dreams."

Standing in the crowd of mourners, Patrick Swift removed his flat, newsboy's cap as he listened to Springsteen.

As he did each year, Patrick took time away from his iron workers job, to come to the 9/11 memorial and remember his brother, Tom. On this day, Patrick also wore a blue T-shirt with his brother's name and a message: "We will never forget."

As he listened to Springsteen, Patrick recalled how Tom had been so proud of his job on the seventieth floor of the South Tower with Morgan Stanley. How Tom was scheduled to give a major presentation at a meeting on the seventieth floor that morning. How Tom even wore his new college ring that his mother had purchased as a gift after Tom had completed studies for a master's degree in business administration.

But as Patrick often reminded himself over the years, Tom was the only worker on the seventieth floor who was killed on 9/11. Twenty years later, Tom's remains had still not been identified.

Patrick sighed and tears rolled down his cheeks as Springsteen finished, slowly singing the song's last lines: "For death is not the end. And I'll see you in my dreams."

"My brother knew every word of every Springsteen song," Patrick said as he wrapped his right arm around the shoulder of his wife, Evonne.

From the stage, Patrick's nephew, Peter, read names of the dead. Peter had not yet been born when the 9/11 attacks took place. But he wanted to pay tribute to his Uncle Tom.

As Peter finished his list, he repeated Tom Swift's name and added his own message about joining someday in heaven: "I can't wait to meet you."

In the crowd, Patrick Swift added another message to himself.

"There is a God," he said.

* * *

Like Patrick Swift trying to cope with the fact that his brother's body was never found, others affected by 9/11 or its aftermath found themselves searching to resolve the pain or uncertainty that had enveloped their lives.

James Yee, the Army chaplain at the Guantanamo Bay terrorist detention center who had been accused—and cleared—of espionage charges, wrote poetry and joined an artists' collective where veterans were encouraged to express how their time in the military had affected them. Yee ended up creating murals with pieces of his Army uniforms that he cut into small pieces and converted them into pulp.

John Ryan, the Port Authority police lieutenant who led underground searches for bodies in the Ground Zero rubble and supervised much of the clean-up of debris, later became the department's chief. But Ryan asked to step down. He did not want to be an administrator. He wanted to focus on counterterrorism investigations. Later, in his retirement, Ryan made several trips to the Guantanamo Bay detention center to support victims' relatives who were attending court hearings there for some of the top al-Qaeda leaders who had been captured.

Joe Connor, who lost his father in a terrorist bombing in 1975 by Puerto Rican nationalists and later lost his cousin in the 9/11 attacks, also traveled to Guantanamo to attend the hearings. Like Ryan, Connor felt a calling to support the victims.

In Nyack, New York, Tamara Duker, who lost her sister, Sara, in a 1996 suicide bombing in Jerusalem by the Palestinian terrorist group, Hamas, volunteered to help war refugees. After 9/11, she took a temporary leave from working in her office in Chicago that was across the street from the Sears Tower skyscraper because of her fears of being attacked by terrorists. Not long afterward, she moved back to the East Coast and became a nutritionist and author. She also married and became the mother of twins. Now known as Tamara Duker Freuman, her life, she figured, was settled.

Then she learned that a group of Afghan war refugees who settled in Albany, New York needed shoes. Duker Freuman felt she could not leave her home and family to volunteer in person with the refugees in Albany. But she felt a calling to do something. The terrorism of 9/11 and its aftermath of war in Afghanistan and Iraq—not to mention the loss of her own sister to other terrorists in 1996—had left behind many scars.

The refugees had come to America with just sandals on their feet. For the cold winters of Upstate New York, they would need something warmer. So after talking with several women from her synagogue, Duker Freuman created a national registry on Amazon where people could donate shoes and boots to the refugees.

"I really just felt the plight of these poor people who were trapped," Duker Freuman said. "What must it be like to be a mother of children who can't keep your kids safe? I think it speaks to my biggest anxiety as a person, as a mother. I just had this appetite to do something."

"We were all affected by political violence and extremism," she added. "We were affected by it from very different places, but we were all affected by the same force and we're much more on the same side of history than on the opposing sides of it. This is the circle. This is what human beings do for other human beings."

* * *

By the spring of 2022, the battle between 9/11 families and Saudi Arabia took a dramatic turn. Saudi Arabia launched what many of the 9/11 families considered an insulting public relations campaign.

The Saudi investment fund, which was closely connected to the kingdom's government, decided to underwrite a new professional golf league known as LIV.

In America, LIV needed golf courses for its tournaments.

It turned to Donald Trump.

Trump was now out of the White House. He made no secret of the fact that he was considering another presidential campaign in 2024. But in the summer of 2022, he hosted LIV tournaments at two of his golf courses—including one in New Jersey where 700 residents had perished in the 9/11 attacks. The Saudi investment fund had publicly committed hundreds of millions of dollars to professional golfers who agreed to join the LIV tour. Phil Mickelson, one of America's top golfers at the time, was reportedly paid $200 million just to show up at LIV tournaments. Other top golfers received multi-million-dollar bonuses.

The 9/11 families who had filed suit against Saudi Arabia felt undermined once again—this time by a former president who had invited them to the White House only a few years before. They felt that the Saudi Arabian government was merely engaging in a slick marketing scheme by spreading money to boost a popular American sport as a way to clean up its poor image that not only included the accusations of its links to 9/11 but a harsh justice system that allowed for public beheadings of criminals. The families came up with a name for what they felt Saudi Arabia was doing. They called it "sport washing."

And in late July 2022, the small town of Bedminster, New Jersey, became a very public showdown between the families and Saudi Arabia—with Donald Trump now in the middle.

Terry Strada knew the town well. She also knew Trump's golf course that was located on some 600 acres of rolling hills in Bedminster that had once been the estate of the flamboyant auto-maker, John DeLorean.

Terry's husband, Tom, a former professional golfer, had played at Trump's course many times before he was killed on 9/11. Terry also played there with her husband. And after her son recovered from a brain tumor, Terry staged several gatherings at the golf course to raise money for research on childhood cancer.

But now, with the shocking news about Trump's partnership with the Saudi-funded LIV tournament, Strada was in no mood for golf or staging a charitable event. On a humid Tuesday morning in July, four days before the tournament was scheduled to start, Strada stood on the front lawn of the Bedminster Library, a short drive from the well-guarded gates of Trump's course. She did not mention the former president's name. She didn't have to.

"Offensive, disrespectful," Strada said of Trump's support for the LIV tournament. "A multibillion-dollar public relations stunt," she added—all aimed to "sports-wash" the alleged Saudi connection from 9/11.

Standing with Strada that morning was Alison Crowther. Her son, Welles, wearing a red bandana to keep the dust from his nose and mouth, had died in the collapse of the twin towers while trying to save other office workers. Afterward he achieved legendary status after survivors described him as the "man in the red bandana."

After Strada spoke, Crowther reached into her purse and pulled out a red bandana that resembled the one her son wore on 9/11, She stared at it for a second or two, then said: "Sometimes I think our government is more interested in protecting everyone else and has forgotten us."

* * *

Such was the beginning of a week-long series of bitter public relations skirmishes.

Two miles down Lamington Road, past the Rocking Horse Farm and a sign that advertised sheep and lambs for sale, another kind of scene was evolving at Trump's golf course. There was no criticism of Saudi Arabia. No mention of "sport washing." The course brimmed with the good feelings, smiles, and pride of a suddenly successful business venture. Some workers drove golf carts. Others checked on the LIV marketing signs that proclaimed "Golf, but louder" and "Don't blink." Still others set up stands to sell hamburgers and beer as the golfers gathered on a practice putting green or at the driving range.

A few days earlier, in response to criticism of golfers taking money from Saudi Arabia against the backdrop of criticism of the kingdom's possible role in 9/11, Trump posted a message on social media. "Take the money," it said.

On that morning, when Terry Strada spoke in Bedminster as her own form of protest, Trump had left town. He flew to Washington, DC—his first trip to the nation's capital since leaving office eighteen months earlier—for a speech at the America First Policy Institute, a think tank formed by a group of his former aides to promote his policies. In the speech, Trump, who had hinted in previous appearances elsewhere that he planned to run for the White House again in 2024, did not talk about Saudi Arabia's link to 9/11. But in an interview beforehand with *The Wall Street Journal*, Trump praised what he believed to be positive publicity for Saudi Arabia for its decision to pour millions of dollars into the LIV Golf series.

"I do think that the publicity that they've gotten, more than anything, has been a great thing for them," Trump told the *Journal*, "I think the publicity they've gotten is worth billions of dollars. It's one of the hottest things to have happened in sports, and sports is a big part of life."

Of the 9/11 victims and their relatives, Trump added: "I don't know much about the 9/11 families. I don't know what is the relationship to this, and their very strong feelings, and I can understand their feelings. I can't really comment on that because I don't know exactly what they're saying, and what they're saying who did what."

A day after Terry Strada came to Bedminster, Brett Eagleson arrived with another group of relatives of 9/11 victims. One of them was Juliette Scauso.

Scauso was only four years old when her father, Dennis, a firefighter assigned to the FDNY's elite Hazmat 1 unit, perished at the Trade Center. Her father's remains were never found. At his memorial service on that Monday after Thanksgiving in 2001, it was Juliette who held a US flag that had been folded into a triangle.

She had spent years since that funeral trying to hold on to her memories of her father—how he loved to treat wounded animals, how he had become known for being able to repair most any kind of gadget, how she loved to be hugged by him.

Juliette was now twenty-five years old and studying to become a physician at a medical college in Ireland. But the lack of answers to the questions about the suspected Saudi links to 9/11—and her father's death—had begun to bother her.

After Eagleson and others spoke that morning, she stepped forward. She remembered her father's attempts to make Mickey Mouse pancakes for her and how he used duct tape to reattach the heads of her broken Barbie dolls. And then she asked one of the most searing questions that anyone could ask in that odd week that juxtaposed a former president at his golf course accepting money from Saudi Arabia while victims of the 9/11 attacks continued to ask whether Saudi Arabia was linked to those attacks.

"How much money does it take to turn your back on your country?" Scauso asked, adding: "Or the American people?"

Then she mentioned her father again.

"My father wasn't the type of person who could be bought," she said. Then directing her message again at Trump and the golfers, she said: "I just want you to know that if you were there that day, my father would have run in to save you without a second thought."

The next day, the stream of golfers at Trump's club was continually asked why they accepted Saudi money amid the allegations of Saudi involvement in 9/11. Each golfer seemed to have the same answer—one that seemed drawn from a public relations manual.

They said their "hearts go out" to the families who were in their "thoughts and prayers."

When Trump appeared, he was asked about the Saudi link to 9/11 and why he, as a former president, would accept Saudi money to run his golf course.

"Well, nobody's gotten to the bottom of 9/11," Trump said.

* * *

A few weeks after the controversy at Trump's golf course in New Jersey, mourners again gathered in Lower Manhattan, some fifty miles away.

They again heard the bagpipes and the reading of the names of the dead.

But they now heard another somber footnote to the tragedy of 9/11.

More than 60,000 people who responded to the attacks in Lower Manhattan or worked in the variety of offices and other businesses nearby—as well as those living in apartments—now suffered from cancer. Thousands more battled respiratory problems.

But, incredibly, that wasn't the worst news.

As America and the world approached the twenty-fifth anniversary of the attacks of September 11, 2001, we learned that the number of people—many of them police, firefighters, and other first responders—who had died from being exposed to toxins released by the collapse of the twin towers had now exceeded the death toll on 9/11.

We also learned that in future years the numbers of dead would continue to grow.

And for those left behind, the scars remained—still painful and unhealed.

The South reflecting pool, with the 9/11 Museum in the background, is part of the 9/11 Memorial Plaza in New York City. A similar pool across the plaza was built on the footprint of the Trade Center's North Tower. Names of nearly 3,000 people killed at the Trade Center on 9/11 are listed on a bronze parapet that surrounds each of the pools. Photo by Andrew Holbrooke/Corbis via Getty Images.

Roses and a US flag are placed next to the name of one of the 9/11 victims listed on bronze parapets on the perimeters of the North and South reflecting pools at the 9/11 Memorial Plaza in New York City. Photo by Mike Segar-Pool/Getty Images.

Epilogue

Stepping Back

I often think of that first day when I crossed the Hudson on the tugboat, with the police and firefighters and priests—all of us staring in silent, collective shock at the smoke that billowed from the fallen towers. I remember the gray ash that covered the streets and sidewalks like snow, the burned scraps of financial reports, receipts, memos, and other pieces of paper that had been blown from the twin towers. I remember the seemingly endless debris field of steel beams and pipes that had been twisted like spaghetti and the concrete that had been broken like cookie crumbs.

But mostly, I remember the people and the wounds they carried—the human cost of 9/11.

On an afternoon in October 2023, I was reminded of how those wounds remain unhealed despite the passage of time.

I received an email from a now-retired NYPD detective, Martin Davin.

"I would like to speak with you," he wrote. "This is an important matter to me. Please reach out to me."

In the email, he reminded me that we met on the afternoon of September 11, 2001, on the corner of West and Murray Streets. As a journalist trying to make sense of the 9/11 tragedy, I had been walking toward the massive rubble pile a few hundred yards away—the remains of the once-majestic twin towers. Davin had been assigned to guard the corner and watch out for looters.

I remembered how I had approached Davin that afternoon. We chatted for a minute or two. I jotted down his remarks in a notebook, then kept moving in search of others to interview. Hours later, after walking many blocks to find a cellular signal, I phoned in Davin's quotes to a rewrite reporter back in the newsroom who assembled a long article with observations about the attack from dozens of ordinary people.

Davin and I had not spoken since then. Our meeting on 9/11, in fact, was just a chance encounter that would have never happened if I had been walking on a different street or he had been assigned to a different corner.

But now, all these years later, Davin needed me to help solve a problem.

His health was failing because he breathed in too many toxins at Ground Zero, first on September 11, 2001, and then on subsequent days when he volunteered to search for his dead colleagues in the massive rubble pile. But the NYPD was holding back the payment of special health and pension benefits that Davin was entitled to receive. As I later learned, Davin was not the only first responder facing this problem.

The NYPD told Davin he had to prove he had been at Ground Zero in order to receive his benefits. Amid the chaos of that first day and in the subsequent days, Davin did not stop to fill out a log book or some other sort of record of where he was going. As it turned out, many police, firefighters, and other first responders did not bother with such details on 9/11—or even in the following days and months. They knew they were needed at what turned out to be the most devastating crime scene and fire of their careers. They simply ran out the doors of their police stations, firehouses, ambulance stations, and homes because their country needed them in a crisis. And they kept going back—even on their days off. But now, many, including Marty Davin, were being forced to prove that they actually responded. And, like Davin, many had no official record that they were among the first responders to Ground Zero on September 11, 2001 or thereafter.

Davin decided to do something. So he found me.

Helping Davin was easy. I merely checked my notes and confirmed that I had interviewed him. Then I wrote a letter to the NYPD and recounted the story of our meeting.

While Marty Davin can now rest a bit easier because he has the medical and pension benefits he rightly deserved, he can't do anything about his health. He is another wounded veteran of 9/11—still bearing painful scars. His ordeal is one chapter in the much longer history of the human cost of the 9/11 attacks.

Over the years since the 9/11 attacks, I learned of many people who quietly bear the scars of that day and its aftermath. A middle-aged man still cries each time I speak to him and we talk about the wife he lost. A police officer still carries the handcuffs of a colleague who never left his post in the Trade Center as he guided thousands of workers to safety. A son who lost his father finds after all these years that he can't jetison the deep anger in his heart because he feels that a series of presidents and others in Washington refuse to examine the alleged role that Saudi Arabia may have played in the attacks.

One third of the nearly 3,000 people who perished on September 11, 2001, at Manhattan's World Trade Center have never been identified. Their bodies were pulverized into dust, burned into ash, or vaporized. After twenty years, modern science has still not been able to decipher all of the often-miniscule DNA material found in the dust and ash and other remains found in the rubble.

I routinely showed up at memorial services and funerals, seeking some measure of context or meaning that would help to explain why so many innocent people had been killed in the name of someone's God. As I completed a mid-career graduate degree in theology, I spent months reading the warped spiritual tracts of Islamist militants—all in the hope that I might find some sense of how they might justify their bloodletting. I never found anything other than a self-centered nihilism.

On far too many days over these last two decades after I wrote columns and other articles about some aspect of 9/11, I was left with a troublesome series of questions: What really is the best way to mourn so many deaths? What can be done with the stream of anger that continues to flow from the memory of 9/11 from victims' relatives and survivors? How can the relatives of the victims and the survivors find a sense of peace while knowing that their loved ones and friends died so ruthlessly?

One morning in late August 2025, a few weeks before the twenty-fourth anniversary of the 9/11 attacks, James Yee, the US Army Muslim chaplain who was wrongly charged with espionage, imprisoned for seventy-six days, and threatened with the death penalty, returned to his alma mater, West Point. It had been two decades since Yee was charged—and then quickly cleared—of mishandling classified documents and espionage. Many within the Army's ranks—and at West Point—felt that the case against Yee was amateurish, probably grounded in a deep distrust of Muslims.

Yee's soul was still wounded. But he still wanted to serve. On that August morning, he came back to West Point to participate in the annual march by alumni to welcome new cadets at the military academy. Most Fridays, he now drives to West Point to lead a prayer service for Muslim cadets.

Phil McArdle, who retired from the FDNY after being diagnosed with respiratory problems from breathing in too many of Ground Zero's toxins, also still wants to serve his fellow firefighters. He worries continually about the families of the nineteen men from his fire house who were killed on 9/11—and for another firefighter who later committed suicide and still others who have died from Ground Zero's toxins. McArdle's concerns about the growing health problems for first responders deepened even more when his brother, John, an elite NYPD emergency services lieutenant who came out of retirement to respond to the 9/11 attacks, died in 2023 from cancer that was linked to the contaminated air and rubble he encountered at Ground Zero.

Last year, after hearing of another suicide by a firefighter who wrestled with the emotional scars of 9/11 that he still carried, McArdle wrote a letter to the FDNY, asking if firefighters who survived the collapse of the twin towers on 9/11 or others who participated in the search and recovery in the rubble could be acknowledged in some way.

"It might be a way of letting them all know that they were not forgotten," McArdle wrote.

* * *

As the twenty-fifth anniversary of the attacks approached, Mark Rossini, the former FBI agent who worked with the CIA and tried to sound a warning after noticing that two al-Qaeda terrorists had slipped into the US, found himself in trouble again with the law.

In 2007, Rossini had been forced out of the FBI after he illegally searched through an investigative file at the request of a woman he knew. By 2022, he faced a much more serious charge. He had been arrested and charged with acting as a go-between in an alleged bribery scheme involving the former governor of Puerto Rico.

On August 27, 2025, after striking a plea bargain with federal prosecutors, Rossini pleaded guilty to a reduced misdemeanor charge of violating the Federal Election Campaign Act. On January 15, 2026, while still awaiting sentencing in the case, Rossini was pardoned by President Donald Trump after a relative of one of Rossini's co-defendants reportedly donated $1 million to a fund linked to Trump.

Was Rossini's flawed judgment, negligence, and recklessness that landed him in so much trouble with the law linked to his bitter and guilt-ridden experiences before 9/11 and in the tumultuous days afterward? The question continues to trouble Rossini. But after so many years, he concedes that he doesn't really understand why he let himself take such risks in violating the law and allowing himself to fall from grace the way he did. Even his close friends find it difficult to explain what he did—and why. The tragic legacy of his story is that his once-respected credibility as a counterterrorism expert has been tarnished. Few in America's law enforcement and intelligence communities bother to listen to him anymore.

* * *

Tim Sorbanelli was in third grade in a New Jersey elementary school when the 9/11 attacks took place. On April 15, 2013, he was a student at Boston's Berklee College of Music and a street musician with an acoustic guitar, entertaining spectators and runners near the finish line of the Boston Marathon.

Two bombs exploded. Sorbanelli was knocked to the ground. The wounds to his body were minor, easy to heal. But the wounds to his soul were much deeper.

He needed years of therapy to recover. Each time he walked Boston's streets, he felt a sense of danger and dread—and flashbacks. If he was a soldier, he might have been diagnosed with post-traumatic stress disorder (PTSD). But as a civilian—another witness to terrorism—he carried his wounds quietly, wondering how to recover. He eventually moved from Boston—to a remote town in the Nevada desert, south of Las Vegas, where he found peace.

* * *

Dereck Lovell, the security guard on the seventieth floor of the World Trade Center's South Tower who heroically guided a group of Morgan Stanley workers to safety, carries another set of wounds.

"The memories," he told me on a recent afternoon near his new home in Brooklyn. "They're too painful."

I had not seen Lovell since 2011 when we met for lunch in Washington, DC, where he worked as a security guard for the World Bank.

It was now May 2025 when we met again. I walked up the stairs of a subway station in Brooklyn after stepping off a train from Manhattan. Lovell waved from a nearby corner.

He said he was battling prostate cancer that his doctors told him was linked to the toxins he was exposed to at Ground Zero. He was still working, but only part time as a driver who chauffeured dogs and other pets to a spa and day care for animals. By the end of the summer of 2025, he would learn that cancer had spread to his kidneys and that he had been placed on a list of patients who needed a kidney transplant.

We sat across from each other in a booth in a coffee shop and Lovell's thoughts seemed far away as he tried to imagine the future and how his life might change. On 9/11, he was not yet an American citizen. (That would come later.) But that day, he became an American hero. Morgan Stanley awarded him with two medals for his bravery.

Lovell knows that his heroism on 9/11 helped to save people's lives. He carries that memory with a quiet sense of pride. But almost a quarter-century after 9/11, Lovell still nurses a deep regret. One of the Morgan Stanley staffers on the seventieth floor, Tom Swift, died in the collapse of the South Tower. Swift's remains were never found. A variety of witnesses say he likely perished after he tried to take an elevator to safety.

"I still feel bad that I couldn't save Tom Swift," Lovell said.

Lovell told me he usually avoided walking near Ground Zero when he traveled to Manhattan. Even seeing the new memorial and its waterfalls reminded him of the fire and smoke of 9/11 and the frightening moments he spent helping people escape.

But one day, he returned.

Lovell searched the bronze parapets that list the names of the nearly 3,000 people who died—finally stopping at Tom Swift's name.

Lovell placed his hand on Swift's name and paused in silence for a second or two.

"I just wanted to remember him," he said.

* * *

One afternoon in late September 2025, I visited Ground Zero again.

The air felt cool as it often does there, even on warm days, because of the breezes off the Hudson River. Tourists posed for selfies by the bronze parapets that listed the names of the dead. A few visitors placed flowers by a name of someone they knew. Some visitors stopped at a kiosk that sold T-shirts and coffee cups to raise money for the memorial. Others sat on benches and talked.

A few weeks before, a federal judge in New York City rejected efforts by lawyers for Saudi Arabia to throw out the lawsuit by 9/11 families. The ruling by US District Judge George Daniels was considered a major victory in the two-decade legal campaign to hold Saudi Arabia accountable for the 9/11 attacks. But it was not the end of the long fight. Much more needs to be resolved. In his forty-five-page opinion, Judge Daniels did not say that Saudi Arabia was guilty. But he wrote that it was "more likely than not" Saudi government operatives provided "essential support" to the 9/11 terrorists. The judge did not specify what form that support took. But his ruling allows the case to go forward, for now.

It may take years to reach some sort of verdict. No trial date was set. Interviews with witnesses still continue. Meanwhile, Saudi Arabia's lawyers pledge to appeal the ruling—and probably every future decision in the case. In short, the long and winding path to unraveling of these allegations will take even more unraveling, more time.

And over time, I have found that the wounds do not heal.

* * *

With most stories I cover, I can usually sense a finish line of sorts—a verdict in a trial, for instance, or a winner and a loser in an election. Some news events are tense and unpredictable, filled with mystery and surprises. But even when America's political, social, cultural, or economic gyroscopes have seemed to wobble amid the forces of war, scandal, or tragedy, I have always felt that the nation would find its balance again. After all, this was America. We have experienced plenty of hardships, from hurricanes to floods to mass shootings—even a Civil War and centuries of slavery, followed by decades of institutional racism. We always seemed to find a way to land on our feet.

Now I wonder.

After a burst of unity following the 9/11 attacks, our politics has devolved into gamesmanship. Far too many of us live in political echo chambers where we only listen to viewpoints that we agree with. In some cases, lies are interpreted as truth—and truths become lies.

On that September afternoon, after visiting Ground Zero and the memorial again, I walked toward the Hudson River and stepped onto a ferry to cross back to New Jersey and the town I call home.

As the ferry left the dock, I turned and looked back toward Ground Zero. The smoke and rubble were gone, of course, replaced by a gleaming skyscraper, nicknamed "The Freedom Tower," that rises 1,776 feet above the landscape that was the scene of so much death. Other magnificent structures had risen nearby such as a subway station that seemed to have bird's wings and a new Greek Orthodox church that replaced one that had been flattened by debris on 9/11.

Sunlight bounced off the Freedom Tower's glass sides, golden and hopeful. Down the river, the Statue of Liberty held her torch aloft as she has for almost 140 years.

Life seemed ordered.

As the ferry cruised toward the middle of the river, the current became choppier. I thought back to that river crossing on September 11, 2001.

A quarter-century has passed since then. But when I look back and recall what I saw that day, I find that I'm still on a boat of sorts, bobbing on a river of uncertainty over why so many innocents died and why countless others—many of them brave first responders who tried to help in some way—now carry such deep scars on their bodies and souls.

I remember how the smoke and fire of terrorism that day blotted out a perfect blue sky and a golden sun.

I still fear that the smoke and fire may return someday.

But I will keep looking for blue sky and that golden sun.

Notes on Sources

Much of the reporting for this book comes from my own observations and interviews with participants over various points during the last twenty-five years. My research goal was not merely to rely on people's recollections in these later years, but to try to capture their thoughts and actions as they happened.

To augment my reporting and interviews, I relied on transcripts of hearings, statements, published and unpublished writings by various characters, other media reports, and videos to understand a person's mindset in different years—and how that perspective may have changed over time. The descriptions of many scenes in this book are based on my in-person observations. In other cases, I relied on the observations of someone being depicted, police and fire department reports, and recollections by other witnesses. The various characters depicted here offered hours of insight in numerous interviews. Many also willingly gave me personal writings and videos and patiently endured my fact-checking.

My reporting took me from Ground Zero in New York City to an apartment in Kuala Lumpur, Malaysia, where several members of the 9/11 terrorist plot met, to Washington, DC, the Middle East (five times), Northern Ireland, Iraq, Kenya, the US Naval Base at Guantanamo Bay, Cuba (twice), and to the Cuban mainland. Other reporting spots ranged from courthouses and congressional hearings to churches, synagogues, mosques, firehouses, police stations, cemeteries, and military installations in New Jersey, Pennsylvania, New Mexico, Texas, Iraq, and Guantanamo Bay, Cuba.

A number of books and memoirs were especially helpful and deserve mention here for other researchers interested in pursuing the implications of the 9/11 attacks. Listed alphabetically, by author, these include: *Who Owns the Dead* by Jay Aronson; *United States of Jihad* by Peter Bergen; *Wake Up Call* by Kristen Breitweiser; *After* by Steven Bill; *Divided We Stand* by Eric Darton; *City of Dust* by Anthony DePalma: *Every Day is a Gift* by US Senator Tammy Duckworth; *The Watchdogs Didn't Bark* by John Duffy and Ray Nowosielski; *102 Minutes* by Jim Dwyer and Kevin Flynn; *Governor Tom Kean* by Alvin S. Felzenberg; *Watching the World Change* by David Friend; *The Price of Terror* by Allan Gerson and Jerry Adler; *Twin Towers* by Angus Kress Gillespie; *The Only Planes in the Sky* by Garrett M. Graff; *Firehouse* by David Halberstam; *Shattered Lives* by Jeff Ingber with Joe Connor; *Without Precedent* by Thomas H. Kean and Lee H. Hamilton; *Closure* by William Keegan Jr.; *American Ground* by William Langewiesche; *The Hunt for KSM* by Terry McDermott and Josh Meyer; *Faces of Ground Zero* by Joe McNally; *The Cell* by John Miller, Michael Stone with Chris Mitchell; *Portraits: 9/11/01* by The New York Times; *A Heart, A Cross, and a Flag* by Peggy Noonan; *Ordinary Heroes* by Joseph Pfeiffer; *The Long Road Home* by Martha Raddatz; *The Red Bandana* by Tom Rinaldi; *America's Trial* by John Ryan; *Who They Were* by Robert Shaler; *The Commission* by Philip Shenon; *Report from Ground Zero* by Dennis Smith; *Beyond 9/11* by Time Magazine; *The Eleventh Day* by Anthony Summers and Robbyn Swan; *The Looming Tower* by Lawrence Wright; *For God and Country* by James Yee; *Fall and Rise* by Mitchell Zuckoff; *The World Trade Center Building Performance Study*; and *The 9/11 Commission Report*.

* * *

A Brief Note on Terminology

Regarding the spelling of "al-Qaeda":

There are several ways to spell the name of the militant terror group, founded by Osama bin Laden. These spellings range from "Al Qaeda" to "al Qaida" and "al Qa'ida." For simplicity and to remain consistent with the style of spelling of other Arabic names in this book, I have opted for "al-Qaeda."

Regarding the spelling of "counterterrorism":

Both counterterrorism and counter-terrorism are correct and acceptable. I'm using counterterrorism to remain consistent with the spelling in various US government reports and with the style of major US media outlets.

Regarding usage of the term, "Islamist":

I have utilized Islamist and, in a few cases, Islamism, throughout this narrative to refer to a particular form of terrorism—and terrorist—who uses the Muslim faith as an illegitimate and immoral excuse to commit political violence. Increasingly, Muslim theologians and scholars from other faiths, along with historians, intelligence analysts, and a variety of media sources, now make a point of using the terms, Islamist and Islamism, to draw the distinction between the religion of Islam and political terrorist groups—notably al-Qaeda, Hamas, Hezbollah, and the so-called "Islamic State" known as ISIS—who distort Islamic principles to justify violence against a political system and non-Muslims.

Additional Notes

Prologue: First Steps

- Scene with first responders on tugboat as it crosses the Hudson River on September 11, 2001: Author's on-scene reporting.
- Confrontation with Puerto Rican nationalist bomb-maker Guillermo "Willie" Morales in Havana, Cuba: Author's on-scene reporting. September 2015.
- Scene with relatives and friends of Pan Am 103 terrorist bombing victims leaving notes for President George H.W. Bush on fence of the White House: Author's on-scene reporting, 1989.
- Descriptions over time of pursuit of justice by families and friends of Pan Am 103 victims: Author's reporting.
- Courtroom scene, 1993, with accused Islamist terrorists who set off a bomb in the garage of the World Trade Center in New York City: Author's on-scene reporting.
- Descriptions of impact of terrorism in Belfast, Northern Ireland; Nairobi, Kenya; Israel, Gaza, and West Bank: Author's on-scene reporting for several projects with *The Record.*

Part One: Day Becomes Night

Chapter 1: Dawn

- Description of activities and escape by Morgan Stanley staff from seventieth floor of World Trade Center South Tower on morning of September 11, 2001: Extensive interviews by author in 2002 for project entitled "Journey Through Shadow," published in *The Record*, September 8, 2002. Also, material drawn from author's follow-up reporting with Morgan Stanley staff in later years.
- Accounts on September 11, 2001, of Bert Ammerman, Kristen Breitweiser, Martin Davin, Tamara Duker Freuman, Brett Eagleson, James Egan, David Handschuh, Brian Jordan, Thomas Kean, Nancy Kennedy (and Morgan Stanley staff), Peter Killeen, Mark Rossini, John Ryan, Juliette Scauso, Frank Silecchia, Tim Sorbanelli, Terry Strada, James Yee: Author's interviews, augmented in some cases with media reports, written statements, and published and unpublished memoirs and other writings.
- Background on the building of the World Trade Center and other milestones there, including high wire crossing between towers in 1974 by Philippe Petit: Various media reports and books about the Trade Center, including *The World Trade Center Building Performance Study* and 2008 documentary film, *Man on Wire.*
- Comment to FBI by Ramzi Yousef, leader of 1993 World Trade Center bombing: from official account assembled for archives by the National September 11 Memorial and Museum, New York.
- Rescue of Morgan Stanley staffers by security guard Dereck Lovell: Author's interviews with Lovell in 2002, 2011, 2025, augmented by interviews with Morgan Stanley staffers.
- Account of FDNY Hazmat 1 Firefighter Phil McArdle: author's interviews, personal notes and writings by McArdle, and FDNY records from 9/11 attacks.
- Timetable of hijacked flights on September 11, 2001: Official report by National Commission on Terrorist Attacks Upon the United States (9/11 Commission), augmented by records from Federal Aviation Administration.
- Account of September 11, 2001, and other events by Joseph Connor: Author's interviews over the years with Connor as well as personal writings by Connor and 2018 memoir, *Shattered Lives,* by Jeff Ingber with Joe Connor.

Chapter 2: Collapse

- Description of 9/11 attack by Joseph Connor: Author's interviews
- Escape from seventieth floor of South Tower by Morgan Stanley staffers: author's interviews for "Journey Through Shadow" project, *The Record*, 2002.
- Description of phone call to Terry Strada from her husband, Thomas: Author's interviews with Strada, augmented by her own writings and various statements.
- Description of experience on 9/11 by Kristen Breitweiser: author's interviews with Breitweiser over the years, augmented by her 2006 memoir, *Wake Up Call*, and her various public statements.

- Description. of experience on 9/11 by David Handschuh, as well as his injuries: Author's interviews with Handschuh, his writings and statements, augmented by FDNY reports, media reports, and his reflection, "Stories of Hope," published on website of National September 11 Memorial and Museum.
- Account on 9/11 with FDNY Hazmat 1 Firefighters Phil McArdle and Jeff Borkowski: author's interviews with McArdle, augmented by FDNY reports and FDNY citation to McArdle and Borkowski for heroism.
- Account of rescue of Silvion Ramsundar: Author's interviews in 2002 and 2011 with Ramsundar, interviews with Morgan Stanley staffers Doug Brown and Stan Kapica for "Journey Through Shadow" project, and other media reports.
- Account of 9/11 experience at CIA with FBI special agent Mark Rossini: author's interviews with Rossini over the years, augmented by notes and writings by Rossini shared with author.

Chapter 3: Dust

- FDNY Firefighter Phil McArdle's survival experience in rubble. Author's interviews. FDNY reports.
- Experience on September 11, 2001, of retired FDNY Chief Larry Byrnes and FDNY Probationary Firefighter Antonios Benetatos. Author's interviews with both, 2001.
- Accounts of various other heroes on September 11, 2001, and afterward: various media reports and archives from National September 11 Memorial and Museum.
- Experience by Tamara Duker Freuman: Author's interviews, augmented by his 2014 book, *The Bus on Jaffa Road.*
- Experience of Brett Eagleson: various interviews with author.
- Experience of Father Brian Jordan: Author's interviews. Jordan's own accounts for archives of September 11 Memorial and Museum and Jordan's 2017 memoir, *The Ground Zero Cross.*
- Experience of NYPD Detective Martin Davin and author at Ground Zero: Author's interviews 2001 and in 2022, 2023, 2024, 2025.
- Experience of Joseph Connor on 9/11: author's interviews.
- Reaction to 9/11 attacks by FBI Special Agent Mark Rossini to 9/11 attacks. Author's interviews.

Part Two: Fire and Rubble

Chapter 4: Ground Zero

- Statement by President George W. Bush: White House transcript.
- Options considered by President Bush, from his 2010 memoir, *Decision Points.*
- 9/11 terrorists in United States and warnings ahead of time by various US officials. Report by 9/11 Commission and author's own reporting.

- Remarks by Rev. Jerry Falwell on *The 700 Club* television show hosted by Pat Robertson, September 13, 2001: transcript from broadcast and various media reports.
- Frank Silecchia's discovery of "Ground Zero Cross" and reaction by Father Brian Jordan: author's interviews with Silecchia and Jordan, augmented by memoir by Father Brian Jordan and various statements each has made.

Chapter 5: Twenty-five Funerals a Day

- Experience of Kristen Breitweiser after 9/11: author's interviews over the years, augmented by her 2006 memoir, *Wake Up Call.*
- Process of identifying 9/11 victims by New York City Medical Examiner: Author's interviews.
- Health problems for NYPD Detective James Zadroga and impact on overall concerns about health of first responders at Ground Zero. Statements by NYC mayor's office and NYPD, augmented by author's ongoing interviews with health experts and author's coverage of Zadroga funeral and aftermath with his family, including extensive interviews with his parents who cared for his daughter after his wife also died.
- Underground search team experience at Ground Zero. Author's on-scene reporting, augmented by interviews with Lt. John Ryan, Ground Zero tour commander for Port Authority police.
- Experience and observations by Peter Killeen: Author's interviews over the years.
- Memorial service for Thomas Swift. Author's interviews with various Morgan Stanley staffers and several members of the Swift family.
- Memorial service for NYPD Hazmat 1 Firefighter Dennis Scauso. Author interviews with Phil McArdle and Juliette Scauso, augmented by memorial service program and video of the service.

Chapter 6: Let's Take 'em To Court

- Experiences and observations by Terry Strada, including her assessment of Ron Motley. Various author interviews and Strada's writings and statements.
- Description of Wilentz Law Firm conference room: author's follow-up reporting.
- Background on Ron Motley: various media reports and biography supplied by his law firm.
- Background on Wilentz Law Firm: Law firm's website and various media reports.
- Background on Saudi Arabia's alleged link to 9/11: Various documents from FBI, findings by Joint Congressional Intelligence Committee Inquiry, and findings by 9/11 Commission.
- Bush family links to Saudi Arabian government over years. From various media reports and 2004 book, *House of Bush, House of Saud* by Craig Unger.
- Background on Bojinka Plot: FBI documents and various media reports.
- Statement by Terry Strada in Washington, DC, after filing of lawsuit: video of event and transcript, augmented by author interviews with her.
- Background on filing of lawsuits against foreign nations. Author's interviews with various attorneys in recent years, augmented by research for his 2014 book, *The Bus on Jaffa Road.*

Chapter 7: What Safety Net?

- Testimony by Kristen Breitweiser before House and Senate Joint Inquiry into Intelligence Community Activities Before and After the Terrorist Attacks of September 11, 2001. Transcript and video of testimony, augmented by author interviews, Breitweiser's writings and various media reports.
- Background of the "Jersey Girls": Author interviews 2003 and 2004, media reports, and 2006 memoir, *Wake Up Call* by Kristen Breitweiser and interviews in 2016 and 2025 with Breitweiser.
- Prediction by Richard Clarke of "something spectacular" to happen. Joint Inquiry report. Transcript of hearings 2002. 9/11 Commission.
- Discussions between White House and 9/11 Commission. Research based on White House documents and author's reporting, augmented by various media reports and the books, *The Commission* by Philip Shenon and *Wake Up Call* memoir by Kristen Breitweiser.
- Meeting with Henry Kissinger and "Jersey Girls" and other relatives of 9/11 victims: based on author interviews with various participants, augmented by various media reports, Kristen Breitweiser's *Wake Up Call* and Philip Shenon's *The Commission.*
- Appointment of Thomas Kean to replace Kissinger as head of 9/11 Commission. Author's extensive interviews with Kean on this subject, augmented by Kean's 2006 book, *Without Precedent*, co-written by Lee Hamilton and Benjamin Rhodes, and 2006 biography, *Governor Tom Kean* by Alvin S. Felzenberg.
- Other research from 2004 inspector general report: *A Review of the FBI's Handling of Intelligence Information Prior to the September 11 Attacks.*

Chapter 8: The Commission

- Presentation of 9/11 Commission report in Washington, DC. Author's on-scene reporting, augmented by transcript and video and interviews with various participants.
- Background on Kean's bipartisan strategy with 9/11 Commission. Author's interviews with Kean. Also background interviews during Commission's investigation with Alvin Felzenberg, Lee Hamilton, Philip Zelikow, and various 9/11 Commission members.
- Kean's view of importance of "Jersey Girls": Author's interviews with Kean, beginning in 2003 and continuing in 2025, augmented by the books, *Without Precedent* and *Wake Up Call.*
- Kean's reluctance to return to politics. Author's interviews with Kean, augmented by books, *Without Precedent* and *Governor Tom Kean.*
- Kean's remarks at memorial for 9/11 victims of Fiduciary Trust. Author interviews
- Kean's opinion of Roger Stone: Author's interview with Kean, augmented by author interview with Stone.
- Reaction by Kristen Breitweiser to release of 9/11 Commission Report. Author's interviews over the years with her. Breitweiser's memoir, *Wake Up Call.*
- Background on 9/11 terrorists Khalid al-Mihdhar and Nawaf al-Hazmi: author's reporting, augmented by documents from the 9/11 and the FBI and review of intelligence reports.

- Kristen Breitweiser's concern about Footnote 44 in 9/11 Commission Report: author's interviews with her, augmented by Breitweiser's memoir, *Wake Up Call.*
- Mark Rossini's reaction to 9/11 Commission report: Author's interviews with Rossini and Rossini's written reflections shared with author.
- Background on Saudi nationals, Omar al-Bayoumi and Fahad al-Thumairy: Author's reporting of 9/11 Commission, augmented by analysis of FBI documents released in recent years and report by Joint Inquiry on Intelligence Activities.
- Background on Prince Bandar's alleged links to 9/11: from previously classified documents known as the "28 pages," augmented by various other court documents.
- Mark Rossini's mindset. Author's interviews with him.

Chapter 9: The Chaplain of Gitmo

- Background on Captain James Yee: Author's interviews with him, augmented by interviews with other veterans who knew him and his attorney, Eugene Fidell, as well as series of articles by Ray Rivera, published in *The Seattle Times* in 2005.
- Description of detention facilities at US Naval Station at Guantanamo Bay, Cuba, based on various government reports, media reports, and author's visit in 2004, as well as *America's Trial* by John Ryan.
- Reactions to Yee prosecution by Generals Hill and Miller: media reports and public statements they released.

Part Three: The Remnants of Reckoning

Chapter 10: The Pit

- Description of tenth anniversary ceremonies at Ground Zero: based on author's on-scene reporting, augmented by other media reports.
- Description of memorial to firefighters and suicide victim from fire house in Maspeth, Queens: based on author's visit, interviews with various FDNY Hazmat 1 Firefighter Phil McArdle, other firefighters, and reports on suicide by FDNY and NYPD.
- Background on growing health problems for 9/11 responders. Based on author's reporting at Mount Sinai Medical Center as well as reports by FDNY and NYPD.
- Reflections by Frank Silecchia: based on author's interviews with him in 2011 and 2025 as well as various media reports.
- Health concerns by NYPD Detective Martin Davin. Based on author's interviews with him in 2023, 2024, 2025, augmented by background interviews with his attorney, Timothy McEnaney.

Chapter 11: The Crucible of Memory

- Reflections in Texas ten years after 9/11 attacks by Stan Kapica and Doug Brown: author's on-scene interviews
- Scenes from escape on 9/11 by Morgan Stanley staff and background on Thomas Swift: author's interviews, 2002.
- Dispute over Ground Zero Cross: Interviews with Father Brian Jordan and Frank Silecchia, augmented by media reports, Jordan's book, *The Ground Zero Cross.*
- Controversy over so-called "Ground Zero Mosque" and its imam: Author's reporting in New York City and in Union City, New Jersey, for investigation in *The Record* by the author, along with Jean Rimbach and Peter Sampson.
- Mark Rossini's resignation from FBI and link to investigation of Anthony Pellicano: Various official statements by FBI and Department of Justice, as well as interviews with Rossini and background from John Miller, former assistant director for public affairs for FBI.
- Port Authority police psychologist Peter Killeen's analysis of psychological issues for police from trauma of 9/11: based on author's interviews with Killeen in 2011 and 2025, augmented by media reports on the issue.
- Scenes from 9/11 memorial on tenth anniversary: Author's on-scene reporting.
- Reflections by Dereck Lovell on tenth anniversary of 9/11 and his heroism: Interview with author, 2011.

Chapter 12: A Law Called "JASTA"

- Description of introduction in US Senate of bill, Justice Against Sponsors of Terrorism Act (JASTA). Based on author's review of Congressional Record, augmented by various statements by senators and media reports.
- Explanation of importance of JASTA: based on author's reporting with a variety of legal experts.
- Reflections by Tom Kean: based on author's interviews with him.
- Reflections by Kristen Breitweiser: Based on author's interviews with her over the years.
- Reflections by Brett Eagleson: Based on author's interviews with him, augmented by public statements and reviews of media reports and video.
- Background on lawsuit against Saudi Arabia: Interviews with various attorneys and study of court documents.

Chapter 13: Unfinished Business

- Efforts by relatives of 9/11 victims to persuade Trump and Biden administrations to release FBI documents—and eventual decision by President Biden to declassify those documents for public consumption. Reporting based on documents submitted by FBI and Biden administration, statements by Presidents Trump and Biden, interviews with various relatives, in particular Brett Eagleson and Terry Strada.

- Summary of legal case against Saudi Arabia. Reporting based on court documents and background interviews with legal experts.
- Scene at twentieth anniversary of attacks: Based on author's on-scene reporting and interviews.
- Accounts by Patrick Swift, James Yee, John Ryan, Joe Connor, and Tamara Duker-Freuman: Based on author's interviews.
- Description of Controversy over Saudi-sponsored LIV golf tournament at Trump National Golf Course, Bedminster, New Jersey: based on author's on-scene reporting.

Epilogue: Stepping Back

- Update on health problems with NYPD Detective Martin Davin: author's reporting.
- Return to West Point by James Yee: Author's on-scene reporting and interviews with Yee.
- Update on Mark Rossini and pardon by President Trump: Documents from Department of Justice, the White House, interviews with Rossini, and various media reports.
- Update on Tim Sorbanelli: author interviews in 2013, 2014, and 2025.
- Update on Dereck Lovell: author interviews, 2025.

Acknowledgments

No book is written alone. I was helped and encouraged by many. But one person stands out—my wife, Judy.

Amid the horror and confusion of September 11, 2001, and continuing all these years since then, Judy supported me in pursuing all aspects of the 9/11 story. She was an immense help to me in writing this book.

Likewise, our daughters, Michelle and Anne, not only listened patiently as I retold stories (often as a form of informal therapy for myself) but they continually posed questions to me that pushed me to dig deeper into the mysteries of 9/11.

My literary agent, Tim Hays, who has represented me for three decades, has always been a bulwark of motivation and friendship. All authors would be lucky to have an agent like him.

Michael Kerns, the editor at Bloomsbury Publishing who shepherded this book to its completion, was always a source of encouragement, along with his assistant, Madeline Jenkins.

Sally Rinehart's evocative cover design captured the book's emotional threads. Bloomsbury's managing editor for production, Tricia Knight, patiently steered me through computerized page proofs. Veronica Dove and Paige Papandrea offered marketing advice. Peter Perez guided publicity with an eye towards the sensitivity of the characters. In India, V. Arun Kumar supervised production with his team from Amnet Content Source: D. Arockia Rajan, K. Baskaran, H. Muthukumaran, P. Sivakumar, B. Ramesh, K. Manikandan, I. Solomon, S. Guruprasath, and B. Stephen.

My newspaper, *The Record*—and in recent years, *The USA Today* network—supported my work and ideas as a columnist and project writer. I am especially indebted to Malcolm Borg and the Borg family, who were long-time owners of *The Record* and never flinched in dispatching me across the globe and America on assignments.

Many journalists encouraged me along the way. These include the editors-in-chief of *The Record* who have guided my reporting on terrorism for the past quarter century: Vivian Waixel, Frank Scandale, Martin Gottlieb, Deirdre Sykes, and Dan Sforza.

Other journalists who supported my work and, in many cases, made it better or inspired me by their own coverage of 9/11, include: Jim Anness, Peter Bergen, Richard Benfield, Dana Cardullo, Dan Christensen, Michael Daly, Susan DeSantis, Julie Dunlap, Jim Dwyer, Scott Fallon, Ed Forbes, Thomas Franklin, Carmine Galasso, Rich Gigli, Peter Grad, Rick Hampson, Peter Haskell, Will Lamb, Art Lenehan, Joe McNally, John Miller, Martha Moore, Tim Nostrand, Chris Pedota, Martha Raddatz, Danielle Richards, Ray Rivera, Tim Scheld, Janny Scott, Philip Shenon, Tyson Trish, Lindy Washburn, Richard Whitby, Jim Wright, and Lawrence Wright.

Lawyers such as James Kreindler, Andrew "Duke" Maloney, Alan Gerson, and Steve Perles steered me through many complexities of terrorism law. Jay Winuk, who lost his brother in the attacks and went on to co-found the non-profit group, "9/11 Day," which organizes a national volunteer day of service each year on the anniversary of the attacks, opened many doors to 9/11 victims and generously offered insight into the trauma of losing someone in the attacks. Attorney Tim McEnaney was a guide in my journey to assess the legal problems of first responders in trying to obtain health benefits that were supposedly guaranteed to them by the Zadroga Act. Robert Haefele of the Motley Rice law firm in Mount Pleasant, South Carolina, and Lynne M. Kizis of the Wilentz, Goldman, and Spitzer law firm in Woodbridge, New Jersey opened important doors for research on the original lawsuit involving Saudi Arabia. Eugene Fidell expertly explained the intricacies of military law in the case of Captain James Yee.

Thomas Kean, the chairman of the 9/11 Commission, along with the Commission's executive director, Philip Zelikow, and other staffers such as Alvin Felzenberg, John Farmer, and Douglas MacEachin were often readily available to answer the smallest of questions.

US Senators Richard Blumenthal and Robert Menendez were especially helpful, along with Representatives Christopher Shays and Carolyn Maloney, in explaining the complicated politics of passing anti-terrorism legislation.

The doctors, nurses, and other medical staffers at Mount Sinai Medical Center in New York City are a credit to their profession for their dogged and deeply kind efforts to keep track of the startling number of first responders and others who have become sickened from Ground Zero toxins.

Members of the New York City's police and fire departments, as well as the Port Authority Police Department, not only opened doors for me to deepen my reporting but often took me along with their recovery searches at Ground Zero. In Iraq, members of the New Jersey National Guard kept me safe and offered much freedom in reporting on the war's impact on soldiers.

The staff of the National September 11 Memorial and Museum in New York City brings grace and dignity to the annual 9/11 commemoration services, and were always available to assist with background research. Mary Fetchet, a kind and gifted social worker who lost her son, Brad, at the Trade Center and founded the group, "Voices of 9/11," opened my eyes to the mental health challenges for 9/11 victims and survivors. Various members of the advocacy groups, "9/11 Justice" and "9/11 Families United," also helped me to understand the trauma of 9/11 for so many ordinary people.

Finally, to all those profiled in this book: In many cases, we've spoken numerous times over the past two decades as you've allowed me to bear witness to your personal and painful journeys in the wake of the 9/11 attacks. As I wrote in the author's note of this book, you allowed me to walk into the "sacred ground" of your lives. Thank you for trusting me.

Index